Two-Track Training
Sex Inequalities and the YTS

YOUTH QUESTIONS

Series Editors: PHILIP COHEN and ANGELA MCROBBIE

This series sets out to question the ways in which youth has traditionally been defined by social scientists and policy-makers, by the caring professions and the mass media, as well as in 'common-sense' ideology. It explores some of the new directions in research and practice which are beginning to challenge existing patterns of knowledge and provision. Each book examines a particular aspect of the youth question in depth. All of them seek to connect their concerns to the major political and intellectual debates that are now taking place about the present crisis and future shape of our society. The series will be of interest to those who deal professionally with young people, especially those concerned with the development of socialist, feminist and anti-racist perspectives. But it is also aimed at students and general readers who want a lively and accessible introduction to some of the most awkward but important issues of our time.

Published

Inge Bates, John Clarke, Philip Cohen, Dan Finn, Robert Moore and Paul Willis
SCHOOLING FOR THE DOLE?
The New Vocationalism

Cynthia Cockburn
TWO-TRACK TRAINING
Sex Inequalities and the YTS

Andre Dewdney and Martin Lister
YOUTH, CULTURE AND PHOTOGRAPHY

Dann Finn
TRAINING WITHOUT JOBS: NEW DEALS AND BROKEN PROMISES
From Raising the School-Leaving Age to the Youth Training Scheme

Angela McRobbie and Mica Nava (eds)
GENDER AND GENERATION

Forthcoming

Philip Cohen and Harwant Bains (eds)
MULTI-RACIST BRITAIN

Philip Cohen and Graham Murdock (eds)
THE MAKING OF THE YOUTH QUESTION

Angela McRobbie (ed.)
RECORD COLLECTIONS
A Youth Reader

Kevin Robins and Frank Webster
NEW TECHNOLOGY AND EDUCATION

Two-Track Training

Sex Inequalities and the YTS

Cynthia Cockburn

MACMILLAN
EDUCATION

First published 1987

Published by
MACMILLAN EDUCATION LTD
Houndmills, Basingstoke, Hampshire RG21 2XS
and London
Companies and representatives
throughout the world

Photoset in Times by
CAS Typesetters, Southampton

Printed and bound in Great Britain by
Anchor Brendon Ltd, Tiptree, Essex

British Library Cataloguing in Publication Data
Cockburn, Cynthia
Two-track training: sex inequalities and
the YTS.—(Youth questions)
1. Sex discrimination in employment—Great
Britain   2. Youth Training Scheme
I. Title   II. Series
306'.36   HD6276.G7
ISBN 0-333-43288-6 (hardcover)
ISBN 0-333-43289-4 (paperback)

Series Standing Order

If you would like to receive future titles in this series as they are published,
you can make use of our standing order facility. To place a standing order
please contact your bookseller or, in case of difficulty, write to us at the
address below with your name and address and the name of the series.
Please state with which title you wish to begin your standing order. (If you
live outside the United Kingdom we may not have the rights to your area,
in which case we will forward your order to the publisher concerned.)

Customer Services Department, Macmillan Distribution Ltd
Houndmills, Basingstoke, Hampshire, RG21 2XS, England.

To Claudi and Jess

Also by Cynthia Cockburn

The Local State, 1977
Brothers: Male Dominance and Technological Change, 1983
*Machinery of Dominance: Women, Men and Technical Know-
how,* 1985.

Contents

List of Illustrations

All photographs by Cynthia Cockburn

Preface

When young people step out of school at sixteen the world they step into is deeply stereotyped by sex. Most women are expected to be working in typically feminine jobs or at home looking after the household. Men are expected to be working in manly professions, crafts or labouring jobs when they are not queueing at the unemployment benefit office. In 1983 the British government instituted a new Youth Training Scheme that was intended as a 'permanent bridge between school and work'. Within a few years it would be providing for up to half a million young people. Here was an unprecedented opportunity to break down the sex-segregation that was producing such persistent inequalities in life experiences, in earnings and career prospects between adult women and men in Britain. Statistics on YTS in its first few years, however, have given rise to fears that the scheme is reinforcing rather than shattering the mould of sex inequality. This book looks at what has gone wrong and how YTS could change to serve young women better.

The account that follows reports on a research project that was set up to look at this tendency for young people on the Manpower Services Commission's Youth Training Scheme to be found in training for sex-traditional occupations. It was to assess the progress being made by MSC in enabling young women (and young men) to cross into gender-contrary areas of training and work – young women into male manual trades, perhaps, and young men into such occupations as typing, hairdressing and nursery nursing. I was to look at the difficulties in the way of young people wishing to try out such non-conforming occupations and to consider how the breaking down of occupational sex-segregation on the Scheme might be supported.

The methods of the research included interviews and observation, as well as a study of published sources. In addition to an examination of MSC's national orientation on women in YTS, as it was expressed in the Commission's headquarters in Moorfoot, Sheffield, policies on women outside the centre in four MSC Training Division Area Offices were examined too. One of these offices was in London, the other three in areas with contrasted economies. The research then focused on one of the four segments into which Greater London was at that time divided for administrative purposes by MSC.

In this Area a number of MSC officers and members of the local Area Manpower Board were interviewed. Fourteen schemes were visited, four of them frequently as the subject of detailed case studies. These four were: an 'umbrella' scheme making placements in many small local businesses; an employer-based scheme operating among printing firms; a training workshop offering a range of subjects from catering to carpentry; and an Information Technology Centre (ITEC) where trainees were learning about electronics and computers.

Several firms providing trainees with work experience were visited. Thirty-two managing agents, supervisors, teachers and training officers were interviewed, including the coordinator of the local Accredited Training Centre. Questionnaires were sent to all schemes in the Area. Because of the important part played by the Careers Service in recruitment to the Scheme, two local careers offices were included in the study and seven careers officers interviewed. Finally, periods of participant observation and simple observation were undertaken in three of the case-study schemes. Ultimately, seventy-two trainees were interviewed and a majority followed up either with a second interview or a telephone call. Of the trainees, thirty-one were female and forty-one male; fifty-one were white, seventeen Afro-Caribbean and four Asian. (In the account that follows I will sometimes refer to the two latter ethnic groups together as 'black'.) The interviews were all semi-structured and wherever feasible were tape-recorded and transcribed.

The intention in selecting schemes for case-study had been to identify situations in which young people of both sexes were attempting to enter non-traditional occupations for their sex. One particular instance of gender innovation that was significant for the study was of young men training for work in the 'caring professions'.

These are rare as gold dust: a scan of the London segment produced only one young man currently in such a situation and available for interview. I therefore made a decision to break out of the original research frame for this purpose and seek out young men who had been in training for nursery work in previous years of the Youth Training Scheme. In this way I interviewed six young men in caring roles, five white and one Afro-Caribbean. One was a current trainee, aged 16. The others were past trainees, aged 17 or 18. Their experience is described in Chapter 8. Where I discuss the trainees as a whole, as in Chapter 2, I include these six.

The research was carried out during the second and third years of the existence of the Youth Training Scheme. Though some of the case studies were begun in 1984/5 I have taken the third year, 1985/6, as the base year for statistics of the Scheme. I tried to gain contact with at least some of most kinds of people involved with YTS – both sexes, adult and young, white and black, administrators, trainers and trainees – and to gain a first-hand understanding of their ideas and practices. The schemes which I got to know well seemed to me, in context, to be of average quality. I heard of some that were better and some far worse. There was one way however in which the research 'patch' was certainly untypical: it was in London. London and the South East are privileged in comparison with many other areas of the country, particularly Wales, parts of Scotland and the north-east. To make some comparison with other areas I visited Wales, where I heard of conditions in the former mining valleys of Mid-Glamorgan, and Birmingham, where the collapse of the metal industries has led to disastrous levels of unemployment. By contrast, I attended a conference in the MSC's Buckinghamshire and Hertfordshire area where the industrialist's complaints of skill shortages sounded more like the 1960s than the 1980s. These visits showed that YTS means different things in different areas. In London we can afford to ask how YTS is affecting the youth labour market. In many areas YTS now *is* the youth labour market. In such areas it is dishonest to represent YTS as likely to lead to a permanent job. In London the employer-based schemes do frequently lead to a proper job; indeed in some cases, as we shall see, the placements are a job from the outset. By contrast, in some areas even considerable talent cannot guarantee a school-leaver immediate employment, and here one would expect YTS to be recruiting even those youngsters with good GCE O-level results. In London

YTS recruits more from 'the bottom of the academic barrel' as one officer put it.

London itself of course sometimes seems like two different cities, with prosperous districts not far from pockets of unemployment almost as bad as in the worst-hit areas of Britain. Within London therefore I was at pains to see projects in the deprived inner-city area as well as in the better-off suburban fringe. YTS as a whole is extraordinarily various and it is impossible in a one-person, eighteen-month research project to cover all kinds of scheme. The Large Companies Unit at the MSC deals with 200 very large firms that run their own YTS schemes. They are not included here. Private Training agencies (PTAs) also abound in YTS. Well-known for instance are *Sight and Sound* offering keyboard training, and *Link*, organising youth training in the distributive trades. None of my detailed case studies covered such a PTA, though I did visit some. I did not see a college-based scheme or a local authority scheme in any detail. I did not visit a scheme for the disabled, nor for English as a Second Language, though I did see a workshop for ex-offenders. I was governed in choice of case-study schemes mainly by the wish to see instances of young women and young men who were innovating by training for occupations that were not traditional for their sex. This, being quite rare, limited the choice. The research, then, is not exhaustive of the YTS experience and can only be indicative of probabilities in the Scheme. YTS is, besides, still a minority experience. Only a quarter of the age group in Britain as a whole are on the Scheme. On the other hand YTS, beyond being a focus in its own right, provided a useful context, a terrain on which to observe gender relations among young people in training and the processes involved in sex-stereotyping and sex-differentiated occupational 'choices'.

The research ended in the spring of 1986 just as a revision of the Youth Training Scheme was about to be put into effect. The MSC's two-year scheme, or 'YTS-2' as it came to be known, will change some of the parameters within which I worked. For example, the Scheme will now to be open to both 16- and 17-year-olds, with provision for two years of training. An attempt is to be made to ensure that all trainees can work towards a recognised vocational qualification, or part of one, while on YTS. The 'managing agents' through which YTS was delivered in its first three years are now being required to submit themselves for assessment according to certain agreed criteria. If acceptable they will become 'approved training organisations' (ATO) and will thereafter be more autonomous than were the managing agents. A new inspectorate, a national 'training standards advisory service' is to be established, to monitor 'outcome performance'.

During the early years of the Scheme, MSC's funding of YTS was bi-modal. Most provision was sought from employers or groups of employers, who acted as managing agents. They provided work experience, combined with on-the-job training. And they were responsible for obtaining for each trainee thirteen weeks off-the-job training too, normally purchased from an educational institution. This was Mode A. In some areas and for some purposes, however, it was recognised that employer-based schemes could not provide all the training places required. Some schemes therefore were not designed around a particular employer or group of employers but based on a community project, a training workshop or an Information Technology Centre. Here the trainees were to experience a simulated working environment and from here they were to be sent out for short periods of work-experience on employers' premises. This was 'Mode B' provision. The payments for trainees on Mode B schemes was higher than on Mode A in recognition of their higher costs. This funding system is being replaced, in 'YTS-2', by a single, uniform mode. All approved training organisations will receive a similar management fee to be paid at the start of each year and a basic grant for each trainee on the Scheme, payable in monthly instalments. ATOs will be less able to afford empty places on their schemes. In place of Mode B there will be 'premium grants' payable to any kind of ATO where an individual trainee can be shown to be in some way disadvantaged and to have 'special training needs'. In other words the additional funding for the disadvantaged will not in future attach to particular kinds of scheme but to particular kinds of young person. The terms Mode A and Mode B become redundant. Finally, the funding of the Scheme by MSC under 'YTS-2' is not intended to be sufficient to cover the whole of the ATO's running costs. Employers are to be expected to contribute some of the cost of the trainee's grant.

Readers may, then, find the terms I use somewhat out of date. I have to continue to refer to managing agents, for that is what they were at the time of the study. I try to minimise the use of Mode A and Mode B and speak instead of 'employer-based' and 'workshop-

xiv *Preface*

style' schemes. It is not always possible however to avoid the original MSC terminology. The fact that YTS has developed in the way it has does not in any substantial way invalidate the findings of the research: the basic principles and processes of YTS remain unchanged.

The book was researched and written while I was a research fellow in the Department of Social Science and Humanities at the City University, London. It was funded by the Equal Opportunities Commission and the Economic and Social Research Council. The views expressed are my own, and do not necessarily reflect those of any of these bodies. I would like to express my appreciation to all three organisations for their support.

I would also like to express my thanks to all those who helped me, both with the research and with the book. People were generous with their time in interview, and I especially appreciate the participation of the trainees with whom I was in touch. Young people always have pressing demands on their time and their enthusiasms do not often coincide with those of social-science researchers. I was therefore especially grateful to those who gave me their time and attention. Thanks, also, to the many trainees who helped with the photography and to the following who agreed to their images appearing in the book: André, Cynthia, Denise, Donna, Garry, George, Hassan, Jane, Joby, Kerry, Leon, Loretta, Marina, Mesut, Pushpa, Rachael, Rachel, Roger, Ruth, Stephen, Steve, Tony and Yvonne. In addition, my special thanks are due to Phil Cohen, John Eversley, Dan Finn, Christine Griffin, Sally Griffin and Pam Janes who read and commented on this book in manuscript, to Angela McRobbie who was a helpful guide in the role of series editor, and to Elizabeth Black and Keith Povey for the copy-editing. If the finished work has any merit, much of it is due to them. Its shortcomings are my own responsibility.

C.C.

1

Inequalities in the Making

One in four young people aged 16 in Britain in 1986 was on the government's Youth Training Scheme. Just under half of them were young women, and it is with their position and achievements on YTS that this book is mainly concerned. However, it is logically impossible to consider what is happening to young women without taking notice also of the experience of young men, since the lives of both sexes intertwine. What men do has a considerable bearing on what women do. What follows then is an account of the young, as they leave school at the minimum legal age, and experience the transition from school to adult life, to work, non-work and training. But it is specifically about gender relations between young people in that context.

There are no metaphors that adequately describe gender. It is possible to describe masculine and feminine as 'two faces of a single coin'. But that image shows the faces dissociated, staring away from each other. In reality the genders are deeply implicated one with the other. The masculine and feminine influence and shape each other. For every masculine 'face' there is a necessary feminine one. With this in mind one could describe gender relations as like the mould and the object that is cast in it. In this metaphor the masculine is seen to form the feminine as a negative of its own outline. That is perhaps nearer the truth. But it implies that the feminine is merely passive. In reality, although masculinity may dominate gender relations, women fight back; they manoeuvre. Masculinity is partly formed in response to women's resistance to its hegemony. Gender relations and the forms of the two genders are also subject to historical change and they differ from one culture to another.

Perhaps after all gender has to be described without the aid of metaphor. As we shall see it is itself a metaphor for other things.

Human society begins with a species, *homo sapiens*, which exhibits a modest degree of biological sexual dimorphism: female and male are similar in most respects but show small physical differences and complementary reproductive functions. These physical phenomena are used in human culture as a prompt, a cue for the creation of an elaborate social system of difference, a dichotomy in which all that is associated with the male excludes and contrasts with everything associated with the female (Oakley, 1972; Kessler and McKenna, 1978). Masculinity is expressed in one set of terms: it may be associated at one moment with physical strength and aggressiveness; at another with intellectuality and reason. Always the feminine will be expressed in contrasting terms: now woman is weak and passive; now she is physical and emotional. Never mind that many of the supposed attributes of one sex are mutually incompatible or have little regard to observed fact, or that the actual range of variation within one sex is observably greater than the differences that divide the two. Logic is not what gender is about. The complementarity of gender has become a keystone of our societies and all else must fall into place around it (Cockburn, 1985).

Biology is not a powerfully prescriptive factor in human life. There are few attributes and few activities that are not possible to either sex. It is gender that has supplanted sex-difference and become dictatorial in the distinctions it specifies between men and women. It is used to justify men's power over women, their greater wealth, high status, wider freedoms. It legitimates women's subordination in marriage, women's lack of training and of certain skills, and the particular form taken by the exploitation of women at work.

Gendered behaviour has to be taught and learned, however. From the moment of birth and the identification of a baby's sex, the process of gendering begins. The baby, then the child, is treated always 'as though' it is one gender or the other. Except when things go 'wrong' we grow up to live out a gender-identity, masculine or feminine, and indeed to desire one. We participate, some willingly and some less so, in the perpetuation of a sex/gender system. Gendering does not stop at adolescence. Indeed it intensifies and even as adults our experience of life, including training and work, very often continues to reinforce and embellish our gender identity. When situations undermine it, in ourselves and others, we experience it as painful. We pay a social price for dispensing with it or rejecting it. Gender is a form of apartheid – pink and blue, perhaps, instead of black and white – and as with other forms of social separation and differentiation – of class, race or nation – it is the basis of domination. Being social however gender relations can and do change. Being taught, gender can be unlearned.

Sex and age: divisions at work

The second theme in the book is the sexual division of labour, the activities women and men characteristically do and for which they are trained. Here is the first occasion to use gender itself as a metaphor. Take the tendency for men to become the family breadwinner and for women to do the greater part of the support tasks in the home. Those two sets of activities are complementary: because his tasks are thus, hers must be so. Take paid employment likewise. Thousands of separately-specified occupations are related to each other in a system of power not unlike a gender system. Occupations form and deform each other, create and destroy each other. One climbs up by pushing another down or colonises those that are adjacent. This is influenced both by the employer who creates occupations and by those who inhabit them. Personnel managers define the role of the receptionist: it may include looking sexually alluring and making the tea. Scientists and technologists design and introduce machines that transform other people's jobs (Gorz, 1976). The mobility of a salesman's job creates the immobility of that of his secretary, back at base (Cockburn, 1985). The former's relatively high earnings partly determine the latter's relatively low pay.

The relational character of work makes it particularly suited to research by ethnographical methods – where actual people and their class, race and gender relations are in view – because onto the relations between jobs is mapped the relation between men and women and between white and black. Men and white men in particular, are found in the jobs that most dominate and influence the jobs of women, and particularly of black women. A pattern of employment produced by the economic system, with its thrust to capital accumulation, takes practical expression in terms of a system of class, racial and sexual inequalities. Capital saves on labour costs while ensuring the skill levels it needs by creating differentiated internal labour markets (internal, that is, to firms or organisations). Work is organised into 'core' jobs with relatively high pay and secure conditions and 'peripheral' jobs in which pay is low and workers may be laid off at will (Doeringer and Piore, 1971; Friedman, 1977; Edwards, 1979).

Employers' current cry is for flexibility in their manpower management and they are in part achieving this by recourse to electronic control systems combined with part-time and temporary employment policies (Atkinson, 1984; Caits, 1986). In the ten years to 1983 the proportion of part-time workers in the labour force increased by 50 per cent. Temporary, insecure employment is also growing: about one-third of vacancies filled by Jobcentres in 1984 were for temporary posts. These are sometimes called the 'demand' factors contributing to occupational sex- and race-segregation, for almost all the part-time workers and many of the temporary workers are women. The separate sub-markets within the labour market operate by different rules and tend not to compete with each other. Segmented labour markets are gendered systems and by and large women do not compete with men for the same job (Barron and Norris, 1976; Rubery, 1980; Reich *et al.*, 1980; Kenrick, 1981).

The main reason why women can be treated differently in the labour market is the social difference imposed on them outside the workplace. Because they have more time-consuming domestic responsibilities, women more often than men need part-time work and sporadic work. They need flexibility for their own purposes, but are forced to take it on employers' terms. Besides, their childhood at home and at school has sometimes developed in women certain skills (sewing, cleaning, caring, being neat and tidy) that can be serviceable in obtaining certain kinds of work. These are among the 'supply' factors tending to occupational sex-segregation (some of the extensive literature is reviewed in Amsden, 1980; Holland, 1981; Beechey and Whitelegg, 1986).

Another factor too can influence employers in sustaining a sexual division within employment. Sometimes they keep women out of certain jobs in deference to their male employees' claim to property rights in particular skills. Trade unions have been instrumental in ensuring that certain trades are seen and maintained as masculine (Hartmann, 1979; Phillips and Taylor, 1980; Cockburn, 1983). Most employers of course are men – and mainly white men. They often act less as 'pure' capitalists and more like their male employees: on masculine prejudice and preference. In a survey of management attitudes in recruitment Audrey Hunt found that for every single positive attribute she listed, a majority of managers thought it more likely to be found in a man than a woman (Hunt, 1975). This prejudice among those with the power to hire-and-fire results, as found by a more recent survey of recruitment, in 'widespread, blatant and potentially unlawful direct discrimination between men and women' (Curran, 1985, p.50). Discrimination against black people in the labour market is similarly endemic, so that black women are heavily disadvantaged (Commission for Racial Equality, 1978; Braham *et al.*, 1981).

As women have their own special place in the structure of employment, so, in their own way, do young people. Teenagers, fresh from school, can hardly compete with 'prime-age' workers, especially white males, who are educationally qualified and work-disciplined. Like women, therefore, they have 'supply-side' qualities that locate them in the secondary labour market (Osterman, 1980). There is some disagreement however over the extent to which, within the secondary labour market, young people form a distinct segment. Some labour market analysts have questioned whether there is any such thing as a youth labour market operating separately from other sectors of the economy. They argue that very few jobs are held only by young people (OECD, 1977). In contrast others suggest that young people occupy their own segment and compete less with adults than with each other (Doeringer and Piore, 1971). It is clear that young men in Britain in their early years in the labour force are concentrated heavily in construction, distribution and various statistically 'miscellaneous' categories of work, while young women are found mainly in clothing and footwear, distribution, insurance, banking and finance (Makeham, 1980). Certainly for many kinds of job youth are 'at the end of the hiring queue' because employers expect that their productivity will be low and the firm may need to invest in training them. Where school-leavers are unqualified or where they lack credentials, employers find difficulty in applying useful recruitment criteria (OECD, 1977). Young workers are particularly liable to lose their jobs. This is not always because they are sacked through their own fault, but often because employers treat them as casual labour, exploiting the fact that they are often unprotected by trade union membership (Evans *et al.*, 1984). In a period when industry is enforcing increased flexibility in employment practices, temporary youth trainees are an ideally flexible resource. Ageing alone of course tends to carry young people out of the youth labour market. Training and qualification however will ensure the process and females who, as we will see, get less training at work than males, are in greater danger of getting 'locked in' to secondary work (Ashton *et al.*, 1982).

Separate spheres

The outcome of the employers' demand for differentiated labour power and the subordination of girls and women in society is a marked patterning of occupations by gender. It is not only people that are gendered. Jobs become gendered in association with the sex that normally does them. Something of the gender character of the job rubs off on the person who does it. When women move into a new kind of occupation, through changes in employers' demand, in the labour process or simply by pushing for it, that job tends to slip relatively downwards in the moving system of related occupations. When men begin to enter an occupation it can be observed to hoist itself up a notch or two. For convenience we refer to jobs as sex-stereotyped, or, for short, sex-typed, though these terms over-simplify the process just described.

Occupational sex-segregation has persisted relatively unchanged over long periods of time (Hakim, 1979, 1981). And though actual stereotypes differ from one country to another, sex-segregation itself crosses national boundaries (United Nations, 1980).

In Britain a separation of the sexes is clearly visible even in school. At GCE O-level in 1984 girls accounted for only 5.1 per cent of those gaining technical drawing qualification, 27.6 per cent in physics and 26.9 per cent in computer studies. On the other hand boys gained only 36.4 per cent of sociology passes and a tiny 2.6 per cent of cookery passes. At A-level the separation becomes yet more pronounced, with girls having only 3.1 per cent, 21.0 per cent and 18.0 per cent respectively of passes in technical drawing, physics and computer science. At A-level boys have fallen to less than 1 per cent in domestic subjects.

The nearer the world of work we get, the greater the sex-typing of subjects (Equal Opportunities Commission, 1986, Table 2.1). While 58 per cent of boys with two or more A-levels went into full-time further and higher education, only 46 per cent of girls with these qualifications did so. Six times as many girls as boys, however, joined teacher-training courses. Among the 16-year-old school-leavers, among pupils with O-level and CSE passes, girls were substantially more likely than boys to go into full-time further and higher education, the difference being accounted for to a large extent by the numbers of girls joining secretarial courses (Equal Opportunities Commission, 1986, Table 2.3). In non-advanced further education we find that 82.3 per cent of students of medical/health/welfare subjects are female, while only 6.1 per cent of engineering/technology students are. At the advanced level in further education these figures are 71.0 per cent and 4.9 per cent respectively, illustrating that while men may progressively penetrate female fields at higher levels, women tend progressively to withdraw from male fields (Equal Opportunities Commission, 1986, Table 2.6).

In employment, women and men continue on the whole to do different jobs. In 1985 women were only 0.4 per cent of the labour force in construction/mining; 4.5 per cent in metal/electrical processing work; 4.6 per cent in transport operation; 9.5 per cent in farming and fishing. On the other hand they were 74 per cent of clerical workers, 76 per cent of those in catering/cleaning/hairdressing and other personal services, and 68 per cent of 'professionals and others' (particularly 'others', no doubt) in education/health/welfare. No less than 77 per cent of women full-time workers and 90 per cent of part-timers work within four categories of employment: selling; catering/cleaning; clerical; and education/health/welfare (Equal Opportunities Commission, 1986, Table 3.4). Men by contrast are spread more evenly across a very much wider range of occupations and particularly fill the more specialised and senior niches (Equal Opportunities Commission, Table 3.4). These figures, besides, grossly underrepresent the true extent of occupational sex-segregation. The more precisely occupational categories are defined the greater is seen to be the separation between the sexes (Martin and Roberts, 1984).

Occupational categories not only unfold into differentially powerful or subordinated posts and positions, they also emerge as having unequal earning potential. In 1985, ten years after the Equal Pay Act became operational, the average gross hourly earnings of adult women working full-time (excluding the effects of overtime) were only 74 per cent those of men. If we include the effects of overtime and look at average gross weekly earnings, women's performance falls yet further behind that of men: in 1985 women earned £6 for every £10 earned by men (Equal Opportunities Commission, 1986, Tables 4.1

8 Two-Track Training

and 4.3). It is now recognised that these persistent earnings differentials are largely due to the fact that women and men continue to be found in different occupations.

The sexual division of labour also entails an unequal distribution of training in and for work. Of all women in full-time employment, 25 per cent have received some full-time, on-the-job training during paid working hours, but for four-fifths of these women the cumulative duration of all such training was less than one year. For men the comparable figures are 30 per cent receiving training and half of these getting more than a year (Institute for Employment Research, 1982, Table 3.11). Only one in five of the 16-18-year-olds given day-release from their employment for training is a girl (Benett and Carter, 1983). The outcome of all these disadvantages is that women often appear, to themselves and others, to be *unable* to be competent production engineers, accountants, airline pilots – even taxi-drivers. Yet, given the chance and the training, women can do most jobs as well as, if not better than, men.

Sexual divisions in YTS

The occupational segregation by sex that characterises employment at large is faithfully reproduced in the Manpower Services Commission's Youth Training Scheme. MSC classifies its YTS places according to a system of 'occupational training families', or OTFs. There are eleven such OTFs, as will be seen from Figure 1.1. OTFs were never intended to be used as statistical categories for defining the occupations for which young people were training. They are created by the Institute of Manpower Studies for the MSC precisely to be broad and encompassing, 'a tool for the organisation of work experience/training by setting up coherent learning objectives for a wide family of occupations' (Hayes and Fonda, 1983, p.7). They are thus deliberately unspecific. MSC took no steps to ensure that OTFs were compatible with the standard occupational classifications, such as CODOT/KOS, used by the Department of Employment and the Office of Population Censuses and Surveys. Yet OTFs, inadequate as they were, were sufficient to reveal a distribution of female and male trainees by occupation in the first three years of the Scheme that was remarkably and consistently skewed.

9

Figure 1.1 *YTS 'starters' in the period April to December 1985, nationally (all trainees, distributed by sex to the 'occupational training families' of their placements)*

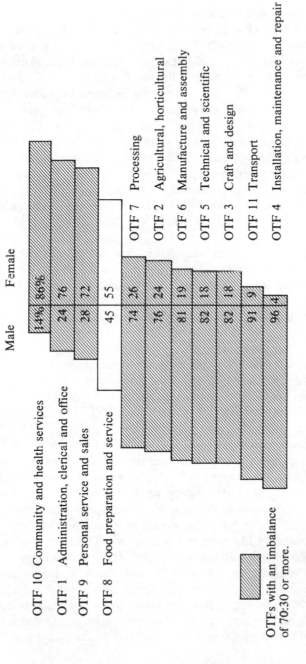

Male   Female

OTF 10 Community and health services   14% 86%
OTF 1   Administration, clerical and office   24 76
OTF 9   Personal service and sales   28 72
OTF 8   Food preparation and service   45 55

OTF 7   Processing   74 26
OTF 2   Agricultural, horticultural   76 24
OTF 6   Manufacture and assembly   81 19
OTF 5   Technical and scientific   82 18
OTF 3   Craft and design   82 18
OTF 11 Transport   91 9
OTF 4   Installation, maintenance and repair   96 4

OTFs with an imbalance of 70:30 or more.

Note: Figures cover approximately 89 per cent of all trainees. Excluded are those who are not reported by their managing agents as allocated to a specific OTF.
Source: Manpower Services Commission, 1986.

Occupational segregation by sex can be measured in two ways (Hakim, 1979). One method is to group occupations according to the sex ratio observed in each. The bar chart in Figure 1.1 is a representation of this kind. An accepted standard for designating an occupation sex-typed is where the ratio of the sexes is more extreme than 70:30 (Hakim, 1979). The Youth Training Scheme by this measure is highly sex-segregated, with ten out of the eleven OTFs sex-typed. In OTFs 1, 9 and 10, women are 72 per cent or more of the trainees. These three, involving mainly work with people (and with paper), were clearly female. Seven OTFs on the other hand were strikingly sex-typed male. Men were 74 per cent or more of trainees in OTFs 2–7 and 11. These were occupations dealing with things (mainly machines). No less than 79 per cent of all women trainees were in OTFs sex-typed female, while 75 per cent of young men were in OTFs sex-typed male.

If we look again at the figure, bearing in mind that young women in fact represent somewhat less than half (44 per cent) of all YTS trainees, it will be evident that the preponderance of young women in 'female' OTFs is somewhat understated in the diagram and their relative absence from 'male' OTFs slightly overstated. The number of OTFs that are sex-segregated, however, remains unchanged.

A second method of expressing occupational sex-segregation is by determining the degree to which one sex is concentrated in a relatively small number of occupational categories. Seventy per cent of female trainees were found in 'office' and 'sales' OTFs, while only 42 per cent of all filled places on the scheme were in these OTFs. On the other hand a mere 8 per cent of all women trainees were in six 'male' OTFs, representing in total 32 per cent of filled places.

My encounter with four MSC Areas produced local OTF statistics just as strikingly gender-skewed as the national figures. Moreover, OTFs, being so broad, considerably under represent the true extent of sexual divisions in YTS. The nature of YTS places and the MSC's system of record-keeping did not allow of a closer analysis. But officers reported that familiarity with individual schemes showed that, for instance, whereas male trainees might be about a quarter of office trainees, such trainee placements could be divided again into those involving typing and secretarial work and those being more generally administrative. Only a tiny proportion of young men were to be found in the former, while the great majority of young women were there. Among the places of OTF 10, I was told, young men cluster in relatively active and adventurous community work placements, working with young teenagers or in community action projects, while young women work in caring roles with the ill, elderly and children.

Most officers I interviewed knew quite clearly which 'jobs' were in practice masculine and which were feminine and could number on the fingers of one hand the youngsters doing the non-traditional thing. A study of young women in YTS by the Fawcett Society reported that 'girls doing non-traditional work... are *very* difficult to find' (Fawcett Society, 1985, p.6). The authors suggest that only one in 250 youth trainees in construction skills is female (see also National Union of Students, Women's Unit, 1985; Women in YTS, 1983; Pollert, 1986). YTS of course, is only one of a stable of MSC schemes. The Commission's adult training activities including the Community Programme show a similar lack of achievement in breaking-down sex-typing (Dickens, 1983). In the Youth Opportunities Programme (YOP), YTS's predecessor scheme, sex-typing was 'almost total' and when one looked in more detail at the actual activities carried out within placements 'there was generally little overlap between the sexes save for a necessary part of many other activities: *cleaning*' (Brelsford *et al.*, 1982, p.15). Teresa Rees has shown how sex inequalities have been reproduced in state training schemes in Britain and Northern Ireland since the 1930s (Rees, 1984).

The research project, then, was not about showing that sexual divisions existed within YTS: that was already clear. MSC itself was aware of the problem and its publicity continually emphasised – in the hope of encouraging young people to break out of sex-stereotyping – that all the Scheme's training places were 'open to all regardless of sex'. The research aimed rather to explore the mechanisms by which sexual inequalities were nonetheless being perpetuated year by year. We need not assume that there is a direct one-to-one relationship between sexual divisions in YTS and in employment thereafter. Yet all the indications are that YTS presages a future inequality. If women are to avoid the channelling process that produces the two-tone, pink and blue pattern we have seen in the adult world of work, a definitive *refusal* has to take place. If the refusal is not made at 16 it becomes progressively more difficult to make. Once she has said 'yes' to hairdressing or typing, even on YTS, the young women trainee can be pretty sure that in ten years' time she will be earning only £6 or £7 for every £10 earned by the young man who said 'yes' to photography, engineering or business studies. She can be sure that he will have good reason in his higher earnings and better prospects to see that his wife, not he, is the one to stay home with the babies. Besides, he will not have learned the skills needed to work with those in need of special care, his own children included. She will have sealed her own fate, besides, as the future over-worked and under-paid combination worker/mother. There is scope within the Youth Training Scheme for supporting young people in the needed refusal. Many YTS workers are putting courage and imagination into the task. Yet the political and economic context of YTS render it, in spite of their best intentions, a vast machine mass-producing the age-old inequalities.

In approaching the subject of the sexual division of labour in YTS I supposed that the normal 'demand' and 'supply' factors would be at work, pulling men into this kind of training, pushing women into that. But I also supposed that another kind of factor would be at work: an *experiential* factor. What young people were actually experiencing on the Scheme would be influencing the distribution of the sexes to different kinds of training place. My previous work and that of other researchers on the labour process has suggested that occupational 'choice' is governed by a strong reality principle. In particular, people know that jobs are, in a sense, gendered as they themselves are. Women know full well that certain jobs are 'for' them and if they seek to do jobs that are 'for' men they will experience, at worst, hostility and ridicule, and, at best, discomfort and a persistent pressure to step back into line (Cockburn, 1985). Male and female act on each other, sustaining gender complementarity and difference. The people with whom one works are a major source of positive and negative experiences that modify the possibilities that seem to exist (Laws, 1976, pp.48–9). As Anne Stafford has put it, 'it is partly *in their daily interaction with each other* that boys and girls are brought to accept different things about themselves and ultimately come to embrace very different futures' (Stafford, 1986). There is a feedback from actual to anticipated experience. A report on one project for young women in the building trades noted recently:

> Those young women who are discriminated against at the outset, those who drop out because they can't stand the isolation and those exceptional young women who survive all have tales to tell, and word gets around. Young women listen to their friends (Young Women's Plastering Project, 1986).

An experiential focus of this kind has two advantages. It avoids the 'immaculate conception' of women's oppression: that it occurs but no-one actually *does* it. It introduces the agents of oppression, employers and colleagues, real men and masculinity. Second, it opens to view factors on which the MSC, and government policy generally, might be expected to act.

Youth unemployment and the Manpower Services Commission

The question that faces anyone concerned with 'equality' in the Youth Training Scheme is of course whether one can logically approach the Scheme and its promoters with any such expectation. Politically the MSC is a queer fish. Ostensibly it is a 'quango', a quasi-autonomous-non-governmental organisation. It nonetheless has the power that normally accrues to the state apparatus alone. Yet though it has this authority it is not answerable directly to a body of elected representatives. The Commission is an appointed body and Parliament has access to its work only via the Secretary of State for Employment. Much of the cost of the MSC's Youth Training Scheme is found from outside the national budget: it comes from the European Economic Community's Social Fund. MSC is structured as a tripartite body with built-in participation by industry, the trade unions and the education service. A central statutory labour-market body was something the unions had been demanding since the Second World War. At the outset therefore it was seen as a creature of the labour movement. The effectiveness of participation by the representatives of labour however declined over time.

The Commission was created by a Tory Employment and Training Act of 1973. In its early years, as developed by Labour and influenced by the Trades Union Congress, the Manpower Services Commission was a reformist body, relatively modest in scale and aspirations, seeking to compensate for the inability of the labour and job markets to move in synchrony. Its functions included 'to make such arrangements as it considers appropriate for the purpose of assisting persons to select, train for, obtain and retain employment suitable for their ages and capacities and to obtain suitable employees' (HM Stationery Office, 1973, Section 2(1)). It had responsibility for Jobcentres and increasingly concerned itself with training. As recession pushed up the unemployment level from 2.6 per cent in 1973 to double that rate four years later Labour was obliged to call on the MSC to deliver temporary work programmes and other special measures for the unemployed. Its size and influence mushroomed. As the scope of the MSC increased, so did worries about the lack of any real control either by trade unions and educationalists sitting on the Commission, or by Parliament (for a critical history of the MSC see Benn and Fairley, 1986). The duty of the Commission was clearly set out. It was 'to give effect to any directions given to it by the Secretary of State', to 'ensure that its activities are in accordance with proposals approved by the Secretary of State', and 'to submit to the Secretary of State from time to time particulars of which it proposes to do for the purpose of performing its functions' (HM Stationery Office, 1973, Section 2(3)). Whatever the growing doubts of the labour movement, however, it was by now thoroughly embroiled and co-opted into the doings of the MSC.

It was during the 1970s that youth unemployment became a policy issue. The report of a working party set up by the National Youth Employment Council voiced concern about the predecessors of today's YTS generation: the unqualified minimum-age school-leavers (Department of Employment, 1974). A number of factors were behind the rise in youth unemployment. Official sources tended to emphasise demographic and attitudinal influences. It was suggested that the important factors were the emergence from school of more young people, the progeny of the 1960s' baby-boom; and the tendency for more married women to seek a return to employment. It was also suggested that young people were more work-shy than they had formerly been and that they were 'pricing themselves out of work'. In fact, although the wages of the under-18s did rise, in most developed countries, in the early 1970s relative to those of adults (and young women's rose more sharply than young men's) by the mid-1970s this rise had more or less halted, while youth unemployment continued to go upwards (OECD, 1977). A further argument sometimes put forward to explain youth unemployment was that changes in the nature of work and the decline of certain industries had adversely affected young people's chances of getting a job. Michael Jackson, reviewing the evidence for these trends, concludes that though young people did suffer from a loss of service sector jobs in this period they were not in fact heavily concentrated in the industries that failed. He argues instead that the overriding factor in youth joblessness is a low general economic activity rate: young people are more quickly and more seriously affected by any deterioration in economic conditions than adults. In other words, youth unemployment is structural (Jackson, 1985, p.75). 'Youth shoulders a major part of the burden of adjustment to economic change' (Evans *et al.*, 1984, p.23).

A rise in overall unemployment from 2.6 per cent to 6.9 per cent between 1970 and 1980 was accompanied by a rise in unemployment for under-18s from 2.5 per cent to 11.0 per cent (Jackson, 1985, p.35). Young women's unemployment increased even faster – at three times the rate of overall female unemployment. When there was a remission in the rise in adult unemployment in the late 1970s, youth unemployment continued relentlessly upward. By 1981 whereas males under 25 constituted 30 per cent of all registered male unemployment, young women constituted 52 per cent of all female unemployment. In particular, long-term unemployment had increased proportionately far more among young than among older workers (Rees and Atkinson, 1982, pp.3–4). Whereas only 4.9 per cent of the unemployed under-25s had been out of work more than a year in 1976, the percentage had more than doubled by 1979 (Jackson, 1985, p.36).

The Labour government however shied away from analysing youth unemployment as permanent or structural, arising from long-term developments in capitalist production. Caught up in the right-wing ideology of the so-called Great Debate in education, it defined youth unemployment instead by a 'deficit model' of young people. The finger was pointed at schooling (Finn, 1987). Employers, ignoring the fact that they themselves were becoming more choosy, complained that the youngsters coming out of school were undisciplined, unlettered, ill-kempt and unmotivated for work. Labour's answer to youth joblessness was a string of temporary and piecemeal programmes – the Work Experience Programme in 1976, the five-year Youth Opportunities Programme in 1978 – designed to 'lick kids into shape', make them notionally employable, regardless of whether the jobs were realistically there for their employment.

So identified was the MSC with Labour statism that the initial reaction of the incoming Thatcher government in 1979, with its commitment to 'rolling back the state' and affirming the primacy of the market, was to cut the Commission's budget. Increases in youth unemployment persisted however, so that by 1981 of all under-18s almost one in five was unemployed. The rate for West Indian young men was twice as high as for white young men. The rate for Asian young women was twice that for white women in their age group (Jackson, 1985, p.44). A wave of uprisings occurred in major cities in 1981, and in these the jobless young were visibly involved. In the early 1980s therefore the Tories were obliged to turn to a revamped MSC and its Youth Opportunities Programme to see them out of trouble. With Norman Tebbitt newly installed as Employment Secretary, well teamed with David Young (now Lord Young) in the chair of the Commission – he liked to call himself a 'free market man' – the MSC was converted into an important instrument for the Conservatives' complex project: appearing to mitigate the distress of youth while also laundering the unemployment figures, subduing the trade unions and forcing the working class to lower its expectations.

The MSC today is an embodiment of the contradictions faced by the Tories as they attempt to govern a capitalist nation during economic crisis and recession. Similar problems face governments of all Western countries. A report of the Organisation for Economic Co-operation and Development (OECD) on youth policy confirmed that between 1980 and 1984:

> the youth unemployment problem... has grown in scale and intensity. Unemployment rates and employment-to-population ratios indicate further deterioration. Recent work by the Secretariat on flows into and out of employment paints a bleaker picture than before of the duration of jobless spells, and the consequences of protracted spells of joblessness. There is also new evidence of segmentation in the youth labour force, marked by distinct differences between the experience of males and females, and between teenagers and young adults (OECD, 1985, p.14).

The 1979 oil shock and the subsequent slide into recession had had 'devastating' effects on youth unemployment. It had increased by 50 per cent in the seven largest OECD countries between 1979 and 1982, to a point where the most seriously affected country, Spain, had a youth unemployment rate of no less than 37 per cent. What is more, this OECD report found that 'though an economic recovery has begun to take hold in most OECD countries, it holds out only limited hope for young people... contrary to all past experience with youth unemployment in the OECD area, the current economic recovery is not expected to yield appreciable dividends in increased employment opportunities for young people' (OECD, 1985, p.15).

To the effect of world-wide recession must be added the fact that the Conservative government's uncompromising monetarist strategy for the UK involved a purposeful 'shaking out' of 'under-employed' labour. Unemployment soon reached levels far surpassing those presided over by Labour. A million and a quarter jobs in manufacturing industry and the service sector were lost in the first year and a half after the Conservatives returned to office in 1979. The aim was to discipline the unions, bringing 'over-priced and over-organised' labour to heel, and to liberate British employers to compete effectively in world markets. Such policies entail high political risks and massive resentment. With its remit of delivering measures for the unemployed the MSC was called on to appear caring while collaborating in ruthlessness.

At its height in 1980–1 the Youth Opportunities Programme covered 360 000 young people annually, providing six to twelve months' work experience with rudimentary training. The programme quickly fell into disrepute. The low level of the training allowance and the poor quality of training made it a slave-labour scheme in the eyes of young people. Trade unions detected that a large proportion of YOP trainees were being substituted for paid labour. And youth unemployment simply continued upward. It was officially recognised that by September 1984, without policy intervention, with another year's school-leavers on the streets, 57 per cent of 16-year-olds and 48 per cent of 17-year-olds in the labour market would be unemployed. Something had to be done for an estimated 300 000 minimum-age school-leavers who would otherwise walk through the school gates direct to the dole queue (Manpower Services Commission, 1982, p.8). YOP could not be abandoned but there was widespread pressure for an improved alternative.

The Youth Training Scheme: new look in 'youth opportunities'

The Youth Training Scheme which replaced YOP in 1983, heralded by a £1m advertising campaign by Saatchi and Saatchi, was met with suspicion but generally acknowledged to be an improvement on its predecessor. This Scheme was proclaimed as no temporary unemployment measure but a 'permanent bridge between school and work'. It offered a year's training to all 16-year-olds and eventually also 17-year-olds leaving school and failing to find work or a place in further education. The training was to be mainly on-the-job, and mainly provided by employers on their own premises (Mode A). There was to be a fall-back formula where the work experience would be in training workshops, community projects and Information Technology Centres (Mode B). This alternative would fill the gap where the employer response was insufficient. All trainees were to have a training programme and a log book, and their training was to be closely monitored. They would receive a certificate on completion, and some might get a recognised qualification or at least part of one. They would receive a training allowance and they were to be given thirteen weeks' off-the-job training in work-related skills and in personal and life skills. A core of maths, English and computer studies was mandatory.

In 1985/6 – the third year of its operation – 389 000 young people took up places on YTS. Of these 44 per cent were female. We will see exactly how the Scheme works in later chapters and the relationship between young women's and young men's experience on it. Meanwhile we should look at some of the problems that affect all trainees, of both sexes, inherent in the Youth Training Scheme as it developed between 1983 and 1986, for it is only by taking account of its nature as an expression of Conservative policy that we can plan our response, as women. Should we put our energies into struggling for an improvement of the position of women within YTS? Or should we simply, as some would propose, turn our backs and put our energies elsewhere, on the basis that, even if young women achieve equality in the Scheme, they would nonetheless be better off unemployed?

Though YTS was undoubtedly an improvement on YOP it soon came to be widely criticised in its turn. From the outset there had been a discrepancy between, on the one hand, the humanely worded proposals of the Youth Task Group commissioned by the MSC to flesh out the Scheme, and, on the other, the government's official White Papers (HMSO, 1984; HMSO, 1985) and the yet-more-revealing pronouncements of Tory politicians. The latter made it clear that YTS was a magic wand they intended to wave to convert an actual unemployment problem into an apparent training problem. It was part of a strategy that combined bringing about a fall in youth wages; improving young people's 'employability', which meant in the main motivating them to submit to work discipline; and simply reducing the numbers that appeared to be unemployed. Training for genuinely useful abilities and skills was a secondary matter. Creating new jobs was not on the agenda. The following are some of the main criticisms that have been levelled against YTS by young people, trade unionists and many of those who work on the Scheme. Many of the points were confirmed to me in interview.

The Youth Training Scheme was originally conceived within the context of a plan to transform training for both adults and young people, outlined in the White Paper on *The New Training Initiative* (HMSO, 1981). YTS thus had a somewhat better pedigree than YOP, which had been more frankly an unemployment measure. The NTI was part of a far-reaching reform of the education system as a whole. During the 1970s right-wing educationists had drawn the educational world into a 'Great Debate' on the state of education. They had castigated the schools for failing to produce the kind of raw recruits employers believed they needed. The return of the Tories to power in 1979 hastened a move away from liberal, pupil-oriented teaching, with reliance on the professionalism of teachers, towards the direct satisfaction of employers' demands for disciplined, work-ready school-leavers. The MSC was central to the development of this 'new vocationalism' as it came to be called (Finn, 1987). It included a transformation of school curricula for 14–18-year-olds, in the shape of the Technical and Vocational Education Initiative and the Certificate of Pre-Vocational Education, and making work-experience a priority during school years.

The New Training Initiative dealt with post-school training in a similar spirit. A key feature of the NTI was the proposal to phase out time-served and trade-union-regulated apprenticeship and replace it by a modular system of training, open to people of any age and leading to recognised qualifications. Trade unions read this as an attack on their historical influence over recruitment and training, as indeed it was intended to be. The new policy certainly coincided with a precipitous decline in the number of apprenticeships. The NTI was, besides, accompanied by a move to throw back the onus of training onto individual firms. A system of Industrial Training Boards had been created by the Industrial Training Act of 1964. ITBs had been given a mandate to take an overview of training for their sectors, levying funds from firms to finance training in the interest of the industry as a whole. Trade unions had been represented on these Boards. Now most of the ITBs were abruptly abolished, another move that reduced union influence over training. The upshot was contradictory however. Some could not help but feel that opening up vocational training at last to women and to black people – groups that had long been excluded from apprenticeships and neglected in ITB strategies – was bound to offer some gains. Even as the NTI threatened an overall decline in the quality and quantity of vocational training, it paradoxically enhanced possibilities for women and blacks (Goldstein, 1984; Wickham, 1985 and 1986).

The NTI focused on three kinds of training: for adults, for potential skilled workers entering direct from school, and for the remainder of the under-18s. It was a concern with this last group, the least-privileged school-leavers, the potential unemployed youth, that the new YTS was designed to meet. From the start, therefore, the Scheme was predicated upon, rather than pitched against, class inequalities. The post-school routes of young people are correlated with social class. The MSC's own study, made in 1976, of 3000 16–19-year-olds showed that of those staying on at school or in other forms of education beyond the age of 16, a majority came from families in the upper social class brackets (A, B and C1). Only 28 per cent of those in employment at this age were from these higher social groups. 80 per cent of the unemployed 16–19-year-olds were from classes C2, D and E (cited in Ball and Ball, 1979). It is from among such unemployed young people that the clientele of YTS in London is drawn.

For these reasons, YTS has been described as part of a new manifestation of selective streaming, a 'tertiary modern' sector, narrowly vocational, aimed at unskillable working-class youth in contrast to the more privileged tiers of apprenticeship, further and higher education. Within YTS itself there is a hierarchy of schemes. At the top are those in which YTS has now become the first year of an apprenticeship. In the middle are the general run of Mode A employer-based schemes. At the bottom (in the punters' perception) is Mode B. Even within Mode B are somewhat more prestigious schemes – ITeCs for example – and less prestigious, such as workshops for ex-offenders.

In the employer's interest

It is widely argued that YTS is a scheme that gives priority to the interests of employers. It accepts the employer's contention that the problem lies in the poor quality of young labour power and a high youth wage. It is an employer-led scheme in which employers have the right to pick and choose their trainees, to terminate a training agreement at will, to keep on or dismiss a trainee at the end of the training period. Young people are led to compete with each other during what amounts to a year-long interview for the few permanent jobs available at the end. There is generous scope for employers to practise their prejudices in the recruitment of trainees.

Trainees are frequently taken on by employers in place of workers on a proper wage. The MSC has no mechanism for preventing, nor even for monitoring, such substitution. The Labour Party has complained of it; trade unions are certain it takes place, the MSC admits that it occurs in an unquantifiable proportion of cases. There is evidence of it in the ensuing study. Some of the substitution is for adult workers of either sex but most is believed to be substitution for other young people who would have been employed at a proper wage (Socialist Society, 1983).

The Scheme is attacked by unions for undermining wage agreements and trade-union organisation in the workplace (Eversley, 1986). Though the Trade Union Congress supports and indeed helps to run the Scheme and the majority of unions felt obliged to accept it, however unwillingly, some unions have refused to cooperate unless the terms of traineeships accord with existing apprenticeship and training agreements and unless the training allowance were topped up to an agreed union rate. YTS schemes in unionised workplaces must have the written support of recognised trade unions before they can be approved by Area Manpower Boards. However, very often schemes and trainee places are so broadly defined as to fall outside the legitimate concern of any one union – a fact happily utilised by managing agents to argue that there is no relevant union to consult. Very many YTS places are provided by small employers that are positively anti-union. Although trade unions are represented on Area Manpower Boards, the problem of monitoring outstrips their resources (Greater London Training Board, 1983).

YOP and YTS have succeeded in the government's intention of undercutting the wages of young people in employment. Between 1980 and 1985 the percentage of 16-year-olds paid at the (lowest) adult rate fell from 16 to 7 per cent in the case of young women and from 7 to 2 per cent in the case of young men. Earnings of adult males rose by 10.4 per cent in real terms between 1979 and 1985 but the real earnings of males under 18 fell by 1.2 per cent. The figures for women are similar: a 14.7 per cent rise for adults but a minimal 1.2 per cent growth for young women under 18 (Labour Research Department, 1986). Many employers hesitate to take on a young person in a permanent job, covered by employment protection legislation, for a living wage, when a youth trainee is offered free and entails no more than a little tedious red tape.

The Scheme also has to be seen in relation to other government measures with a similar but more obvious wage-cutting intention. In January 1982 the government introduced a Young Workers Scheme that paid £15 a week subsidy to employers for every employee kept on low pay – that is to say, earning a gross wage of less than £40 a week. This scheme has since been dropped, but the principle continues in the New Workers Scheme covering 18–20-year-olds. In 1986 the protection of the Wages Councils was withdrawn from half a million young workers, and it is recognised that it is precisely the areas not covered by wages councils where young workers' relative pay fell most in the early 1980s (Labour Research Department, 1986). The government has been quite unambiguous about its policy of forcing young people to 'price themselves into work'.

The Scheme then is inevitably compounding the damage done by unemployment to young people's independence and self-respect. The very low trainee allowance (£27.50 in 1985) gave 16-year-olds a standard of living that was actually lower in real terms than that afforded by YOP. The training allowance is little more than pocket money. The government has made it clear that families are now expected to subsidise all 16–18-year-old offspring. YTS prolongs the twilight zone of transition from school to work that the raising of the school-leaving age in 1973 had already stretched by one year. Worse,

the long-term implication of the Youth Training Scheme is an end to 'work' for youth up to eighteen years. As a result it will enforce a financial and therefore psychological dependence on the family not known since the 1930s (Socialist Society, 1983, p.10).

The White Paper on the NTI and early ministerial statements proposed changes to the social security system so as to compel young people to take part in YTS. The threat was posed again by the Prime Minister in December 1984. However, opposition to coercion on the part of employers as well as young people and their advocates has been so outspoken that the government has so far felt unable to persist. YTS does retain some coercive elements however. The Department of Health and Social Security treats the refusal of a YTS place in the same way as a refusal of a job offer: the claimant had benefit reduced for six weeks – thirteen weeks since October 1986. YTS trainees also lose six weeks' benefit if they leave a traineeship before it is completed.

Uneven quality, unfair access, undemocratic control

There have been serious criticisms of the quality of training offered by the Scheme. YTS was rushed into existence and expanded with great speed over a period of three years. In its fourth year of operation – as we've seen, far too soon in the view of many Area Manpower Boards and not a few MSC officers – it is being extended to become a two-year Scheme. This has over-stretched MSC Area Offices responsible for monitoring and approval of schemes. In day-to-day practice managing agents are expected to monitor their own work-experience providers. MSC's coverage even of managing agents is 'patchy', according to an independent survey (Incomes Data Services, 1983). Monitoring is against rudimentary minimum criteria and even by these many schemes are known to fall short. Not all trainees receive quality training in the workplace. Many complain of being stuck in 'dogsbodying' activities with little to learn. Some do not get their full thirteen weeks off-the-job training. Sometimes when they do it is not related to the job, and it has been the exception rather than the rule that a scheme leads to a recognised qualification. MSC's own figures confirm that the quality of YTS training is very variable. At the end of January 1985 30 per cent of all Mode A programmes did not meet the Commission's own quality standards (Labour Research Department, 1985, p.10).

The content of YTS has been developed on guidelines from the Institute of Manpower Studies, whose vocational orientation was favoured by MSC over the more liberal educational principles being pressed by the Further Education Unit of the Department of Education and Science.[1] In practice however the content of YTS training is neither educational nor vocational so much as empty of meaning. The Institute's 'transferable skills' (Hayes *et al.*, 1983) are so basic as to lend themselves to parody: learning to push, learning to pull. Learning to stand up without falling over? Life and social skills, intended by the MSC to be a core element of all YTS schemes, are widely regarded as a patronising slur on young people's personal qualities. Under this theme they are invited to improve their appearance, their interview techniques and their approach to authority. The implicit message is that their unemployment is their own fault, and the implicit promise is that they will thereby get a job (they will only of course compete better with the next young person for the same dwindling stock of jobs). 'That' as Phil Cohen puts it, 'is the savage presumption behind the humanistic idioms of social-and-life skilling' (Cohen, 1984, p.119).

The situation of black youth with regard to YTS has given rise to widespread concern. Young black people of course are discriminated against in the youth job market itself. In a study of the experience of black and white young people in the first five years after leaving school, Shirley Dex found, in the 1970s, that West Indian young women and young men encountered more difficulties and disadvantages in their transition from school to work and in the early years of employment than white young people. She found that West Indian girls in particular often responded to rebuffs by determinedly continuing to apply for jobs, by postponing marriage longer than white young women, and by getting more training and education. Yet all these efforts could not defeat prejudice and discrimination. They could not equalise their chances with those of white girls, only improve them relative to other black girls (Dex, 1982). More recently, in Coventry, white youngsters have been shown to be seven times as likely as Afro-Caribbean and three times as likely as Asian youth to get jobs on leaving school (West Midlands YTS Research Project, 1985). The pattern persists in YTS. MSC reports 'recruitment figures have steadily shown a fifteen percentage point gap between white and ethnic minority participation in Mode A schemes (Manpower Services Commission, 1986d).[2] No less than 40 per cent of Asian males and 51 per cent of Afro-Caribbean males as against 27 per cent of white males are clustered in Mode B in 1985/6. A report from the West Midlands confirms this picture in more detail, concluding that the underrepresentation of black young people in Mode A schemes is partly the result of discrimination by careers officers, managing agents and employers and partly the effect of the difference between YTS in different localities (West Midlands YTS Research Project, 1985). After YTS, about one in two white young people obtain work, but only one in three black young people. That this is only partly due to their relative absence from employer-based schemes, and mainly due to prejudiced recruitment, is shown by the fact that even among Mode A trainees, after YTS 68 per cent of whites find jobs, as against only 47 per cent of Afro - Caribbeans and 44 per cent of Asians (Manpower Services Commission, 1986d).

Finally, and most fundamentally, the MSC and its Youth Training Scheme are felt to weaken democratic control of training. MSC, a nominally non-government body and not directly controlled by Parliament, is being given increasing power over schools' curricula and non-advanced further education, at the expense of local education authorities. YTS employers, being free to shop for their off-the-job training in the cheapest market, can oblige further education colleges to compete with each other and with private training agencies (PTAs) to win their favours. It is estimated that 30 per cent of Mode A provision in YTS is by means of this new profit-motivated kind of training body. Studies have shown that many PTAs have dubious business records (NATFHE, 1984; West Midlands County Council, 1985).

The Scheme is in effect training by sub-contract to the private sector. 'YTS cannot be seen as a state training scheme. It is a scheme where privatisation of both training and administration is built in and will pose severe problems for teaching and civil service unions' (Allum and Quigley, 1983). The real deliverers of YTS are not MSC's Area Offices but over 100 000 'managing agents'. This was the only way the MSC could create such an enormous project so rapidly. Besides, it matched the Tory philosophy of market freedom. Paradoxically, however, control of this multitude of agencies brought into existence a highly centralised structure. Area Manpower Boards lack the power to impose a local character on their schemes. Expressions of independence by AMBs have been overruled by the MSC. Board members may not visit schemes unless accompanied by an MSC officer and must give notice in advance. Local authorities are limited by financial constraints imposed by central government in the extent to which they can themselves run high-quality schemes (Greater London Training Board, 1983).

Young people are virtually excluded from running and monitoring the Scheme. They are not represented on AMBs and there is no requirement on managing agents to involve trainees in the internal decision process of schemes. Very few do so (National Youth Bureau, 1984). The government has banned the inclusion of political material

in off-the-job training, specifically matters relating to 'the organisation or functioning of society'. It is cynical that MSC require the
inclusion of a training component they call 'life and social skills' while
defining this to exclude any exploration of the political and economic
processes young people are caught up in (Batsleer, 1985/6).

At the time of writing in the summer of 1986, MSC is embarking on
its expanded scheme, YTS-2. Many young people will now remain on
YTS from their sixteenth to their eighteenth birthday. In the second
year, though the training allowance will go up marginally (to £35) all
trainees are intended to be on employers' premises and so will in
effect be working for a 'wage' far below the cost of their own
maintenance. By cutting its funding of the training allowance MSC is
forcing approved training organisations to recoup part of the cost of
the Scheme from employers. This gives the MSC less authority to
impose requirements on employers concerning, for example, positive
action for black trainees and young women. Particularly worrying is
the increased financial pressure on the training workshops and
community projects that have developed in response to MSC's
funding under Mode B in past years. Many are expected to close
down. Others will be unable to afford education authority rates for off-
the-job training. The substitution for Mode B of 'premium places',
attached to the individual trainee shown to have special needs, is
invidious. It will be doubly insulting in that 'premium place' trainees
will undoubtedly be offered to employers at 'cut price' because of the
subsidy received for them from MSC. A further worry about the loss
of Mode B schemes is that, while they were less popular than Mode A
as being further removed from a 'proper job', they have demonstrated
themselves to be far more sensitive and forward-looking on matters of
race and sex (Edmond, 1986). It is widely believed that the effect of
YTS-2 will be to raise to 19 the age at which a young person is
expected to enter the labour market as a proper worker. MSC's aim
has been to change the arrangements within the Scheme, without
tackling its context. There is still no acknowledgement that the real
need is for more and better jobs for young people, and that no training
scheme can of itself create them.

In summary, then, there is a sizeable credibility gap between the
published aims and objectives of the Youth Training Scheme,
especially in the more liberal interpretation of the Youth Task Group
and the Youth Training Board, and the tough reality perceived by the
average trainee. Above all, YTS does not and cannot have any effect

on the real underlying evil: the lack of jobs for young people. Dan
Finn points out:

> By 1986 more than half of under-18-year-olds and a quarter of
> under-25-year-olds were unemployed. One in three young men aged
> 18 and 19 were without work. Over 600 000 under-25-year-olds
> had been unemployed for more than six months and just under
> 350 000 had been continuously out of work for more than a year.
> There were over 300 000 young adults who had never had a job
> since leaving school. It was these realities, and the quality of many
> YTS places, *not* young people's alleged idleness, which were
> seriously undermining the credibility of the Scheme and provoking
> the different reactions of young people to it. For many the YTS was
> a preparation for the dole, not a permanent bridge to work
> (Finn, 1987).

So clearly is the Youth Training Scheme deficient, so clearly is it an
instrument of a capitalist, racist and patriarchal state, that there are
frequent calls to boycott it altogether:

> The YTS is a class instrument, an integral part of the Tory strategy.
> Its purpose is to shape and cow the next generation of workers in the
> interest of high technology capitalism and as such it should be
> vigorously opposed by the whole labour movement (Scofield *et
> al.*, 1983).

A boycott position is difficult to justify in practice however. The
training system the NTI has replaced never served women – or black
people – well. The education system has always been élitist and
unfair. We cannot simply call for a return to the past. Besides, the
trainees and low-paid scheme workers would be unlikely to be
participating in YTS if they saw any better alternatives. Should they
be abandoned? There is a danger that to boycott YTS is to ignore the
real current problems of those most in need of training, while those
lucky enough to climb into and through the further and higher
education systems carry on unaffected. It would be for those in work
to write off those without work. If a Labour government is returned in
the late 1980s it will inevitably continue with some kind of a training
scheme for 16–18-year-olds. The important thing is to know how we
want that scheme to work.

This book is based on research that asked 'Is YTS perpetuating or is it counteracting sex divisions in work?' To ask such a question already carries us beyond a boycott position. If we have a detailed concern about the progress of young women in YTS we are already implicated in an analysis of how their position could be improved. Through the detailed examination of relations within YTS that follows, however, we need to be aware of the limits to reform. We are no longer anticipating, we are living within, a law-and-order state, the caring arm of which is being rapidly dismantled (Cole and Skelton, 1980). A person-centred and often voluntary provision for youth, oriented to individual growth and development, that with all its contradictions allowed some scope for progressive interpretations, has given way in the past ten years to a national state youth policy involving increased policy powers, greater stringency over social security benefit rules and even threats of compulsory 'community service' – a single-minded thrust to control and contain the young (Davies, 1986). It would be naive to see youth training provision except as it exists in that context.

Notes

1. The Further Education Unit exists to give curriculum leadership to the further education colleges. The 'new vocationalism' is necessarily in conflict with much that the FEU had come to represent in educational philosophy (Searle, 1984).
2. MSC's handling of racial definitions has been unsatisfactory. Its original fourfold classification system comprised: white European; Afro-Caribbean; Asian; other. The 'European' was then dropped and the first category became simply 'white'. Managing agents completing trainee 'start' forms with information about new recruits to YTS were instructed to complete the racial information in consultation with the trainee. It was intended that a group such as Greek, Turkish or Cypriot would be entered under 'white'. Many may have been entered under 'others'. Besides, the 'other' category was used by many managing agents wishing to resist categorising young people at all. From 1986 and in the context of YTS-2 the classification has been changed to: white; black/African/Caribbean; Indian sub-continent; none of these; 'I prefer not to say'.

2

Turned Sixteen

What is it like to be a 16-year-old school-leaver in London in the mid-1980s? I interviewed seventy-two young people, with all the inhibitions such interviews normally entail: the young have no place to call their own, and neither they nor you can feel at ease in the college canteen, the local Wimpy, the parents' front room or the manager's spare office. I also however spent days alongside many of them at college or in their training workshops and this filled out the picture.

In terms of family background, almost all these young people were working class. There was of course a difference between those from the inner-city area where my two workshop-based YTS schemes were located and the relatively suburban outer-London district from which the employer-based scheme drew its trainees. Even in the outer-London area, however, although there were one or two people who came from families with professional or managerial fathers, it was the norm to have a father who was a skilled or semi-skilled manual worker – a rather high proportion drove vehicles for a living. Mothers often had a part-time job in cleaning, cooking or office work. In the inner-city group there were more young people from single-parent families, and more with unemployed parents. Almost all the young people had been through the local comprehensive education system and normally it had been a mixed-sex school. Inner London however has a higher proportion of single-sex schools. In the inner city, too, there were more young people who had been to 'special' schools because of some family or physical problem.

There was a racial difference between the two groups of trainees. The suburban group were predominantly white: twenty-seven white, two Afro-Caribbean and no Asian trainees were interviewed. This reflected the composition of the population in these outer-London boroughs where less than one in ten is black (Afro-Caribbean or

Asian). In the inner city white and black were more evenly balanced. I interviewed twenty-four white, fifteen Afro-Caribbean and four Asian trainees. Again this reflects the nature of these inner-London boroughs where one in four or five of the population is black[1].

The interviews necessarily focused mainly on how the young people had come to be in their current placement on YTS and what they were feeling about it. But we covered other things too: school, home, hopes of work. A picture emerged of young people tentatively inhabiting an in-between world. What sociologists know as 'the transition' from school to work used to be no more than the sliding interface between the classroom and the workplace. Today government youth schemes have stretched it out to six months, then a year, now to two years. It is this limbo that YTS trainees inhabit. They are also of course in another kind of temporary space – since most of them will get married within a few years of leaving school. Consciousness of this other 'transition' was much sharper among the young women I interviewed than among the young men.

Seeing the back of school

So much of the literature on youth cultures shows young people at their most active and, in the case of 'the lads', necessarily also their most destructive. As Angela McRobbie has said:

> attention has been paid to young people in the school, on the dole and on the street, all sites where they are immediately visible to the social observer. This has had the effect of reducing the entire spectrum of young people's experience implicitly to these moments, neglecting almost totally those many times when they become viewers, readers, part of an audience or simply silent, caught up in their own daydream (McRobbie, 1984, p.141).

The young people I met on the Youth Training Scheme spent a lot of their spare time at home. Young women, particularly, passed their weekends more often than not watching TV or holed-up in their room, listening to music, playing with the dog or talking to a friend. Male pastimes were much more active than female. If a young man mentioned 'music' it was usually to play it. A young women meant listening to it. Very few of the young women from the outer suburbs mentioned sports, even fewer of those from the inner city. The young

men went out and about more, liked football, snooker and pool. Many
had motor bikes. No young woman in the study had the mobility or the
access to technology conferred by owning a motor bike. Few were
even regular riders of a pedal bike.[2]

However, the fury of male youth subcultures depicted by writers
like David Robins, Philip Cohen, Paul Corrigan and others, a
violence that resonates out of their book titles – *Knuckle Sandwich*,
Schooling the Smash Street Kids – was not burning through the
accounts of most of these young Londoners (Robins and Cohen,
1978; Corrigan, 1979). What my particular research focus brought to
light was a more hesitant set of youngsters, diligently picking their
way through the mess of hope and despair with which their elders have
landed them. Frank Coffield, Carol Borrill and Sarah Marshall who
spent time with young north-easterners, also in and out of 'govvy
schemes' like YTS, would have recognised this lot (Coffield *et al.*,
1986). Some nastiness, yes. A bitter distaste for independent women
surfaced in a few of the young men, a subterranean racism in some
whites. But any muscling bravado among the 'lads' seemed
compounded with a kind of innocence and disquiet.

Despite a good show of courage, most of these 16-year-olds felt
apprehensive, anxious to prove themselves adult, worried about not
getting a job, worried about how they would hold one down if they did.
Of course it is great not to be driven by legal compulsion to school
each day. It is a relief not to have to tramp those crowded corridors,
rattling up and down the familiar concrete stairs, in and out of the
same old classrooms. It is something not to have to choose between a
draughty playground and smelly toilets for a quiet chat. And as one
walked out of the gates for the last time it was a relief to have escaped
for a moment from an environment where authority and control are
the rigid backbone of social relations between young people and
adults, where 'having a laugh' is always at risk of exploding into blame
and punishment. One long school holidays: 'Me? I couldn't wait to
get out'.

There are losses though. The patterns of friendship until now have
been organised round school and the school playground, round
nearby chippies and the local tobacconist. Now everyone is going
different ways, some staying on, some hanging about home all day,
the luckier ones going to the 'tech' or, luckier still, to a job. To meet up
with friends you used to see every day, now, you have to make an
arrangement. 'I felt glad to go' one young man said in interview, 'My

mates all left. But now we'd all of us rather be back there.' Others said, 'At first I was pleased to leave. But then you miss all the laughs.' Some were already regretting failed exams: 'I wish I could do it again and put right all my mistakes. I wasn't listening and was always wondering what to do next and generally fooling about.' 'I wish I could go back right now. Because I wasted most of my time. I wasted a lot of time. And now, my little brother, I've told him not to do what I done, which was to come out of school with no qualifications.'

When you leave school, which has been a home of sorts for ten years, home itself becomes more important. For all the stories of runaway teenagers and conflict with parents, most 16-year-olds are close to parents, especially to mothers. Besides, few have any immediate hope of leaving home. This is a class-specific reality. For young working-class people in London there is no question of flat-sharing with mates. That, if it exists at all today, with the precipitous decline in private rented accommodation, sky-high rents, and a tightening-up of the squatting laws, is for older and better-off young people. As David Robins and Phil Cohen have pointed out, the scope of youthful independence falls on:

> [a] fundamental class divide. On one side, those who embrace studenthood, accept continued wageless dependence, on their families or State grants, and whose struggle is for *a place of their own to be who they like in*. On the other, those who take for granted the fact of continued domestic dependence, because their target is *a wage of their own to do what they like with* . . . They use their wage to buy substitutes for the thing they lack (Robins and Cohen, 1978, p.9).

For the YTS generation of 1985 the only way to a home of your own is the interminable Council list, only effectively speeded on by a pregnancy. Meanwhile, what they want is less to leave home than to move into a new relationship to it, to contribute financially, to pay their way and get some respect for that.

Gendered experiences: school

Early years at home and school are a profoundly differentiating experience for girls and boys. 'It all starts' as one adult in this study put it, 'with the colour of the Baby-gro.' By three or four, children have learned an appropriately gendered way of playing, dealing with adults and peers, responding to life's ups and downs: girls cry, boys grin and bear it. There are few schools that do not use a distinction between male and female as a protocol for organisation: girls and boys form different queues in the canteen, wear different uniforms, use different playgrounds and play different sports.

A survey in 1975 of the curricular differences of girls and boys found that traditional assumptions about the 'proper' sphere of the sexes were being worked out through the curricular patterns of secondary schools. It found acceptance for these patterns by the majority of teachers, parents and pupils. The authors warned 'a society that needs to develop to the full the talents and skills of all its people will find the discrepancies disturbing' (Department of Education and Science, 1975). In the same year an independent study of 1204 pupils in nineteen secondary schools in different areas of England found the sexual distribution so marked that they wrote of 'gendered' subjects. 'Male' subjects were chemistry, geography, maths, physics, handicraft and technical crafts. 'Female' subjects were art, language, biology, history, music and housecraft (Ormerod, 1975).

A skewed distribution of sex to subject is still apparent in national statistics of education today, as we saw in Chapter 1, and it was reflected in the school history of the young trainees I interviewed. In London schools (those of the Inner London Education Authority particularly) it has become common to require youngsters of both sexes to take both the 'male' handicraft subjects and 'female' domestic subjects in the first three years of secondary education. Once the option system takes over for the fourth and fifth years however very few pupils indeed opt for the 'wrongly'-gendered subject. 'When we was at school they did encourage people to do, like, opposite options' said one trainee, 'Like, boys to do child-care. None of them did!' Talking of metal-work and carpentry one young woman told me 'We did them for first and second year. I think it was good to have an opportunity to have a go. It was something different. But I didn't get on all that well with it. Some girls do. But I didn't. I wouldn't have taken it after.'

Beyond subject choice there is the 'hidden curriculum' of school, which again operates to the detriment of girls. It is there even in primary school where:

teachers tailor the subject content of lessons to boys through the ostensibly non-sexist curricula, through the use of linguistic sexism, through preferences for pupils by sex and through the link between the criteria for according status and sex-appropriate behaviour (Clarricoates, 1978, p.353).

Almost all the adults I met in connection with the YTS study pointed to schools as the main source of gender-stereotyping. Many believed that teachers, and parents too, still push young women one way, young men another, regardless of their individual abilities or bents. Few however pointed to that other pressure to conform that the opposite sex itself – the presence of boys in the system – exerts on girls. Many studies now show that gender polarisation in choice of subjects is greater in co-educational than in single-sex schools. The DES survey cited above showed that while girls-only schools were less likely to offer subjects such as physics and chemistry, when they did so the proportion of girls who took the subjects and passed them was higher than in mixed schools (Department of Education and Science, 1975; and see also Shaw, 1980; Sarah *et al.*, 1980; Arnot, 1983; Deem, 1984; and Mahony, 1985). This of course is partly due to the way teachers and educational administrations structure different kinds of school, but it is also partly due to the *relations* between girls and boys and between girls and male teachers. Katherine Clarricoates has shown how interactions between teachers and pupils and between pupils themselves, even in primary school, are 'suffused with notions of gender'. She concluded 'it is increasingly evident that boys are able to dictate classroom life to their own advantage... pupils are "ordering their own world" on the basis of gender and do, in fact, exert some influence on their teachers' (Clarricoates, 1978, p.363).

   In an older group of A-level pupils, too, Michelle Stanworth found classroom relations to be marginalising girls and reproducing gender inequality. Looking at girls and boys, side by side in the same liberal arts subjects, she found that:

girls may follow the same curriculum as boys – may sit side by side with boys in classes taught by the same teachers – and yet emerge from school with the implicit understanding that the world is a man's world, in which women can and should take second place (Stanworth, 1981, p.58).

...understanding that it's a man's world

Maths of course is crucial, since most scientific and technical work and even business careers today demand maths qualification. No-one may drop out of this subject before the end of the fifth year of secondary education, but the grades achieved heavily determine future career possibilities. It had long been assumed that though girls were as good or better than boys at maths in primary school, they 'fell off' in secondary school. Rosie Walden and Valerie Walkerdine found that, even more disturbingly, girls continued to do better than boys to the fourth year of secondary school, yet fewer were being put in for O-levels. They concluded that gender enters into the way boys and girls are assessed by teachers. In particular, girls cannot retain feminine characteristics (be helpful, kind or pretty, for instance) and show, or be assessed as showing, the sharp and challenging approach to maths supposed necessary for success in the subject. The girls strive 'to achieve a femininity which (nonetheless) possesses the characteristics which are the target of teachers' pejorative evaluations' (Walden and Walkerdine, 1985, p.104). The girls are in a double bind that we will recognise again in YTS. The need they feel

for a recognised gender identity is incompatible with serious achievement in a worthwhile and marketable subject.

To understand the performance of girls, as these authors argue, we
have to see how it is produced and evaluated. Precisely the same
applies, of course, to the performance of different races. The authors
of a book on black women's experience of life in Britain write:

> for Black schoolgirls sexism has, it is true, played an insidious role
> in our lives. It has influenced our already limited career choices and
> has scarred our already tarnished self-image. But it is racism which
> has determined the schools we can attend and the quality of the
> education we receive in them. Consequently this has been the most
> significant influence on our experience of school and society
> (Bryan *et al.*, 1985, p.58).

The hidden curriculum is at work again here. They claim that
teachers' attitudes have done lasting damage to black children's self-
image by denying the validity of their own culture and experience.
Teachers have tended to interpret black children's disorientation and
bewilderment in the face of a negation of their world as a sign of
stupidity. The education system has been a problem to black children,
but it is they who have been treated as a problem by the educational
system. As a result, 'in just over twenty years the British education
system has succeeded only in entrenching our position at the bottom
of the ladder of employability' (Bryan *et al.*, 1985, p.81).

Gendered experiences: domestic life

While the school timetable from nine till three have been giving
teenagers one set of experiences, the surrounding hours of the day
have been affording a parallel set. In a sense, like adult women, girls
do a double shift. They interact as females with males not only in the
mixed-sex school but in the mixed-sex home, where their experience
is again different from, and partly formed by, that of their brothers. At
quite a young age working-class girls are familiar with child care, look
after little sisters and brothers, baby-sit for relatives. They are adept
at many household tasks, know how to shop in the cheapest places
and how to prepare food for the family. They know about washing

clothes and cleaning the house or flat. On the other hand, unlike their brothers, they have seldom been allowed or encouraged to have access to tools or to perform maintenance tasks on buildings or vehicles. Christine Griffin has shown how girls may resent having to do domestic work but nonetheless do it, and often use this as a reasonable excuse to miss classes at school (Griffin, 1985; see also Coffield *et al.*, 1986). Among her young women it was rare to find fathers and brothers contributing to household work. It was accepted that brothers might 'just lie around doing nothing, watching the tele all day'. When boys and men did help out in the home, 'their activities were judged against an assumed baseline of nothing... women's work in the home was taken for granted as normal' (Griffin, 1985, p.38).

There appears to be little change over time in the attitudes to home, marriage and children expressed by either sex. There was no evidence in my interviews that Sex Discrimination laws, a world-wide women's movement or the high incidence of unemployment were making boys re-evaluate their relation to the home. I asked adults too – YTS managers, teachers supervisors and careers officers – for their perception of young people's attitudes to domestic life. They confirmed 'boys are only interested in themselves'. 'Boys are just as sexist as they ever were, really.' Girls though they expect and want to work, do not appear to be rebelling against marriage. 'For some of those for whom education has had little benefit, they find a security in marriage. They are not ashamed to say so. They are quite pleased. It does give them something.' Few girls appear to be thinking in terms of committing themselves to an uninterrupted, life-long career. 'Very few. Maybe none. It's provisional, until they marry.'

Unemployment, which after all is experienced now by both sexes the week after leaving school, is also differentiating young men from young women.

Something happens to young women when they become unemployed that doesn't happen to young men. If they've ever come out of traditional roles, they are forced back into them at an alarming rate by the fact of unemployment. That's what happens. Back into the family. They are required to perform all sorts of duties in the household that young men – it doesn't happen to them. Looking after young siblings, collecting them from school, that sort of thing.

Gendered experiences: a conflict of desires

For the YTS trainees with whom I talked, leaving school had of course meant expectations of a new relationship to the outside world: the street. When it comes to it, however, life on the street is a laugh only as long as you have the right clothes to wear, the weather is fine and you have a fiver in your purse or pocket to give you access to the burger joint or under-age drinking in the pub. 'The key to the freedom of the working-class city is not a birthright, not for free, because the key is still the wage' (Robins and Cohen, 1978, p.8). A YTS training allowance of £27.50, of which perhaps £10 went to parents for 'keep', was not allowing this group of working-class young people much scope for self-expression.

The experience of outdoor life is, in any case, sharply differentiated by race and by sex. Public places do not afford the same kinds of freedom to young women as they afford to young men. It was not only lack of money that made the young women I interviewed rarely list 'dancing' among their pastimes, for instance. Many were rightly cautious, or had parents who were reluctant to give them much freedom to take risks. Male violence against women is a very real danger, with instances of sexual assault continuously increasing. Again, to be Asian on the streets, in a widespread atmosphere of white racial hatred, was very differnt from being white. Reports were showing that anti-Asian racism had now spread from the older Asian ghetto of the East End to the newer suburban communities, including the one from which many of these trainees came. In Chris Griffin's study she found that a black young women among whites, even of the same age and sex, could not necessarily feel secure. 'Some young white women saw verbal abuse and even physical attacks on local black people as an integral part of their leisure activities, and a potential source of entertainment' (Griffin, 1985, p.69). So young black women often have to deal with both racial and sexual violence. White young men frequently administer both, and while women may occasionally be a source of fear to other women, women are not a source of fear to men: that is a significant difference.

At the end of their last term at school, young people find themselves in the long-anticipated job market. What that means for girls, as contrasted with boys, is discussed in the next chapter. Both in and out of school however young women are busy handling another set of deals: those of what might be called the 'romance market'. The relations of the two markets intersect and bear on each other.

To say that girls are preoccupied with 'romance' is not simply to perpetuate an old slander. There are by now many studies of teenage girls which detail the obligatory and demanding nature of hetero-sexual culture, the extent to which girls are compelled to devote their energies and skills to competing and 'succeeding' in the sexual sphere and the adverse effect this has on their education and vocational achievement. Anne Stafford carried out five months of participant observation in a Youth Opportunities Programme training centre in Edinburgh. Although it pre-dated the Youth Training Scheme, the situation was very similar to that of many trainees in my study. Boys were in their 'male trades' workshops, girls in traditional women's areas. The boys were dedicated to the search for meaningful work. 'Real jobs as painters and decorators was what the boys wanted most in the world.' In the male workshops therefore 'boys created them-selves and were created as hard real men with hard real jobs. The franticness and desperation they created around this was also manifest in other aspects of their lives.' Within the culture of the boys' workshops, girls were the subject of collective abuse. They were in effect part of the raw material used in males' relationships with each other. 'In all the time I was with the boys' wrote Anne Stafford, 'I do not think I ever heard a girl discussed in terms of anything other than her appearance or as an object of sex. Girls as people were never mentioned' (Stafford, 1986, p.128).

The girls in their knitwear workshop, for their part, could get no sense of 'meaningful work'. Reckoned by the experience of mothers, sisters and friends, women's work was bound to be boring, irrelevant and without a future. The only escape route from their impoverished lives and dismal prospects, perceived by these working-class girls was attachment to a man. In so far as they thought about a job it was not valued for its own sake but in pursuit of a glamorous life and world. They dreamed not of a knitwear factory but of a hairdressing salon or a smart office. But even such work was seen instrumentally. 'The franticness the girls felt about their lives was transferred, not on to a desperation about jobs but, all too predictably, onto feelings of desperation about boys, boy-friends and relationships.' The sad truth however is that boys and girls are brought up to want very different things of the opposite sex. 'Boys want to score, girls want stable relationships.' In organising their lives and hopes around love, the girls were destined for disillusionment. They might achieve engagement and marriage, but trouble lay ahead: their male counterparts were by no means committed to these things in the same way as the girls (Stafford, 1986).

This Edinburgh study shows how class-consciousness is modified and distorted by gender. The girls were every bit as rebellious, enterprising and assertive in their resistance to the YOP workshop regime as the boys. But unlike boys' lives:

> girls' lives are created out of an early definition and acceptance of themselves as less than boys. They are at the bottom of every power hierarchy. All the forces of capital, the state, patriarchy... bear down on these (as yet) strong and independent girls, creating and recreating daily feelings of failure, stupidity and worthlessness, which eventually lock them into both a lifetime of meaningless work (and unemployment) and into a lifetime of dependence on men (Stafford, 1986, p.233).

Anne Stafford's study was set in the uniformly-white Scottish culture of Edinburgh. In other cultures the exact nature of the interaction between job market and marriage market varies. Chris Griffin from her experience of young women in the Midlands suggests, for instance, that Asian and Afro-Caribbean girls do not experience pressures to get a boy-friend to the same degree as whites, and they can besides draw on stronger cultural traditions of female friendship (Griffin, 1985, p.62). Statistics show that Afro-Caribbean women are more likely to continue to work full-time throughout their lives than white women, though in worse jobs. The pattern is very different for Asian girls, however. They are less caught up in the pressures to 'find a boy-friend' precisely because that is often undertaken for them by the family. For them marriage in fact bears even more heavily on their relationship to the job market. Amrit Wilson writes 'once an Asian girl has finished school, whether she is Hindu, Muslim or Sikh, the threat or prospect of marriage begins to loom over her, casting a blight over her chances of further education' – or of a worthwhile working career (Wilson, 1978, p.100; see also Westwood, 1984, on Asian women in work and marriage).

In subsequent chapters, as we follow the progress of young women and men on the Youth Training Scheme we will continually be forced to remember the significance of sexuality. It is not just the simple fact of sex, the existence of male and female; nor is it just the cultural phenomenon of gender that is important in the lives of 16- and 17-year-olds. It is actively sexual relationships. Sexual relations are not merely physical, they are cultural and gendered. Gender relations are thus a powerful link between the different phases of an individual's life: they mesh her (or his) relationship to production, to consumption, to recreation, to love and desire into a seamless fabric. Getting and maintaining an appropriate gender identity goes on within all these spheres. It goes on at home, on the street or the dance-floor, and it goes on at work. Success or failure in this respect in one sphere embellishes or tarnishes one's image and chances in others.

Sue Lees, in her book on adolescent girls' sexuality, points to the idea of 'reputation' as a key factor in a girl's gender identity. She demonstrates, with painful evidence, how girls are effectively policed (and obliged by the masculine ideology in which they live to police themselves and each other) by the threat of being labelled and dismissed as tight or promiscuous, as 'drag' or 'slag'. Whatever her actual behaviour, a girl is always at risk of being termed a 'slag' so long as she is not attached to a young man as girlfriend, fiancée or wife (Lees, 1986). Amrit Wilson adds to this picture:

> the idea that a girl's reputation is important is almost universal, but for Asian girls it is not just important; 'reputation' is the bane of their lives from adolescence to the early years of their marriage. It controls everything they do and adds a very terrible danger to any unconventional action (Wilson, 1978, p.103).

The effect of this ideology is to limit the expression of women's own sexuality to the confines of marriage. Girls do not necessarily have any illusions about marriage, but they see no alternative.

Beyond 'slag' and 'drag' of course is another damaging label that can be attached to the girl who steps out of line: that of lesbian. It appears that it is only since the emergence of the new women's movement and active politicised lesbianism in the 1970s that 'lezzie' has become a term of abuse in school culture. Now 'lezzie' has joined 'poofter' in the lexicon of insults used in classroom and playground. The universal slur on lesbians drives homosexual feelings under-ground, makes attachment to men compulsory and makes close and enduring friendships between girls difficult. In learning a man's trades and skills, working in a male workplace alongside men, young women take a dual risk. If they are seen to be there 'for the boys' they will be

Wanting different things

labelled slag. If they disregard the boys and show aptitude for the work they will be labelled lesbian. In a world where feminine gender-identity is a large part of a working woman's stock-in-trade 'a man's job' for all the advantages it might promise in the long run is a social hazard.

Not categories but relations

Since the early 1970s flourishing literature on subcultures has developed that throws light on these aspects of the lives of young people. In a seminal essay by John Clarke and others culture was defined as:

> the peculiar and distinctive way of life of the group or class, the meanings, values and ideas embodied in institutions, in social relations, in systems of beliefs, in mores and customs in the uses of objects and material life... the 'maps of meaning' that make things intelligible to its members (Clarke *et al.*, 1975, p.10).

They suggested that culture embodies the trajectory of group life through history: always under conditions and with raw materials which cannot wholly be of its own making. The book from which this extract was taken was, it so happened, a study of *youth* subcultures. This was a concept that had gained importance in post-war Britain as the older generation of a ruling class began to be disturbed by a new phenomenon: Mods, Rockers and Teds (Hall and Jefferson, 1975). A concern with youth was consonant with the way subcultural studies focused on divisiveness in society. 'A complex society involves various subgroups and subcultures in a struggle for the legitimacy of their behaviour, values and life-style against the dominant culture of the dominant class' (Brake, 1980, p.6). Subculture represented 'a challenge to hegemony' on the part of a class or, of course, a race and, as it would eventually turn out, a sex (Hebdige, 1979).

Tacked onto the early collections of essays on youth subcultures were occasional tentative discordant complaints by women about women's silence in the (hegemonic) male monotone of the subculture discourse. Angela McRobbie and Jenny Garber called for an explanation. If girls were not there, perhaps they were somewhere else? 'Marginality of girls in the active male-focused leisure subcultures of working-class youth may tell us less than the strongly present position of girls in . . . "complementary" but more passive subcultures' (McRobbie and Garber, 1975, p.211). A genre of subcultural work on girls and young women began to be published (McRobbie, 1978 and 1984; Walkerdine, 1984; Winship, 1985; Griffin, 1985). Eventually it became possible to deal with both female and male within the scope of the same research without subordinating the one to the other. Frank Coffield, Carol Borrill and Sarah Marshall for instance, in their work on young people in the north-east, write about the lives of young women and young men without giving primacy to the men (Coffield *et al.*, 1986).

Something is still missing however from the subcultural analysis of youth and its absence continues to weaken our purchase on the main issues here: occupational choice and the separation of the sexes in training and work. We need a conception of male and female sub-cultures as related, two facets of a single unitary phenomenon. Just as masculine and feminine are complementary parts of a single gender system, so girls' and boys' subcultures are in reality only two aspects of one subculture, with different implications for the sexes. It was fair enough to propose that girls' culture was *not* merely marginal to that of boys: girls too had something going for them and what girls did and thought and felt was cultural and specific. But it is not enough to interpolate a 'girls' subculture'. Girls lived lives that were complementary to, in relation to, and mutilated by, those of 'the lads'. We need to understand young *men*'s culture as gendered, relational and entailing a certain form of femininity.[3] It is sometimes suggested that, through the subculture of femininity, girls and women 'contribute to their own oppression'. They do not. What contributes to their oppression is living on the dark side of a gendered youth subculture, male-dominated and male-advantaging.

We need concepts that recognise, besides, that much of what young women and young men do can be explained as dealing with, modifying or resisting definitions threatened by the opposite sex, within an overall rampant culture of heterosexuality. This is not to say that women's definitions have an equal valency to those of men, but that women are not entirely passive. The social construction of gender is riddled with resistance and the resistance itself is complex. While some boys may refuse the macho mode of masculinity and pay the price of being scorned as 'a wimp' or 'a poofter', others resist the class-domination of school precisely by means of masculine codes (Willis, 1977; Corrigan, 1979; Connell *et al.*, 1982). For girls, too, the possibilities are contradictory. Some use femininity itself (makeup, stylish or outlandish clothes) as a form of resistance to school and class authority. Janice Winship, analysing the new wave of young women's magazines, points out that many of the images today, stylish though they are, reflect something new happening among young women:

> They express less the customary passive sexuality of women than an assertive strength... Maybe it isn't a sexuality which wholly breaks free from oppressive codes of women as sexual commodities, but neither does it straightforwardly reproduce them (Winship, 1985, p.25).

There is an alternative strategy available to girls however, that rejects glamour altogether. It is an active resistance which undermines conventional femininity and challenges girls' subordination (Connell *et al.*, 1982, p.178). Girls are continually testing out the boundaries of their confinement to get a sense of their possible power. We will see how one way girls have of doing this is to refuse 'women's work' and women's domestic roles and make a bid for 'men's work' and a space for women in men's world.

Notes

1. Figures for the racial composition of borough populations are drawn from the *London Labour Plan* (Greater London Council, 1986, p.106). Within the category 'black' this source appears to include Afro-Caribbean and Asian.
2. This sex difference in leisure activities is confirmed by Griffin (1986).
3. Sue Lees has suggested that 'by avoiding the analysis of gender relations in the subcultural literature on boys, only a partial picture emerges of girls' social world' (Lees, 1984, p.17). What is happening in the study of youth subcultures moves in parallel with what has happened in the study of labour processes. First, men studied men only and without consideration of gender. Then women interpolated the study of women, introducing concepts of gender. Only later did women (and finally also men) start to study men at work, now seeing them with gendered eyes as gendered creatures, having an effect on and being affected by women (Cockburn, 1983 and 1985; Game and Pringle, 1983).

3
Settling for the Youth Training Scheme

Among all the trainees I met there was a sense of urgency about getting work, a pervasive fear of long-term unemployment. In the background was often a parent who, though superficially sympathetic, was showing at a deeper level mistrust and alarm. 'My dad said he wouldn't stand for a useless layabout'. Things are profoundly different for this generation from the school-to-work transition their parents experienced. The delay until 1973 in raising the school-leaving age to sixteen was precisely because of a hungry demand on the part of employers for young workers. Nor was the work available only unskilled work. It was generally believed 'that a vast untapped pool of ability existed among working-class youngsters and this ability had to be released to meet the needs of the economy for up-skilled labour' (Finn, 1987). In the 1960s, even the early 1970s, you could flout stuffy convention by choosing to reject work. No-one today can see something meritorious in being on the dole. The renegade status of 'drop-out' is one more thing that has been stolen from the young.

One source of worry to the trainees was their generally poor results in school-leaving exams. Of the trainees in the employer-based scheme few had more than one or two O-level passes and a little clutch of CSEs. Those in the workshop schemes had at best two or three CSEs in the 'pass' grades. They may have had a go at many more but while they might remember the subjects (with some bitterness!) they had not always bothered to go and find out what grades they had received.

Reflecting on school within a few months of leaving, almost all the YTS trainees with whom I talked could remember having had a clear idea of what they 'wanted to do with their lives'. In many cases this idea had been forming while they were still quite young, but in most it had been considerably sharpened by an impending encounter with careers advisers in the fourth year of secondary school. Relatively few of them now, on YTS, were training for work they had once aspired to do. In one of the workshops, for instance, there were trainees who had had ambitions ranging from 'being an artist', or 'in acting', to 'working in a bank' or 'working with children'. But judging by the section of the workshop in which they had settled, only six of the twenty-four appeared now to be pursuing their original aim. The others had all been deflected, had changed their minds, or had simply 'been brought to their senses' in the light of their school-leaving-exam results. Particularly embittering was the failure of those young women who had wanted to train for work with children. They were certainly destined to spend a good deal of their lives looking after their *own* children. Yet the continually more rigorous entry standards for training courses for this kind of work meant they had no chance of a professional career in it. Instead they were doing cooking or typing. Even within the stereotype of women's work, these young women had had to scale down their aspirations to accord with their class status. Similarly one young woman had talked with friends and concluded 'even if everyone's on about being an air hostess I thought "Oh no, they're just living in a dream world". It's so difficult to get into'.

Dreamers or realists, all alike had now been levelled to the Youth Training Scheme. Some were ashamed of it and saw it as a stop-gap till work should turn up. Some of the luckier ones in the employer-based suburban scheme were in YTS places that were actually jobs, with security and a wage. These however were a minority in this study and are not typical at all of YTS nationally. For most the YTS placement was strictly instrumental, a possible foot in the door to future employment. An FE teacher said of her trainees 'They're really not interested in getting further qualification. If they have a job they're content'. One young man felt demoralised because he had been promised in advance of leaving school 'a proper job in the City'. When he presented himself to take it up he had been told they now had no vacancies. 'It shot me down like a bullet' he said.

The desire for real work was partly the urgent wish for an independent wage. Money was specially important because the work to which this particular bunch of early school-leavers can aspire is normally routine, repetitive, low-paid and heavily subordinated to supervision. It is not work that is generous in the status and self-image it affords. Such activities may have been acceptable as a Saturday job or an evening stint, but they become intolerable when they are done for eight hours a day, five days a week. It has been a commonplace in the sociology of transition that young people change their jobs frequently in the first year or two out of school, even today (Veness, 1962; West and Newton, 1983). The fact should be laid at the door not of youthful irresponsibility but of employers who create labour processes that are impossible to carry on for any sustained period without physical or psychic damage. One young woman said 'I wanted to leave and start work but there are times you get down at work. I get fed up being told what to do, like a dogsbody. I thought "Oh, I wish I was at school".' YTS trainees are, for the moment, in suspension between the degradation and boredom of being unemployed, and the exploitation and boredom of the dead-end jobs that have traditionally been allotted to the working-class young, even in the guise of apprenticeship.

The sham of 'choice'

Today the early theories of 'occupational choice' have a quaint look to them. Born into post-war prosperity they seem to reflect the naiveté of a period that had forgotten unemployment, forgotten the dictatorial directiveness of war, and almost forgotten class inequality. Sex inequalities were certainly pushed well out of sight. Eli Ginzberg, the founding-father of what quickly became a flourishing genre within psychology and sociology, held occupational choice to be 'the result of a compromise, rationally determined'. Each young person, he said, developed through three stages – by means of 'fantasy', to 'tentative' and eventually to 'realistic' occupational choices (Ginzberg *et al.*, 1946). The notion of optimisation that he introduced had a ring of those positive theories of management decision-making that post-war American business was just then pioneering. Donald Super, taking up Ginzberg's 'developmental' theory, saw the vocational compromise as a psychological process, the outcome of reaching a satisfactory 'self-concept' (Super, 1953 and 1957). While later theorists tentatively introduced the notion of constraint and realism (Blau *et al.*, 1963) and began to recognise that not only individual wishes but also 'settings' and 'roles' influence choice (Psathas, 1968), the literature remained open to the criticism of appearing to reflect the experience solely of a relatively privileged white middle class, whose sons could play the job market with confidence.[1]

As the 1970s brought the shock of oil crisis, a deceleration of economic growth and an embittering of class relations, it became impossible to ignore certain 'external social influences and institutions which might play a crucial role in canalizing people toward one occupational stream or another and therefore in affecting the overall distribution of persons between occupations' (Williams, 1974). A class 'reality principle' in occupational choice was now beginning to be emphasised, picking up on earlier class studies of adolescents (for instance Himmelweit *et al.*, 1952; and Ford, 1969). Eventually the work of Kenneth Roberts, examining a careers service on which the 'developmental' theorists had had considerable influence, stated baldly that the emperor was naked: choice can hardly be seen as central to outcomes if individuals rarely get what they want (Roberts, 1972, 1975 and 1980). Systems of qualification and certification, the structure of local labour and job markets and even 'socialisation in the workplace' (what you could expect to become by following the occupation of a professional, a manual worker) are causal factors in occupational segregation. Roberts marked a shift from a concern with 'supply-side' factors in occupational decisions to 'demand-side' factors. Recent data bear out Roberts' contention. Michael West and Peggy Newton, in a recent longitudinal study of transition, have shown that the reasons given for taking jobs are very different from those given for choosing jobs. Young people ending up in occupations different from those they had 'chosen' while still at school gave reasons that were 'overwhelmingly biased in the direction of forced choice . . . desperation was the reason for their decision to take a different job' (West and Newton, 1983).

Constraints on girls

When women first entered the studies of occupational choice and school-to-work transition, their choices were recorded but neither questioned nor doubted. 'It is girls only who show desires to serve others, to be missionaries, to help others, to repay parents for their sacrifices and so on; and only girls speak of working with animals', wrote Joan Maizels, and accepted it as normal (Maizels, 1970). Often in these accounts the adolescent is 'he' throughout, so that it comes as a shock on closer acquaintance to find that one is called Susan, another Annette (Hill and Scharff, 1976).

Sex-stereotyping was increasingly difficult to ignore however as studies began to show children and youth at all ages from pre-school to the university demonstrating an acute gender-consciousness and differentiation (Rauta and Hunt, 1975; Sharpe, 1976; Nemerowicz, 1979; and Pitcher and Schultz, 1983). In the past few years feminist work on schools and transitions has begun to explore and fill out in a more satisfactory way the complicated reality of gender and class in which young people are formed and within which they act. This work has shown how even 8-year-olds envisage occupational choices that are appropriate for both their class and gender (Dahlberg and Holland, 1984). It shows that while working-class girls can imagine themselves as boys doing 'men's work', their male peers refuse to envisage themselves as girls doing 'women's work' (Holland and Varnava-Skouras, 1979; Sharpe, 1976). Research has demonstrated that the older the child grows, the more stereotyped becomes her or his choice (Chisholm, 1984). The reality principle, it seems, tightens

Women's work – how genuine a choice?

over time. Analysing the social relations in Australian schools, R. W. Connell and his co-researchers concluded:

Class and gender don't just occur jointly in a situation. They abrade, inflame, amplify, twist, negate, dampen and complicate each other. In short they interact vigorously, often through the schools, and often with significant consequences for schooling (Connell *et al.*, 1982, p.182).

Intersecting with a consciousness of class and gender, very early in life, a consciousness of race and racist hierarchy is also at work. Children of black ethnic groups soon learn that not all the jobs open to white working-class children are deemed to be appropriate for themselves. Asian girls see their mothers confined to working in laundries and factories; Afro-Caribbean girls see theirs limited to the lower ranks of the Health Service, cooking school dinners and working on buses and tubes (Brooks and Singh, 1978; Lee *et al.*, 1982; and Brah and Golding, 1983 are all cited in this connection by Griffin, 1985). A consciousness of racial identity and difference itself can be positive of course. Mary Fuller's work with Afro-Caribbean fifth-formers in a London comprehensive identified a group of girls making a positive identification with being both black and female. They were committed to study and achievement in a way that showed their group self-identity had allowed them to escape from the ideology that so often leads working-class girls to 'fail' at school, because they reject education as snobbish (Fuller, 1980).

All the young people in my study had been put through the hoop of formulating an 'occupational choice'. They had had group discussions with careers teachers. They had had an individual interview. By the end of their fifth year almost everyone had worked up some plausible answer to the continual adult questions: 'What do you want to do for a living?' 'What will you do when you leave school?' For girls, one of the factors that had determined the 'choice' was their experience of domestic work at home. It had developed certain skills in them that remained undeveloped or atrophied in their male peers. On the other hand it had failed to develop certain practical technical skills that boys had developed. In short it was contributing substantially to the 'supply-side' causes of sex-segregation. Finally, it had developed expectations (even if it had also developed resentments) about a woman's future role as mother and housewife. It had contributed one term of the contradiction all these young women were experiencing: they knew it was important to 'have a career' but they also knew it would prove difficult to sustain one and that its interruption must be anticipated and accepted. Christine Eden and Keith Aubrey, interviewing young people in the south-west in connection with their YTS decisions reported that:

> differences in perceptions and expectations held by boys and girls in relation to the labour market are directly rooted in their respective views of their future role in child care and domestic labour. These views affected the scheme chosen and the dedication to the work associated with it... Their expectations of work are fundamentally tied to and built upon a view of themselves which is rooted in their expectations of their place in the sexual division of labour in the home. The extent to which this creates the framework within which all other decisions are taken cannot be overestimated (Eden and Aubrey, 1986).

The occupational decisions made by the trainees I interviewed had been far more effective negatively than positively. If a girl or boy at school had said 'I'll never work in a factory' or 'I couldn't stand to work in an office', they had normally managed at least to steer clear of this fate. Far less common was to find someone who had said, specifically, 'I really want to be... a nurse, an apprentice engineer, an artist' who had been able to make YTS the first step in this kind of a career. Over and over again I heard of aspirations, even quite modest hopes, that had been abandoned because of the widening gap as school-leaving exams became more competitive and the level of qualifications demanded as the base line for many kinds of training rose ever upwards.

Young people's perceptions of the world of work are very acute. Most of the trainees in my study had had experience of waged work while still at school. They had done paper rounds, casual work in their mothers' places of work, Saturday jobs in local shops, baby-sitting for friends. In his study of fifth-year pupils at school in the West Midlands Dan Finn found that 75 per cent had experience of part-time work and of these 60 per cent had held more than one job (Finn, 1984). Holding part-time jobs increases the information available from adult workers already in the labour market. Robins and Cohen describe a typical young male Londoner:

This lad knew what to expect on the shop floor long before he ever got there from his dad, his dad's workmates, his older brothers and their friends. He could judge his school experience against that measure because he was connected to the informal labour exchange, which circulates information not just about the jobs going, but wages and conditions, what are the good and bad firms to work for, as part of the local grape vine of the working-class city (Robins and Cohen, 1978).

What we have discussed here are the 'supply' and 'demand' factors in the distribution of young people to different kinds of training and work, and the interaction between them. A knowledge of what jobs employers will offer women penetrates back into the schools to limit what school-leavers will ask for. What they do not aspire to they will not get, and that in turn confirms the pattern of recruitment. As suggested in Chapter 1 however there is another factor in job 'choice' – one that often slips out of focus in these discussions. It is the actually existing gender relations within which young people live in school and in the community. The same gender relations persist in employment, and knowledge of them feeds back to young people in school. They are power relations, in which girls and women are subordinated, and they act in subtle and not-so-subtle ways to make it difficult and painful to break gender codes. Almost to the present day it has been the practice to discuss the choices of girls and boys in *parallel*, without recognising the active relationship and dynamic that links those choices. Girls choose one way *because* boys choose another, and vice versa. The breakthrough has come less in the work on occupational choice than in studies of sexual divisions in school, such as those cited previously (Stanworth, 1981; Walden and Walkerdine, 1985; and see also reports on the 'Girls into Science and Technology' project carried out in Manchester schools, in Kelly *et al.*, 1984). These studies show that the relations of school are unmistakably power relations and that an important aspect of the cultural regime within which girls are formed is male dominance. If young people are conscious of the reality of job markets and tailor their choices to them, they must be assumed to be aware too of the real-life nature of different kinds of labour process and work relations; not only whether they will be permitted *access* to certain kinds of work, but whether they could *survive and thrive* within them if they were.

When girls 'choose' typing or hairdressing and do not 'choose' engineering or computer skills, therefore, we cannot assume, as so many adults in YTS implied in the course of my research, that they are making a genuine, free and unconditional choice. Girls must be supposed, along the way, to have generated certain hopes that they have later suppressed; to be making the best of a bad situation; to be doing the only thing that seems possible; to be counting costs.

Careers guidance: less and less to offer

The great majority of young people I encountered had found their YTS placement through the agency of the Careers Service, the exceptions having mainly found it by personal contacts. The MSC's own surveys of YTS show that the Careers Service is the source of recruits in a majority of cases. Careers officers claim that the emphasis which MSC is now placing on employer-based provision means that more employers are advertising and recruiting their trainees directly. Nonetheless the Careers Service plays a crucial role in filling schemes, as it does in the school-to-work transition more generally. Its influence for conformity has been widely criticised.

'Careers Service' is in many ways an inappropriate name for this institution (Ball and Ball, 1979). Careers are progressive occupations with identity and status. Young people with the chance of a real career seldom need to use the Service, which deals on the whole with the lower-achieving school-leaver and the tatty end of the job supply. Careers officers are oddly placed, having two masters. The Minister responsible is a Minister of State at the Department of Employment, where there is a Careers Service Branch. At the same time, under the Employment and Training Act 1973 it is the local education authorities that are responsible for running local Careers Services and the statutory guidance on provision is contained in memoranda to LEAs. Some Careers Service posts are funded by the Department of Employment, some by LEAs and some jointly.

The responsibility for careers guidance is shared by the Careers Service and the schools. While careers officers place young people in work (when they can), the schools careers teachers' role is to prepare them for the transition. The careers officers however have an auxiliary role in schools, 'supporting and assisting' in the development of careers education. The link with teaching is the stronger for the fact that many careers officers were teachers before they went on to take their post-graduate diploma in Careers Guidance. Finally, of course, the Careers Service is expected today to work in conjunction with the Manpower Services Commission which now looms large in the area of youth employment, unemployment, education and training.

The Careers Service runs local careers offices, open to the public, which are visited by a stream of young people seeking advice on work or training. The stream grows to a flood after the end of the Easter and summer school-terms. The age group with which the Service mainly deals is the 16–19-year-olds. (Older people usually find themselves referred to the local Jobcentre.) The Jobcentres for their part advise the Careers Service of any vacancies for young people that come their way, and send over to the careers office most young people who enter their doors. The Educational Advisory Service (administered by the Education Service) is responsible for the guidance of young people who want a place in further or higher education. Employers phone in their jobs vacancies to the careers office, as do YTS managing agents. They may visit the office and discuss their labour requirements with careers officers. Some offices make a room available for local employers to carry out interviews with young candidates. The service is increasingly making use of computers, storing information on applicants, job preferences and vacancies, in order to match labour against job.

A rough division of labour exists within a careers office between those officers who act as 'unemployment specialists' (they are the ones mainly concerned with the Youth Training Scheme) and those who deal with schools. The characteristic practice in the Careers Service with regard to schools work is to begin contact with pupils in the third year of secondary school by attending parents' evenings. This continues in the fourth year. Then in the September of the fifth year the careers officers hold sessions with classes or groups of pupils, describing the service they offer and distributing forms for completion by the young people, setting out their thoughts on what they want to do on leaving school. These forms are gathered together and sorted, and the next step is for the careers officer to go into the school and address groups clustered according to their particular career interest: hairdressing, office work, engineering and so forth. This grouping process makes it difficult for pupils with unusual job preferences to come forward. Subsequently the careers officers try to see as many as possible of the fifth-year students individually in half-hour interviews.

They are available to see parents too. A follow-up to the individual interview takes place in April, when a letter asks each student to call at the Careers Office if they want help in finding work or training.

The quality and level of development of the schools' own careers education system with which the external careers officers find themselves dealing varies markedly, both from school to school, depending on the careers' teacher and the commitment of the head teacher, but also from one local education authority to another. At one end of the spectrum are schools that have no careers teacher, as such, at all. At the other are schools pioneering new careers curricula and teaching materials. In very few is there positive action to counter sex-stereotyping.

During the stage between interview and follow-up the careers officers send students address-lists of places to write for information on their chosen careers. Details of jobs that come into the office are sent off to students. Some young people get fixed up in this way by the time they leave school. The less-lucky majority call at the careers office on leaving. Here they are dealt with by one of the support staff administering the reception desk. The desk officer's role is to listen to the young person's request, give information about appropriate vacancies on the computer or direct them to the display cards on the noticeboard. Only if the young person presses for it, does she or he get an interview with a careers officer, at which career prospects and choices can be discussed at length. Until quite recently the reception desks were segregated, one for girls and one for boys. Index cards were colour-coded pink and blue. Today this overt sexism is gone, but in routine dealings with young people there is no attempt to question the job choices they present or to explore alternatives. Any influence the desk officer does exert tends to be in the direction of conformity, not innovation, for she (or he) represents, above all, realism.

We will see that many of my trainees found their encounters with the Careers Service useless, a 'waste of time', and depressing. Several felt they had been deflected by their contact with careers officers from careers that appealed to them and that they had, often too tentatively, proposed. Other research confirms the low opinion young people hold of the Careers Service. Often the advice places heavy emphasis on technical matters: how to fill in forms and perform well at interview. Many young people feel that careers officers do not listen to them or want to know what their hopes really are, but rather apply a set of preconceptions based on the dismal range of opportunities they know to exist (Benett and Carter, 1982). 'It is probably as well that schools do not consider the development of initiative and self-confidence as a high priority, because the lack of those qualities in school-leavers who come to them suits the Careers Service very well', write Colin and Mog Ball. 'As far as we can see the Careers Service do not strive to encourage the development of these qualities but rather . . . aim to make the 'client' fit the service, not vice versa. This works for some of the clients, some of the time. But it fails an awful lot of them' (Ball and Ball, 1979).

Studies have shown that Asians and West Indians are obliged to rely on the Careers Service more than white youth, because they lack the informal network of contacts in key positions in employment that some white families can use. We know that the Careers Service does not achieve much for these groups, however, from the relatively high levels of unemployment that persist among them in the immediate post-school age group. Consider this description of young Afro-Caribbean women from a comparison of black and white school-leavers: 'West Indian young women... were less successful in obtaining the jobs they desired or some acceptable substitute but this was not... because of more unrealistic or different preferences but because of their colour which appeared to be used as a screening device by employers.' West Indian young women, as mentioned previously, responded to the difficulties they faced by persisting in applying for the jobs they wanted, they married less early and they took up further education courses in greater numbers than white girls. However, 'by increasing their stock of education West Indian young women were only likely to alter their position in the queues relative to other West Indians. They were still likely to be behind whites on the basis of their colour' (Dex, 1982, pp.52–3; see also Brooks and Singh, 1978; Walsall Council for Community Relations, 1978; and Commission for Racial Equality, 1978).

Another option: the placement on YTS

It is the local education authorities that determine the limits of the role their Careers Services may play in the Youth Training Scheme. I was told that for the great majority of local Careers Services their engagement with YTS was restricted to recruiting young people into YTS places and helping them obtain permanent work at the end of their time on the Scheme. In one area near London, for instance, the careers officers were not allowed to be involved in the 'induction' process by which trainees are introduced to their scheme, nor may they visit trainees until they have been in place eight months. Careers offices are receiving less, not more, information about local schemes as time goes by. In early years they were automatically sent a copy of each 'start' form. Under Two-Year YTS however they will receive only a 'scheme information sheet' as a basis for advertising vacancies and an occasional list of new trainees as they come onto the Scheme, though without their addresses or those of their sponsoring employers. A careers officer complained:

> We don't get the facts so we can't play an informed role. The MSC regard the Careers Service as a spare part. No role has been designed for us in the Scheme. Access to sponsoring employers isn't allowed for. On occasions when we have visited employers with YTS placements we have had MSC managing agents screaming at us down the phone, 'Why were you visiting this company? It's no business of yours!' In our area we have had to organise a conference of managing agents and introduce ourselves and what we can do. But the hostility towards us has been terrific. The part played by the Careers Service in most areas is therefore limited to including a knowledge of YTS vacancies on offer to young people along with actual jobs. Managing agents and sponsoring employers are however free to advertise and recruit privately as well.

For all this, YTS has changed the kind of advice a careers officer can give:

> Up till a few years ago you were talking about three options: jobs, and particularly important being apprenticeships; further education; and staying on at school. And you would have been talking about occupations in some detail. And now we find ourselves talking about occupations in less detail and more about the range of *ways* of doing things that are open to the sixteen year old, one of which is YTS.

Influencing the advice are the young person's school-leaving qualifications, the chosen career and the context of local opportunity:

If you have an interview with someone who is a very competent typist, is good at English, has a good range of school-leaving exams and wants to work in an office – then YTS wouldn't be so important. They've got some skills to offer and if they present themselves well in interview they will probably have few problems getting a job in this area. [It was outer-London] YTS might be mentioned, but only as a thing to fall back on. On the other hand, if you have someone sitting in front of you who wants to be a motor mechanic and that is their only interest, then you will mention YTS and full-time college courses, because these are the *only* options today. There are *no* jobs for first year apprentice mechanics now: no choice.

What are the criteria for suggesting a Mode A place, employer-based, or a Mode B scheme – training workshop, Information Technology Centre or community project? 'If I thought a young person could get an apprenticeship, for instance, I'd send them on Mode A. I would tend to send young poeple who I think need more support to Mode B. That's my criterion.'

Officers to whom I talked in both careers offices reported that YTS had a bad public image in the area. 'YTS came in after YOP and with the same money as YOP, and it's quite difficult to get it across to people that it is meant to be something different, a training programme not an unemployment measure.' Some individual schemes have exceedingly bad reputations. In the inner-London Careers Service the occupancy on YTS schemes is very low, because many young people, in spite of high unemployment levels, will 'do anything rather than go on YTS'. School students in this area are often warned off YTS by teachers, many of whom 'are very "anti", and consider the Careers Service to be the handmaiden of the MSC'.

Many careers officers therefore feel themselves immobilised – identified with the worst of MSC's reputation yet unable to influence the working of MSC's scheme. Some had good things to say of YTS: 'Some of the schemes are excellent and I'd have 100 per cent confidence that the trainees would get a good deal on them.' Mode B schemes, workshop-based, were felt to be the best addition to training opportunities created by the MSC. 'Some are very, very imaginative in the way they have interpreted MSC's rules and that is very nice'.

Other careers officers were sharply critical of the Scheme: 'It's a numerical exercise, not a quality exercise.' The allowance was ridiculously low, they felt: 'People who have set up as managing agents have all sorts of backgrounds and all sorts of motivations... Some are very interested in the money, and there's a lot of money to be made.' The careers officers were worried, too, about the introduction of two-year YTS with what they felt was indecent haste and insufficient thought.

When the MSC first announced its Youth Training Scheme in 1982, some careers officers formed a Careers Workers Action Group to protest at features of the Scheme (London Careers Workers Action Group, 1982). Their experience with the Youth Opportunities Programme had led them to fear that YTS was not destined to provide quality training nor to increase the number of jobs available to young people. Above all they suspected that the government intended to make participation effectively compulsory for unemployed school leavers. Not long after these protests the Employment Minister Peter Morrison issued a press statement defending the Scheme and castigating the Careers Service. YTS, he said 'offers the opportunity to review many aspects of the conduct and approach of the Careers Service'. The press release was sent out to all Careers Services for distribution to officers. Not long after this the Career Workers Action Group (CWAG) folded and opposition to the MSC 'shrank to nil, because people were afraid to step out of line'. Many of those who were involved in CWAG now feel that YTS as it has developed has exceeded their worst fears. They are still adamantly opposed to any move by the government to withdraw YTS 'refusers' rights to supplementary benefit. 'I'd resign.' 'We'd never pass on the information to the DHSS.' And young people, they were sure, would never accept it: 'You'd get a bunch who'd just give it two fingers and say "Right!" ' Meanwhile, the more critical careers officers continued to worry about the effect of YTS on young people's wages, on the youth labour market and teenagers' independence. 'Personally I find a lot of it very distressing.'

Responses to sex-stereotyping

One of the careers offices I visited had their records on computer. I asked them to give me some indication of the degree of sex-typing in the job 'choices' of school-leavers. We selected certain revealing occupations and put them through the computer. It showed that, out of a total register of 488 young women and 779 young men, no girl had asked, as either first or second choice, for work in engineering, printing or photography. Only three young women had put 'motor mechanic' as their first choice and a further six had asked for a building trade. As for the young men, only one had asked for hairdressing and two for nursery nursing.

Careers officers frequently cited statistics such as these as evidence that they had little scope for breaking sex-segregation in YTS. They joined the chorus of adults who were saying, 'It's too late at 16. Their minds are made up.' 99 per cent of school-leavers, they said, came into the careers office with a sex-typed decision ready formed: 'By the time they reach us I'm afraid they've already been influenced, by parents largely.' When non-traditional choices do present themselves they are usually tentative and are rarely, in the event, adhered to.

> You do get occasions when a girl comes in and says she wants to do painting and decorating. And you proceed to try and get that kid such a place. And then very often you get a visit or a phone call from her mother saying 'I don't *want* her to do this, thank you. I want her to work in an office.'

This was the experience of one outer London careers officer too. She said:

> Well, out of all the youngsters I've seen in this particular school [she named it] I saw one girl who wanted to be an engineer. Out of say a hundred girls leaving school. She came in and at first talked about other things. Then she said, 'But actually I'd like to work as an engineer'. Very embarrassed about it. She didn't have a mother. Her father had been an engineer. And in fact, when I backed that up and gave her literature about how girls can train to be an engineer, how today they have *more* opportunities than boys because there are special courses for girls – when I explained that to her, she took it all home to her dad. And her dad talked about it with his mates. And she came back and said she had decided 'it wasn't a good idea anyway'. Her dad had decided that even if she went on the course she wouldn't be able to get a job. And she'd get laughed at by the men. Perhaps he was being realistic. But she was the only 'engineer' I saw out of the three schools I went to last year. She said they had laughed at her. On the other hand boys can say they want to be chefs.

The attitude of the careers officer quoted here was sympathetic to gender-contrary choices. Yet young people in my study would have said she was untypical. They felt that careers officers had done little to help the few school-leavers who did want to break out of sex-typed occupations. Other researchers too have found the Careers Service offering bad or inadequate advice to girls wanting to escape the straightjacket of 'women's work' (Benett and Carter, 1982). I tried to find out from careers officers, first of all, what they did when they encountered someone asking for help in getting started in a non-traditional occupation; second, what they did about stereotyped choices.

To the non-conformists, most careers officers said, they would be warmly supportive – supportive *but* realistic: 'Personally I would tend to be over-supportive. But at the same time make the kid aware of possible difficulties. But so as to give encouragement and support to actually try it.' They were less than wholehearted in their support for two reasons. One was that they feared they might not find the necessary training or job openings. 'We are in an invidious position really, because we are the people who actually have to come up with the goods, the job.' They are also wary about allowing young women, particularly, to get themselves into socially difficult situations that they may not have fully thought through. For instance, one careers officer cited a very shy and inexperienced young 16-year-old girl who was interested in a YTS place in a London Transport depot. It would have meant a unionised and long-term secure job. But it would also have meant working in an environment almost entirely elderly, working-class and male. The vacancy was clearly 'meant', she said, for a man: she advised against the young woman taking it. Some careers officers said they would advise workshop-style schemes, where there are sheltered opportunities in a range of trades and a chance to change one's mind. Yet this is an inferior mode of entry to the manual trades. A boy would normally look for an apprenticeship or at the very least an employer-based scheme.

It just so happens that the two local services I visited, and in particular certain of the officers I met (six out of seven were women, all were white) have a reputation as being among the most progressive and energetic in the country, both in promoting the interests of young working-class people, and young women in particular. So these are likely to be among the most favourable of Careers Service practices. A more common response to gender-innovation, say these careers officers, is well-meaning dissuasion. A girl asking for training in the building trades may be asked to consider whether she may be 'jumping on the feminist band wagon', a boy interested in fashion or hairdressing may be gently probed about his 'latent homosexuality'.

It is not surprising then, that if young people turn up with conventional ideas about training and work these are normally accepted at face value. Careers officers hesitate, even if they are aware of sex-typing as a problem to press their views on the young people they help. 'Just because I don't think what they want is right, why should I impose my ideas on them. You know what I mean?' White professionals, if they are sensitive, are hesitant to give young black people advice of any kind that might seem to disrespect their particular cultural traditions. And such is the power of gender-expectations that, if a young person presents herself with a traditional job in mind, few careers officers will feel able baldly to put forward some radical alternative:

> If they are dithering and not really sure, *then* there is a possibility of broadening those ideas... But is is very hard, if someone is sitting there in front of you, say a boy who wants to do motor mechanics, who spends all day tinkering with cars, perhaps had a part-time job in a garage, lives and breathes engines – try to convince *him* of taking an interest in anything else.

Particularly anything feminine – hairdressing, typing or nursing.

With young women, too, a careers officer said 'I've tried. It's difficult to sit there and say "have you thought of manual trades?" That's already been brought up in their careers lessons. They'll laugh, a lot of them, and say "that's a boy's job". And instantly dismiss it.' Another added:

> A lot of the girls are much brighter than they realise, and with the boys it's exactly the opposite. A girl may say 'I'd like to be a receptionist-typist' and I have her teacher's report and *know* she could do more. And I may say 'Have you ever thought about being your own boss?' And she'll go, 'Oh, no I couldn't do it. I couldn't do that.' With boys, they may have nothing more than Grade 5 CSE Maths and yet they'll come barging in and say 'I want to be a company director'.'

Faced with the risk of rejection or ridicule, most careers officers forget the flights of fancy and concentrate on getting the young person the place or job they are asking for, if they can humanly do so. After all, in one sense, it is something to be thankful for when a young person does know or think they know just what they want. Because time and pressure of work militate against the careers officer exploring alternatives. 'We don't have time. [Firmly] There is a time limit. I wouldn't want to open it up in that way' one careers officer admitted frankly. 'If I did they might get interested. I'd have to see them again and I – it's really a question of not enough time. Because you've got the next kid waiting outside.'

So the choices young people appear to be making, through their own apparent inclinations, their parents' pressure, the forces in the job market and the limitations experienced by careers officers, are almost 100 per cent traditional and sex-stereotyped. YTS is doing little or nothing to break this pattern. Does it matter? Perhaps the decision made at 16 can be reversed? 'No, it's crucial' insisted a careers officer. 'There's not an awful lot of opportunity to change, so that once people go down a route, then... it's going to be very, very difficult to move to another one.' The choice will be binding. 'Yes' said another careers officer, 'unfortunately it sets the pattern. We don't have a labour market now where you can leap from one thing to another with impunity.' 'I don't believe that there is any *better* time than 16 for people to make up their minds.'

Dealing with prejudice

If young people's own stereotyped intentions are one side of the immobilising problem for those careers officers who want to be helpful in tackling sex-segregation, the other is the attitudes of YTS managing agents and sponsoring employers. Careers officers are in the front line with a statutory role in combating discrimination in recruitment. The contradiction they face is that both they and the young person need to keep the managing agent and employer happy; they need the work experience that is offered, even by discriminatory employers. It is a juggling act: 'Our priority is to get a job out of them. But not at *any* price.'

As we've seen, not all Careers Services can deal direct with YTS employers. Those I encountered, however, on occasion did so. They had a set form of words to read out to any employer who appeared out of line. 'Do you realise' they would ask, 'that it is an offence under the Sex Discrimination Act to distinguish between boys and girls?' If the employer proved not to be exempt under the law, and persisted in discriminating, then the careers officer would continue 'You are breaking the law. We cannot help you, because we would be contravening the Act.' One officer reported an instance when she had had a head-on confrontation:

> The office manager of a local firm phoned me and said 'I want a girl'. And I said 'You know you can't say that'. And she said, 'Can it have boobs, then? Can it wear a skirt?' She was actually offensive. I said to her, 'I'm a woman, and you are offending *me*. No, you can't say that.' And we actually wrote her a letter, saying we had withdrawn the vacancy until such time as they could guarantee us that any young person we sent along, boy or girl, would be treated in the same way for the vacancy.

The trouble is, of course, that in reality such an employer can continue to discriminate – either by turning down the person of the wrong sex, on interview, or by making them uncomfortable in the job. 'Deep down you are left with the feeling that if a young man had gone along and got the job his life would have been made miserable. Even what things we have at our disposal are weak weapons.'

Employers today have the power that comes of operating in a 'buyer's market'. 'If we go through the motions the employers say to themselves. "Fine, stuff the system. I'll advertise. You people don't matter." ' Because of this, some careers officers compromise with discrimination. 'I find it very difficult' said one officer:

> Because if I've got a lovely young lad who's keen, wants to go, and they say 'I only want a boy. Don't bother sending me girls' I find it very frustrating not to send him. And I must say I try to do it without breaking the policy. Because you can see the kid's face in front of you and you just know that that job would suit him well. I know some careers officers would come down stronger than I do, on that. They come down strongly.

Another added, 'It's very difficult, you see, as one of the Joe Bloggses, to actually [confront them]. And I think perhaps we are guilty of

'Send me a lad.'

acknowledging it but never actually confronting it.'

Careers officers felt that they had far fewer powers, in the YTS context, than the MSC itself. And the Commission was not taking the problem of sex-stereotyping and discrimination seriously.

> Everyone knows the Construction Industry Training Board shows a lot of prejudice towards girls. But the MSC – and this would have to be at national level – would not take the CITB to task. Because it can't afford for the CITB to pull out of the Scheme. So they condone it... And I mean, government aren't really interested in equal opportunities.

The Conservative government had certainly made it clear that YTS was to respond, first and foremost, to employers' view of their needs. The Employment Minister, Peter Morrison, in the press release mentioned above, criticised the Careers Service for what he called 'social engineering'. He reminded them:

the best way to help young people get jobs and training is to act with market forces, not against them. Employers are operating in the real world – the world of profits. *The Careers Service must respond positively to the indications employers give about the sort of youngster they want* (Department of Employment, 1983, my italics).

It could hardly have been more baldly put: if an employer says he wants a girl, boy, black or white, send him what he orders. For a while the Careers Service were on trial, their continued existence dependent on their cooperation with the MSC and employers over YTS (Davies, 1986).

Possibilities for change

Within the Careers Service are many individual careers officers who worry about sex inequality and the adverse implications for both girls and boys of occupational sex-segregation. They are hindered in acting on their concerns however by the structure in which they work. They are given no training in how to act to break down sex-stereotyping, nor are careers officers who are less aware of the problem given any training that would alert them to it. The Inner London Careers Service has a Central Support and Training Unit. Its training activities, however, deal with problems 'out there', such as young offenders. Its courses seldom tackle issues of Careers Service practice such as challenging sexism. The Careers Service Manual is the basis for training in other regions by the various in-service training committees of Careers Service Branch of the Department of Employment. It has a section on interpreting the Sex Discrimination legislation, but, as we have seen, that is only a fraction of the problem. The Manual contains nothing on the subtler and less obvious deterrents to young people pursuing non-traditional options. The Manual is accompanied by a series of booklets, 'Approaches to Careers Service Practice', dating from 1981. It was not until the twelfth such booklet to appear, in 1986, that one took up the issues of equal opportunity. This welcome addition was helpful, and said, 'the first and most essential task for the Careers Service in promoting equal opportunities for girls and boys is to arouse a general awareness of the problems involved amongst all its staff and in all its fields of activity.' It recommended the appointment of an equal opportunities officer in each Careers Service (Department of Employment, 1986). It may be hoped that this is a sign of a new consciousness. The Institute of Careers Officers, however, gives less ground for hope. This is the professional body representing many careers officers. It publishes a series of posters directed to young people to awaken their interest in various kinds of job. I saw these on the wall of the local 'tech' for students to read. The crudeness of the sexism in the images is difficult to credit, given their apparently respectable professional origin. The style is 'comic strip' and the appeal is 'humour'. There are stereotyped curvaceous blonde secretaries with their breasts falling out of tight-fitting dresses. A welder burns his partner's behind, so intent is he on the passing 'bird'. A window-cleaner peering in at a startled women in the bath is addressed: 'Enjoying the work itself?'. And a third illustration reads 'Working at sea isn't all scrubbing decks': the young rating and his officer are leering at the sight of a woman's behind, in frilly knickers, glimpsed through a cabin porthole. No young woman could feel herself addressed in these posters as a manager, welder or potential Navy recruit. In fact the posters could be read as a warning to any woman thinking of stepping out of line and are an act of contempt to women generally.

The Careers Service often describe themselves as a Cinderella in relation to the employment and education services in whose environment they are situated. 'It is not a valued service unfortunately. It is a poor relation... underpaid and undervalued.' We have seen that the Careers Service is not invited by the Manpower Services Commission to play an active part in YTS nor given the information to do it. 'MSC generally has a very contemptuous view of the Careers Service' I was told, 'So has the government.' This bad opinion is mutual. The relationship between the MSC and the Careers Service in the two areas in which I made this study had deteriorated since YTS began. Increasingly, I was told, there is disrespect between the two teams, the MSC programme assessors and the careers officers, each tending to denigrate the other's skills. Much of what the more active and interventionist Careers Services are doing with their YTS work, careers officers feel, is compensating for the shortcomings of the MSC. 'They've been asked to deliver YTS. And deliver it they will' said a careers officer of the MSC. 'I think the situation at the moment is they are desperate to deliver anything. Numbers. To please the minister.'

The Careers Service however does have it in its power to effect change. The evidence for this is in the outer-London Careers Service I visited. Here, by single-minded effort and against the intention of the Service itself and of the MSC, careers officers had succeeded in intervening in YTS to a remarkable extent. They had developed close working-relationships with individual managing agents and schemes. This had allowed them to gain the information about trainees and placements that would enable them to have first-hand contact with employers. They had negotiated with employers to achieve a uniquely high proportion of 'employee-status' placements within Mode A. These placements were proper jobs, the first year of permanent employment, and the trainee was paid a wage of £45 or £50. The employer paid the wage and recouped the training allowance from the MSC. The only difference from a 'real job' was that the trainees had off-the-job training by day-release, had a training plan and log-book to govern their occupations at work, and were monitored. Employers felt that they obtained more committed and industrious trainees this way. In this area careers officers were attending, even organising 'induction' days for new trainees and ensuring that these were used to inform them of their rights. They were writing training manuals to guide YTS employers. They were visiting trainees in their place-ments, compensating for the sketchy monitoring of the managing agents and the MSC's own officers. They would have liked to have the power to organise equal-opportunity awareness sessions with YTS managing agents. 'They don't know how to deal with the sex discrimination they meet. You do need training. The MSC think they have this quality scheme that is going to offer equal opportunity on sex and race, on a shoe-string with no training. It's a disgrace. I feel very angry about it.' This however is an exceptional Careers Service, staffed by particularly aware officers. It has made a role for the Service in YTS which does not officially exist, where it is in fact contrary to expectations. In more typical areas careers officers them-selves would benefit from additional training on sex and race issues.

Even within this 'progressive' Careers Service in outer London, however, very little had been achieved on breaking down sex-stereotyping. The focus had been on the quality of the schemes more generally. A careers officer explained:

Some kids are saying to us things like 'I did 57 hours last week, is that all right?' 'I didn't know I was entitled to a lunch break.' While lots of managing agents passively condone such exploitative practices as that it is difficult to put your energies into pressing for a clean scheme in terms of sex equality, let alone getting into the more problematic area of sex-stereotyping.

Officers felt that if staffing levels were more generous and the pressure on their time relaxed they could do more in interviewing young people to explore more deeply the long-term significance of choices they are making.[2] They could have called the bluff on the concept of occupational 'choice' and begun to reveal all the pressures to gender conformity that were making it not a choice but a 'needs-must'.

When the present Careers Service was formed in 1973 out of the former Youth Employment Service it marked a change towards a more 'client-oriented' working philosophy. Counselling and guidance of young people were seen as more important than assessing their psychological type and matching it to employers' needs (Roberts, 1972, 1975, 1980). Not many years afterwards, however, the 'Great Debate' in education and the 'new vocationalism' it sanctioned were to collide with these liberal principles. A right-wing view of education and the school-to-work transition, given force by the return of a Conservative government in 1979, defined and limited the boundaries of professional autonomy, whether of teachers or careers officers, and legitimised a new 'industrial needs' emphasis. Under the new 'vocational' ethic, as Phil Cohen writes:

> guidance and training of working-class school-leavers had nothing to do with their inner desires, still less with preparing them for a professional calling or career. If they talked about 'dream jobs' this was usually attributed to a passing flight of adolescent fantasy, to be cured by some stern counselling in the reality principles of earning a living and growing up. Instead they were offered guidance and training in how to make the best of a bad job (Cohen, 1984, p.119).

The 'client-oriented' philosophy in careers guidance however also had its own internal contradiction and this too hinged on 'choice'. The ideology was that the young person's expressed choice should be the focus of guidance. To question it was in a sense to deflect the client away from it, and thus to be directive and unprofessional. Yet an understanding of the social relations of home, school, training and work, as we will see, exposes this presenting 'choice' of young people as so subject to the push-and-pull of social pressures as to be a sham. It does not merit the word 'choice'. A careers officer put it this way:

It is not as if there's free choice in the beginning. Because the conditioning and the roles, and all sorts of things, have up till the age they get onto YTS led them to make that choice. Or have excluded choices from them. Because of the stereotyping, conditioning in school, all those things. So it's not as if you're presented with two equal things and then you choose one. Everything leads you towards particular 'choices'.

What is needed, then, is change: change in the formative class, race and gender relations of the early years, change in structure and relations of training and work, and change too in the process of careers guidance. As Inge Bates wrote in her recent essay on the history of careers education, there is:

[a] large group of children for whom choosing between different jobs and their accompanying lifestyles can, in reality, make only a marginal difference to the quality of life... It is not choosing which will answer the problems they experience at work... but changing, changing the conditions of work, changing the society in which they live (Bates, 1984, p.192).

Notes

1. For a review of theories of occupational choice see Clarke, 1980. Debate in the 1960s centred on 'socialisation' and 'rationality'. How free was the individual to choose, how strong were the societal determinants of choice? See in particular Musgrave, 1967; Ford and Box, 1967; and Coulson *et al.*, 1967.
2. A recent action-research project in Sheffield involved a careers officer being given half the usual case-load so as to be able to improve vocational guidance to certain target pupils. In the process of spending more time with each young person, the officer began to develop new roles. She became a consultant to schools on careers programmes, a counsellor to young people, a vocational-guidance specialist, an advocate from the community to the local education authority, and she acted much more as an agent of individual and social change in relation to clients and their choices (Dunn and Grimwood, 1984).

4

The Manpower Services Commission and the Issue of Sex Equality

We need now to turn to the Manpower Services Commission itself, this rapidly expanding creature of government that has been responsible for the form and functioning of the Youth Training Scheme, among many other aspects of manpower and training policy. Where does the sex-equality issue fit into the picture of the developing YTS?

One of the problems identified in the government's Job Creation Programme of the mid-1970s had been the scarcity of provision for unemployed young women, who had constituted no more than a quarter of those benefiting from employment under that scheme (Manpower Services Commission, 1977). The matter of equal opportunities for young women was therefore not entirely neglected in the early thinking on Special Programmes. An MSC paper specifically dedicated to this topic showed that women were concentrated in a narrower range of occupations than men, and in the lower grades of those occupations. They were receiving less training and education than men in preparation for work and also once in work. Their pay was on average considerably lower than that of men and the long-term employment prospects in industries and jobs that traditionally employ women were declining (Manpower Services Commission, 1979).

The Youth Opportunities Programme (YOP) which developed out of the Job Creation Programme, did perform somewhat better in attracting young women, bringing their numbers to nearly half of the total trainees. Just getting females onto YOP, however, proved insufficient. A study commissioned by the MSC from University College, Cardiff, found that:

apart from limited exceptions, girls and boys are almost completely segregated on work experience on the scheme. Boys are concentrated in manual work based in project teams and in (employer-based) commercial/industrial placements. Girls are concentrated in placements doing 'caring' work and in typing and general office work, mainly in the statutory and voluntary organisations (Brelsford *et al.*, 1982).

The researchers also found 'evidence of conscious and unconscious sex discrimination on the part of scheme staff and behaviour which contributed to the maintenance of sex-role stereotypes' (Brelsford *et al.*, 1982; and see Bedeman and Courtenay, 1983).

This knowledge then was available to the Commission as the Youth Training Scheme was designed. It appears to have made little significant impact, finding expression in the founding documents of YTS only in bland and repetitive statements of good intent. Thus in its consultative document on the New Training Initiative the Commission reiterated that 'there are far too few opportunities for girls outside a very restricted range of jobs and occupations traditional for women' (Manpower Services Commission, 1981a). In its later paper, carrying the NTI into an action programme, it mentioned 'people at a disadvantage in the labour market, in particular women, disabled people and members of ethnic minorities' (Manpower Services Commission, 1981b). The Youth Task Group in its definitive report on the new Youth Training Scheme noted that around 35 per cent of 16-year-olds entering jobs receive no training at all and added 'girls fare worse than boys because they often enter service industries which provide less training than manufacturing.' They urged that the new Scheme should not only 'comply with existing legislation forbidding discrimination but, more than this, should provide *positive opportunities for disadvantaged groups*' (Manpower Services Commission, 1982, p.10, my italics). However, in the process of realising the Youth Training Scheme the Manpower Services Commission dropped the commitment to positive action for women. In a policy statement published shortly before YTS began the phrasing of the paragraph on equal opportunity was more slippery. It read 'the Scheme will need to comply with legislation forbidding discrimination but, more than that, should provide *special help for all young people who take part*' (Manpower Services Commission, 1984, p.13, quotes this paper). 'Special help' could perhaps still be interpreted as positive action – but if it was to be for *all* YTS trainees, just what could it mean?

Positive action for women had in fact gone by the board. YTS had instead a simple 'open door' position on equal opportunity, abjuring prejudice and discrimination. The justification given for this was legal. To the surprise of some women, the Sex Discrimination Act of 1975 had been concerned to outlaw sex-discrimination not only against women but against men too. This meant that, just as it ruled out most men-only activities, it ruled out most women-only activities. Under the Act two justifications were recognised for mounting single-sex training schemes or for reserving places for one sex or the other on a training scheme. These were, first, that special needs could be proved, and, second, that the one sex could be shown to be under-represented in existing provision. For either of those reasons it was possible to apply for and obtain 'designation' from the Secretary of State to bring the initiative within the law.

The MSC had taken the advice of Department of Employment lawyers on what it was possible for them to do under the Act.[1] They had been told that only women 'returners' could be seen as having 'special needs' within the terms of the Act. MSC had felt able to offer Wider Opportunities for Women courses and other initiatives for adult women but not for youth trainees. That left the second justification: underrepresentation in particular occupations. Outside the context of YTS the MSC had, for instance, funded some girl-technician schemes and were currently supporting TESS, a scheme for young women 'technician engineers'. The Commission were themselves designated under the Act and when funding a college to carry out such single-sex training the college was accepted as the Commission's agents for purposes of the Act and so was not obliged to apply for individual designation. The Commission's legal advisers advised that in the Youth Training Scheme the Commission's relationship with providers was qualitatively different, less direct than in the case of Further Education. Managing agents wishing to offer single-sex YTS schemes would have to seek designation individually, in their own right. There was another snag. The lawyers advised that, being a 'broad bridge from school to work', the Youth Training Scheme was not sufficiently vocational to justify speaking of 'occupations'. The clause concerning underrepresentation in certain occupations therefore they insisted, could not hold water.

From the moment the government had embarked on its 'New Training Initiative' the Equal Opportunities Commission had been pressing for the inclusion of positive action for girls and women. In its response to the MSC's Consultative Document on the NTI the Commission pointed out that:

> where girls and women have received encouragement to embark upon non-traditional training courses, they have proved themselves generally to be equal to their male counterparts. This has been particularly so where the trainees have had supportive counselling in the initial stages of training.

They urged 'positive action to compensate for the effects of past practices which have been detrimental to girls and women'. They recommended that trainees entering non-traditional courses be paid an additional allowance; that publicity and information campaigns should be organised to reach out to girls in school; that counselling be provided and day-care facilities also associated with training initiatives (Equal Opportunities Commission, 1981). As the YTS got under way in 1983 the Equal Opportunities Commission took issue with the Department of Employment's interpretation of the Sex Discrimination Act. It quoted chapter and verse and claimed 'it is clear from the above that the MSC is allowed to discriminate positively in any of its training courses which comply with the criteria' of the Act. It urged the MSC to take advantage of the opportunity offered to make specific provision for girls on non-traditional training schemes, and offered its assistance in developing this provision (Equal Opportunities Commission, 1983).

None of this shifted the MSC's adherence to the Department's lawyers' exceedingly conservative and unhelpful interpretation of the law. It was only much later with the introduction of two-year YTS in 1986/7 that the lawyers conceded a change of position. YTS-2 was held to be more 'vocationally specific' than the original Scheme and could be deemed to be involving young people in 'occupations'. Positive discrimination would now be permissible. As we shall see, this coincided with a more favourable political climate in the Department of Employment and the MSC. It was supposed, outside the MSC, that political philosophy had not been without effect on legal opinion.

'Special groups' in the Youth Training Scheme

The issue of 'girls in YTS' became the responsibility mainly of a small unit within the MSC's training Division. The unit was at first called AT-2, and was located in the Adult Training side of Training Division, though it dealt equally then, as it has continued to do since, with both adult and youth training. Later it transferred to the Youth Training side where it became known as YP-3. The unit was small in comparison with the scale of the problems faced: it was essentially the rump of a more powerful 'Special Groups Branch' that had withered in the unfavourable political climate of the early 1980s.

YP-3 was not in fact an 'equal opportunities' unit. It inherited from Special Groups Branch a responsibility for the promotion of the needs of particular categories in the labour market. The special groups were defined as the disabled, ex-offenders, ethnic minorities and women. Because men were excluded from the remit of YP-3 (at least white, able-bodied and non-offending men) it could not deal with sex-stereotyping and sex-segregation *as such*. It was unable to deliberate on policy for young men in YTS with regard to their special needs. It could not, for instance, foster the development of skills that young men, taken as a sex, widely lack: caring, nurturing, supportive and expressive skills, for instance. Nor could it consider the gender-significance for young men of their exclusive tenure of certain occupations – engineering, for example. Consequently YP-3 was not led to analyse the problem of sex-segregation itself – only the phenomenon of young women's *absence* from certain areas.

The staff of the unit would certainly have wished from the start to make more positive interventions for young women in Youth Training, but it was limited mainly to an information role. It put out material aimed at schoolgirls exhorting them to think imaginatively about the kinds of work for which they felt they might train. Positive action however was limited to 'preparing guidelines and training material for use by MSC staff and managing agents to help diminish sex-role stereotyping and encourage the promotion of equal opportunities for girls' (Manpower Services Commission, 1983a). The training material in question emerged in the form of a guide to resources for use in training sponsors' staff (Manpower Services Commission, 1983b). But by early 1986, three years after the beginning of YTS, this was the only instruction on equal opportunities for women that had emerged from Moorfoot, and it was directed neither to MSC's own officers nor even to managing agents, the two key groups running the scheme, both of whom as we shall see, badly needed guidance and training. It was directed to participating firms and other work-providers.

Down the line: MSC's Area Offices

At the time of my study in 1985/6 the Youth Training Scheme was delivered by the Manpower Services Commission through the agency of its nine Regions and fifty-five Training Division Area Offices (TDAO), each headed by an Area Manager.[2] TDAOs had two parts: Adult Training and Youth Training, each operated by a separate team of personnel. The officer in charge of administering YTS was in some cases the Area manager, in others a Senior Executive Officer with the designation 'YTS Manager'. In the particular London area with which this research was concerned the YTS team consisted of four Programme Managers (including one woman), each leading a programme team of five or six Local Programme Assessors (LPAs), of both sexes.[3] A team would cover two or three London boroughs and each LPA would handle three or more schemes.

Organising YTS in this area represented a considerable administrative challenge. In December 1985 unemployment for Greater London was standing at over 400 000. The young were hardest hit: while the average unemployment rate in the Greater London area was 10 per cent, the 16–19-year-old group showed rates of 27.4 per cent (male) and 21.6 per cent (female). During the nine-month period, April – December 1985, 20 881 school-leavers joined the Youth Training Scheme. Though London's unemployment rate, at 10 per cent, was less than the national average of 13.5 per cent, there were large differences within London. Two of the boroughs in the segment of London with which this research was concerned had male unemployment rates of 30 per cent or more. Women as a percentage of London's unemployed had risen from 12.6 per cent in 1974 to 30 per cent in 1985 – and that figure excluded an estimated 60 000 unregistered women who were also looking for work. Throughout the London area the rate of unemployment for Afro-Caribbeans was twice the rate for white British (Greater London Council, 1986, pp.187–212).

In our particular segment of London, 6075 school-leavers joined the Youth Training Scheme in the course of the 1985/6 Scheme year. 77 per cent of these joined employer-based schemes (Mode A). 44 per cent were female, and 18 per cent were black (see Table 4.1). In these respects the segment barely differed from Greater London as a whole. Access to Mode A schemes, however, was, as elsewhere, significantly skewed in favour of whites (of whom 86 per cent were in Mode A schemes, as against 30 per cent in the case of black groups), and women (80 per cent in Mode A as against 74 per cent of young men).[4] The Training Division Area Office recorded that occupancy on their schemes, even in December, not long after the annual peak, was low. In the Mode A schemes, employer-based, only 66.5 per cent of approved places were filled; in Mode B1 the figure was 68 per cent and in Mode B2 only 58 per cent. Clearly many young Londoners were giving the Youth Training Scheme a vote of 'no confidence', and one of the Programme Teams' main preoccupations was therefore to win YTS a better reputation for quality training.

A typical slice of London

The wedge of London for which this particular office was responsible consists of three fairly distinct territories, a characteristic cross-section of Greater London as a whole.[5] First, at the hub of London there is the central business district, with thriving employment opportunities in the office sector. This is an area in which relatively few people live, but to which many employees commute daily. There are approximately 300 YTS places provided by a handful of big schemes, all Mode A, mainly in banking, insurance, shipping and other kinds of commercial activity. The majority of places, as would be expected, are in the 'occupational training family' *OTF-1: administrative, clerical and office services*. Whereas only 24 per cent of YTS office places nationally are filled by young men, and 29 per cent in this London segment as a whole, in the central business district over half are filled by males. It seems that the preponderance of males may be connected with the relatively high status of work in the city centre or with the travel-to-work involved.

Second, adjacent to the business centre, there are a number of boroughs with the character of a typical deprived inner-city territory. Residentially it is a decayed and ageing environment that houses a population of mixed race, with communities of Asians, Cypriots and

Table 4.1 Youth Training Scheme 'starts' 1985/6 in one segment of Greater London, analysed by Mode of scheme, and by sex and ethnic group of trainee

Mode and type of scheme	Male	Female	Total	Female as % of total	White	%	African/ West Indian	%	Indian sub-continent	%	Other	%
Mode A	2542	2132	4674	80	1738	86	222	72	101	65	71	39
Mode B1:												
Community projects	329	211	540	39	123	6	42	14	6	4	40	22
Training workshops	343	180	523	34	82	4	25	8	27	17	46	25
Information Technology Centres	76	35	111	32	17	1	7	2	3	2	8	4
Mode B2	128	99	227	43	49	3	14	4	18	12	18	10
TOTAL	3418	2657	6075	44	2009	100	310	100	155	100	183	100

Afro-Caribbeans. Here as in similar areas elsewhere in London there has been a long decline in manufacturing activity, both as industries moved out to the new towns and later as the recession brought closures. In terms of YTS there is some spill-over in employer-based schemes from the central business district. But only 57 per cent of approved places were employer-based in 1985/6, characteristically provided by local councils and local health and education authorities. However some office and service work, small shops and a variety of small production and commercial units (clothing, business machinery) also offer employer-led opportunities under Mode A. 60 per cent of young women and 44 per cent of young men were in Mode A. More characteristic of the territory however were Mode B schemes, responding to the social and educational deprivation in the area. The training workshop described in Chapter 6 and the Information Technology Centre in Chapter 7 were located here. Other Mode B schemes included projects for young offenders and for the disabled. In one of the boroughs, on which I focused particular attention, 55 per cent of trainees were female and as many as 40 per cent were Asian or Afro-Caribbean.[6] (This compared with a local population in which 17 per cent was of these two ethnic groups.)

Third, there is a geographically extensive suburban area on the fringe of London, covering four boroughs. Most of this suburban area is more spacious and better-maintained in its environment and more middle-class in its social structure. Up to 30 per cent of its resident population may travel out of the area to work, mainly to the central business district. There are however several local mini-business centres with office blocks and shopping arcades. To take just one of these boroughs – the location of the scheme described in Chapter 5 – black trainees here were in a small minority: 7 per cent Afro-Caribbean and Asian against 11 per cent in the local population. Employer-based schemes prevailed. No less than 88 per cent of trainees were in Mode A, against 77 per cent nationally. Again women had the greater presence in these employer-based places (93 per cent of the young women were in Mode A as against 83 per cent of the young men). The employer-based schemes included private training agencies, such as secretarial colleges, a 155-place hairdressing scheme linking many local salons, and a 'group training association' serving nearby engineering firms. The borough council here also had its own scheme. One or two firms were large enough to be managing agents in their own right. But as in most areas such as this, many employers were served by large YTS umbrella schemes, organised typically by local chambers of commerce, further education colleges or charitable organisations.

Of particular interest, as we saw in Chapter 3, the borough had a strikingly high proportion of places designed, partly by intervention of the local Careers Service, in a way that somewhat diverged from the Manpower Services Commission's original intention for the Scheme: they were not merely temporary training places but actual employment.[7] The trainees were in permanent jobs and were paid a wage of perhaps £45–50 a week by the employer who recovered the £27.50 training allowance from the MSC by way of subsidy. One in four employer-based trainees in this outer London borough were in employee-status places, as against one in eight in the inner London borough. It is interesting too that whereas females represented 57 per cent of trainees in the outer London borough Mode A schemes they only had 35 per cent of the desirable employee-status places.

Administering the Youth Training Scheme

In 1985/6 when I made this study the work of the Programme Teams responsible for YTS was to a large extent made up of two phases: approving new schemes; and monitoring existing schemes. Organisations or firms that wished to participate in YTS as managing agents first made contact with the Area Office and were sent a copy of the *Handbook for Managing Agents* and other MSC material. They then completed a training proposal form setting out details of their scheme for vetting by the Area Office. 'We regard the managing agents as our sub-contractors, basically', explained an officer. 'They do the work of putting the Scheme into effect.'

There was a notable omission from the training proposal form however. These 'subcontractors' were not required to state their intentions with regard to guarding against sex inequality. Though the *Handbook* contained the usual caution about the law of discrimination, the actual training proposal form asked for information about everything, it seemed, except the managing agent's intentions on equality. A space on the form did request information on 'recruitment factors', and though some managing agents might volunteer in their response that their scheme would be 'open to all, without prejudice etc. etc.', others would read the question as an invitation to emphasise that 'only people willing to wear overalls and heavy boots and to get dirty need apply'. Since it was not even this training proposal form itself, but an abbreviated transcript from it, that was subsequently submitted to the Area Manpower Board for approval of the scheme, there was nothing to prompt Board members to scrutinise the application with sex-equality in mind. Besides, Boards seldom argued with officers' advice. 'Once we have licked [proposals] into shape we put them to the Board, which has the final say. By and large they go along with our recommendations.' Before a scheme is approved it must satisfy the MSC that a relevant trade union has agreed its design. In theory this ought to be enough to ensure compliance with sex-discrimination law and equal opportunities. Many schemes however are in non-unionised situations where there is no trade union to consult. Besides, the unions themselves are by no means trustworthy advocates of women's interests.

Once a scheme had been approved, a Local Programme Assessor from within the local team would take on responsibility for monitoring. Since LPAs had a big case-load they were often out in the field three out of five days in the week. They were assisted in their monitoring work by various written instructions from Moorfoot, as well as by advice from their Programme Manager. The principal guide was the Programme Assessor's *Aide Mémoire*, a pocket booklet with a checklist of questions to bear in mind when making monitoring calls. Nowhere in the *Aide Mémoire* was there a prompt on the presence of young women in the scheme or the incidence of sex-stereotyping. Another important item of documentation for the LPA was the set of monitoring forms kept on file back in the office. (This was known as the MAR system.) One LPA described the use of this system as follows:

This is a series of forms looking at all aspects of a scheme and you put down your priorities of what you are going to be looking for. You put down what date you make each visit, what you are intending to look for on that visit, what you found, what you did, any points that were raised and things to follow up later. If you see something that needs looking into, you put that down... you would do a follow up and see if there had been any alteration. So it covers all the organisational aspects of the scheme. There's a section on health and safety for instance. *It covers all the areas we are supposed to look at.*

Yet the 'minimum criteria' listed in the monitoring pack for assessment of schemes did not include equality of opportunity or absence of sex-discrimination or sex-typing. In September 1985 a memorandum (Manpower Services Commission, 1985) had marked a shift in emphasis in monitoring practice, away from minimum criteria (inputs to YTS) to effectiveness (outputs). This likewise neglected to propose that one of the measures of effectiveness should be the achievement of an equal presence of the sexes on schemes, and in different 'occupational training families' within schemes.

Monitoring is of particular importance because whatever a managing agent says he (or she) will do in the way of training means little until the scheme is in operation. The LPA and sometimes the Programme Manager aimed during the YTS annual cycle to visit all the managing agents in the 'patch' not once but several times. As many work-experience providers as possible were also to be visited. Close liaison was meant to be maintained with the Careers Service. But because of an increase in work without a concomitant increase in staffing by MSC the standards of monitoring, never adequate, had deteriorated sharply in 1985/6. 'The monitoring of places has been cut back quite drastically' said one worried officer. 'The problem is that monitoring is certainly not in-depth and there is not much of it.' To see as many individual trainees as possible they felt was important, too. That way 'you are talking to someone who sees all aspects of the scheme, they can tell you what they think about the managing agent, the college, the work placement, whatever. It is another piece of the jigsaw.' But the current level of trainee contact was only 15 per cent visited during a year. 'I mean we don't work it that way. We used to pride ourselves on seeing every youngster. But we can't now... It's MSC policy (to cut down).' The YTS Manager reluctantly concluded that to attempt 100 per cent coverage of trainees was simply an inappropriate ordering of priorities.

Confronting discrimination: where is it?

I asked officers how often the issue of sex equality arose in the course of their normal business of approving and monitoring schemes. The answer was: infrequently. This was partly because firms providing work-experience were by now relatively alert to the letter of the law and knew all too well how to avoid 'putting their foot in it', while continuing in practice to discriminate. But it was also because it was the managing agent and the careers officer, rather than the MSC officer, who was the one to have most direct contact with employers. Managing agents themselves, like employers, on the whole knew better than to expose to view any prejudices they might have. MSC officers to whom I spoke therefore had not had much experience of countering overt sexism. They were inclined to believe it was 'not a big problem'. This was fortunate, for they felt it could be quite difficult or embarrassing to confront sex prejudice in an employer openly:

> Because you have also got to remember that we're interfering if you like with the managing agent's business. And we could create a lot of problems for them. Not that that would stop me. But I would want to inform the managing agent what I was doing before I created a stink.

However, managing agents cannot be trusted to confront employers either. Another LPA said, 'You don't see it unless you go prying for it. And I don't think the managing agents are prepared to do that quite honestly. They don't get paid if they don't have a trainee [in placement].'

It has to be remembered that most Local Programme Assessors were relatively inexperienced and still feeling their way with YTS. They were also operating with very little guidance on sex-equality issues from MSC head office. I asked the Programme Team members in this London Area Office (the four I interviewed were men, and white) had they had any in-service training with the MSC in connection with their YTS work? Three had received such training, in modular courses varying in length from a few days to a couple of weeks. None however could recall any component of this training having dealt with sex equality. 'I can honestly say there's been nothing, as a topic. I was just made aware when I joined of phrases like "non-discriminatory policy". Not an actual session in any of these courses on how to handle it, no'. Field-staff trainers were not obliged to include equal opportunity material in the courses they ran until 1986.

It should be added here that in addition to training its own staff, the MSC makes provision through locally 'accredited' training colleges for training in YTS procedures and practices for managing agents and sponsoring firms. One of the principal courses used for this purpose is the specially-designed City and Guilds no.924, 'Youth Trainers

Award'. There is no mention of women, gender or equal opportunity anywhere in this curriculum. Nor is the provision of training on equality issues specified in the MSC's contract with its Accredited Training Centres. Any courses on this subject provided (and the ATC in my London area had, unusually, laid on some innovatory sessions on 'women in YTS' and 'working with girls') were organised on local initiative.

Again, I asked officers for evidence of any guidelines on sex equality reaching the Area Offices in written form from Moorfoot. Several mentioned and produced a one-page leaflet boldly titled 'Equal Opportunity and the Youth Training Scheme'. It was designed, it said, for 'managing agents, sponsors and work-placement providers'. This turned out to be about *race* equality only. There was no mention of women. This came as a surprise to the officers, who had not examined it in detail. They searched their memory without success for any similar leaflet that might have dealt with sex equality. 'I'm sure there must be *something*.' There was in fact nothing. Neither did the local Area Manpower Board stress sex equality as a high priority. Board meetings are attended by certain senior officers. Later they hold 'de-briefing' meetings with their staff, passing down the sense of the meeting on various agenda items. Yet, 'I suppose' said one LPA 'I'd have to say it was not particularly high priority with the Board, because I've never been aware of it. And if it had been, we would have been made aware of it in some form or another.' A second officer said, 'One isn't very conscious of the Board at all.'

Sex equality and the Area Manpower Board

This raises the question: just what is the role of the Area Manpower Board? As we've seen, the AMBs are not elected bodies. A Board chairman (I use the masculine noun, since that is MSC practice) is appointed by the Minister. He or she in turn, by agreement with the Regional Director of MSC, extends invitations to Board members, who normally serve for three years. There are five employer-representatives, nominated by the Confederation of British Industry, and five employee-representatives whose names are put forward by the Trades Union Congress. The people chosen are intended to represent the nature of employment in the local job market. In addition there is one education service representative, a professional education representative, one from a voluntary organisation, a chair-person of a Committee for the Employment of Disabled People and, finally, several local council members. An AMB may also co-opt up to four non-voting members to represent 'other important views', including those of women (Manpower Services Commission, 1983c). Getting adequate representation of black people and of women on AMBs has been a problem from the start. In 1985 only 1 per cent of AMB members were black (Hansard, 1985). Only five of the fifty-five AMB chairmen in Britain and only 10 per cent of AMB members were women (Manpower Services Commission, October 1985e). Trade unions have been no better than other bodies in putting forward women. A study in 1985 showed that only 10 per cent of trade-union representatives for Area Manpower Boards were female (Randall, 1985).

The relationship of an Area Manpower Board to an Area Office is by no means a managerial one. It cannot be compared with the relationship of a local council to its council offices. As the chairman of this particular London Board described it:

> it's an advisory body... I honestly think if you were to speak to Board members, including myself, and say 'Do you really believe you are shaping YTS or having a great deal of influence on the nature of the schemes, the financing of schemes, the overall administration of schemes?' the answer would have to be 'No'. I think what the Board probably can do is make sure that schemes do not suffer from the most extreme abuses that they could suffer from... We are a watchdog, but not without teeth.

This is confirmed in the phrasing of the booklet about the Boards, given to new members. It makes it clear that the Boards act only 'within guidelines established by the Commission', and are intended to be not decision-makers but facilitators, forging links between the bureaucracy and the local community (Manpower Services Commission, 1983c).

Agendas of the Board's monthly meeting are taken up more or less equally by business concerning the MSC's Community Programme and the Youth Training Scheme. The latter involves discussion of individual training proposals and monitoring reports, but also includes examination of monthly 'progress reports' summarising the current overall position of YTS for the Area. Data on trainee starts and on leavers are returned by managing agents to the Area Office on a monthly basis. These, along with information on places approved, are the basis of the Area Office's regular reports to Moorfoot, the Region and the Board. The Board in my London area in early 1986 were thus seeing statistics on the cumulative number of trainees starting YTS during the year, the number of trainees currently in training, and analyses of both these by Mode and type of scheme. Data on ethnic origin of trainees were also provided. Statistics included occupancy rates, the number of disabled trainees, and a comparison of ethnic breakdown of trainees in the area with other London areas. Once each quarter this ethnic analysis was also specified by sex.

There was a serious omission however. Clearly when considering occupational sex-segregation and sex-typing in YTS statistics show-ing sex of trainee are of particular importance. Yet the only data specifying sex being presented regularly to the Board were at the disaggregated level of individual schemes, or in relation to ethnicity. Even in these instances sex was related to scheme, but not to occupational training families. What the Board was not seeing each month was the picture of trainees in the various scheme types analysed by sex or the sexes distributed to the various 'occupational training families'. It seems this lack of information was not untypical. A 1985 study of AMB members showed that only one in fifty were able to give the breakdown between male and female on MSC schemes in their area (Randall, 1985). Such statistics were nonetheless readily provided for me on request by the London Region Office, Planning and Monitoring Department, not only for the London Region as a whole but for each segment. They are therefore no doubt available on each Area Office computer, whence they must originate. But the officers were not making it a priority to prepare them, I was not given such statistics, nor was the Board asking to see them. To learn about the position of young women on the Scheme presumably Board members would have had to do as I did: first, do their own sums from the disaggregated scheme sheets; second, ask officers to produce a special-purpose table; or third, ask the Regional Office. There was no conspiracy here; no-one was trying to hide anything. It is simply that the question 'What is happening to young women on the Youth Training Scheme?' was not one that anybody in 1985/6 was finding time to ask.

It has already been pointed out, in Chapter 1, that there are serious problems with 'occupational training families' as statistical surrogates for occupation. As the YTS Manager in my area affirmed, to say that someone is training in a certain occupational training family means nothing. In hotels and catering, for instance:

> you could be waitering, or you could be a hotel management trainee. And you might know a girl and a boy were both in that OTF. But unless you knew the girl was doing service and the boy was a management trainee, you wouldn't be really informed.

True enough. However, until Moorfoot would produce its new more detailed classification of training placements (due in the 1986/7 Scheme) 'occupational training family' was the only basis on which the degree of sex-segregation in YTS could even begin to be appreciated. It is not only 'sex by occupational training family' that was needed however. With so few statistics specifying gender there was no indication how well or how badly young women were represented generally within YTS or how one London Area differed from another or from other parts of the country. There was no evidence that officers or Board members were aware, for instance, that they had such a varying proportion of female trainees from one borough to another; or precisely how well or how badly the two sexes were doing in gaining access to employer-based schemes, or employee-status places. Such figures were only produced later, in discussing this report. Yet without these data officers and Board members were limited to hunch or impression. The failure to draw up regular statistics of this kind was evidence of a low level of alertness to gender-issues in the Area Office and on the Board. Experience in other MSC Areas outside London suggested that this Area Office was not unique in its neglect.

The Board members I met, like the officers, stated clearly that they personally were aware of sex equality as an important issue. 'I don't think there's anyone on the Board that doesn't fight for equal opportunities. People's attitude has always been quite progressive' said one member. A vague policy of 'equality' however, that no-one articulated in any detail, resulted in issues lying buried. 'It doesn't seem to enter [our discussion] very often. People assume, I think, on the Board that equality has already been achieved.' It is significant that Board members are not – any more than officers – assisted in carrying out a sex-equality monitoring role by any guidance, directives or training from MSC head office. The booklet which Board members receive on joining contains no reference at all to women, sex issues or equality of opportunity (Manpower Services Commission, 1983c).

Interrelationship of race and sex

The gap left by the Manpower Services Commission where a strong campaign on sex equality ought to be, is filled by a vague awareness of social injustices engendered by inner-city 'riots', sharpened by the activities of local pressure groups. This consciousness is, perhaps naturally, far more oriented to issues of race than of sex. Women do not riot. Among 'rioters' can be identified young black men. Local ethnic associations are quite rightly quick to press their case on the Area Manpower Board and on the MSC. Political masters in Whitehall are pressing the MSC to deal with what they perceive as a problem of law and order threatened by 'racial minorities'.

The matter is confused by the practice of the MSC of lumping together in its policies all kinds of 'special group', using the phrase 'equal opportunities' to cover issues of race, sex and disablement. Equal opportunity is a term that needs unpacking since within it are certain complexities. Black youngsters in Britain do encounter serious discrimination and prejudice on account of race. There is all-too-plentiful evidence of massive discrimination against black people in the labour market (Commission for Racial Equality, 1978; Walsall CCR, 1978; Dex, 1982). There is no question (as there is with gender) that the people in question are physically able to do the full range of jobs. Three unique worries appear to apply on the race front with regard to the Youth Training Scheme. First, that widespread (if subterranean) racial prejudice results in the failure of black candidates to get placements on YTS. Second, that the youth of certain groups show no enthusiasm for YTS – they boycott it. And third, those black school-leavers who do enter the Scheme come to be disproportionately clustered in community projects and workshop-style schemes (Mode B) rather than employer-based schemes (Mode A). By a two-way process of association they then come to be seen as second-class citizens in YTS. A study in Leicester found that the two forms of discrimination, racist and sexist, do not operate in the same ways. Young black and white people are more likely to be competing for the same jobs than are young women and men, and racism (between same-sex groups) appears to be more prevalent and visible (Griffin, 1986).

Young women by contrast are *not* disproportionately clustered in Mode B in YTS, nor do they have less success in getting jobs when they leave the Scheme. These facts however partly arise from the underlying sex-stereotyping in YTS and in the economy generally: women are in demand precisely for 'women's work'. Sex-segregation appears to popular view as much more 'natural' and 'chosen' than differences in the circumstances of racial groups. The two phenomena call for specific kinds of strategy.

Disabled people for their part also encounter hesitancy and prejudice but in this case there are some jobs (though not as many as often believed) that they actually cannot do, or where the work and training conditions need adapting to their needs. Here the MSC has been prepared to make some, if inadequate, extra provision in Mode B2 schemes, and disabled trainees are also allowed a preliminary thirteen weeks on a YTS allowance to undertake preparatory training.

Many young women in the target age-group of the Youth Training Scheme in London are of groups against which white racism is prevalent. Many are disabled. Special attention to their needs on these counts is vitally important. In addition however for those young women *as women*, and for other young women too, there exist problems that differ from either racial discrimination or prejudice against the disabled, that interact with those phenomena, and that call for positive action. Looking at statistics of youth training from the perspective *both* of race and sex certain things come to light that are otherwise obscured. For instance, young black women do not share to the same degree the tendency to be excluded from employer-based schemes that young black men experience. Of all female Afro-Caribbean trainees entering the Scheme in 1985/6, 68 per cent entered Mode A, as against 49 per cent of young men of Afro-Caribbean origin, but as against 83 per cent of white women. Of Asians, 68 per cent of young women entered Mode A, as against 60 per cent of young men. Both stereotyping and discrimination operate along dimensions of race as well as sex.

In day-to-day practice, however, both in the Area Office and the Area Manpower Board, very much more time and effort was being devoted to race problems. No-one to whom I spoke hesitated to confirm this, although some felt that in the early days of YTS the balance had been more equal. The chairman of the Board said:

> I think if you were to ask me the objective question 'Has the Board spent more time on the problems of ethnic minorities than it has on the question of sex equality?' the answer must be 'Yes' without any shadow of doubt. We have spent a substantial amount of time on the ethnic minorities... I think the nature of this area is such that it leaves the Board no choice, although the Board were very willing to get into that field. But we do have no choice. Because though we recognise the problem of equality of choice for young men and women, the inherent problems of ethnic minorities are so much deeper and so much more difficult to overcome.

While he could recall many meetings between the Board's members and ethnic minority leaders he had to admit 'the only meeting we have had that I can recollect on the specific question of young *girls* was when we met the officers of London Women in Youth Training.' (This was a GLC-sponsored action and research project that existed for twelve months in 1984/5.)

It was not only in London that I found sex equality to be buried deep within an 'equal opportunity' policy defined mainly as race equality. In this and in three other Area Offices it was the same. When I raised the question of equality of opportunity with officers they responded immediately as if I meant *racial* issues. The fact that I meant sex equality had to be continually re-emphasised: I was raising matters that were not often thought about. In a West Midlands Area Office for instance, yes, 'Equal opportunity frequently raises its head on the Board but very frankly in this area the emphasis is always on race.' And in a Welsh Area:

> in the last twelve months there has been little discussion of equal opportunity for girls, whereas there has been considerable discussion of equal opportunities for ethnic minorities. Because it is conceived by the Board to be a more significant problem.

It cannot be emphasised enough that the problem for young women in YTS, being mainly the problem of sex-stereotyping, is a disadvantage of a different kind from racial disadvantage. Its effects do not show up immediately, but in lost opportunities and earnings in later life. It damages women of every ethnic group and it merits specific attention.

Sex-typing: whose problem?

So what exactly was the situation of young women in this London area when the statistics of OTF were analysed? Table 4.2 shows some differences from the national pattern, because of the nature of London employment, but overall a similar degree of occupational segregation by sex. In an attempt to obtain more detail of how many young people are 'crossing' gender-type in their choice of YTS placement I undertook a simple postal census of all schemes in the Area. Approximately a quarter (twenty-five schemes) returned usable replies, covering a total of 2847 trainees, past and present. The picture that resulted confirmed the broader-brush pattern of the statistics for the area. As many as 82 per cent of the 1007 young women mentioned were or had been in office work or hairdressing. Of the 402 hairdressing trainees mentioned, only 8 per cent were young men. Of the 344 retail butcher trainees, only two trainees were young women. All fifty-three trainees in a sports scheme were male. And finally of 942 trainees in building trades, engineering activities and electrical work, twenty were female – about 2 per cent.

More worrying was the degree of complacency about the sex-stereotyping that was clearly occurring. For every scheme that felt it to be a problem there was another that did not. One group-training association with 156 males and not a single female in plumbing, mechanical engineering, motor mechanics and electrical maintenance did not think sex-typing to be a problem on their scheme and did not wish to see any action taken to break it down. A further education college running its own YTS scheme found that, although trainees were obliged to try a range of skills, there was 'no evidence that any trainees find final employment outside their traditional areas'. Nonetheless, their answer to the question 'do you consider sex-stereotyping to be a problem on your scheme?' was answered with a 'No'. Some schemes were satisfied if they had managed to attract a small proportion of the minority sex to non-traditional placements. But others were clearly worried about sex-segregation, and did wish to see more preparatory work with schools and parents, more support from the MSC in combatting it, and an encouragement to employers to take equal opportunity seriously.

Table 4.2 YTS starts April to December 1985 analysed by occupational training family of placement and by sex of trainee. Geographical area covered is the case study segment of London, for which percentages are compared with those for Greater London and YTS nationally

Occupational training family	Number of trainees			Females as a percentage of all trainees			OTF as a percentage of all YTS placements		
	Male	Female	Total	Case study area	London region	National Scheme	Case study area	London region	National Scheme
1. Administration/ clerical/office	511	1277	1788	71.4	70.4	75.6	32.0	31.5	21.0
2. Agricultural/ horticultural/ forestry/fishery	42	20	62	32.2	36.7	24.4	1.1	1.3	5.1
3. Craft/design	340	54	394	13.7	19.5	10.0	7.1	5.0	5.3
4. Installation/ maintenance/repair	608	26	634	4.1	5.6	4.3	11.4	14.2	16.2
5. Technical/scientific	109	29	138	21.0	22.9	18.4	2.5	2.5	2.2
6. Manufacture/assembly	788	81	869	9.3	8.3	19.3	15.6	12.5	16.8
7. Processing	53	2	55	3.6	7.6	25.6	1.0	0.6	0.6
8. Food preparation/ service	141	108	249	43.4	42.0	55.4	4.5	3.9	4.7
9. Personal service/sales	231	692	923	75.0	74.9	71.9	16.5	19.4	21.2
10. Community/health care	74	196	270	72.6	83.8	85.9	4.8	4.4	4.9
11. Transport services	176	24	200	12.0	8.9	9.0	3.4	4.6	2.1
Total	3073	2509	5582	44.9	46.4	44.8	100.0	100.0	100.0
Unclassified trainees and unclassified placements	345	148	493	30.0	39.6	35.2			
Grand total	3418	2657	6075	43.7	45.0	43.7			

In addition to this postal census I asked MSC officers to tell me what instances they knew of in which young people of either sex were training in YTS for work non-traditional for their sex. Characteristic answers indicated both that informally the notion of 'traditional' and 'non-traditional' work for the sexes was very well understood and needed no explanation; and, also, that the instances were very few indeed. One officer mentioned a girl, the first proudly reported by a training workshop's carpentry section. 'I would be struggling to find more examples', he said. 'And if I did, it would be one-off.' Another said, 'We have a few. Single figures. There is a girl doing engineering work I think.' Three other MSC Areas gave me similar impressions: sex-typing is the rule.

Curiously, it is precisely because sex-stereotyping is universal that it is felt not to merit comment or concern during the Local Programme Assessors' monitoring visits to schemes. If a hairdressing scheme or a secretarial scheme is 100 per cent female, well, it is assumed that this is a fact of life. Nothing need be questioned and no blame is involved. Anyway, 'I've yet to find a queue forming of boys who want to be secretaries, or girls who want to be motor-vehicle mechanics.' It is not that officers are not delighted when the odd instance does arise. As the YTS Manager said of the Programme Teams, 'they take pride when they find an instance of a girl doing non-traditional training'. The officers do see it as 'a success'. But it is treated as a chance occurrence and even used instrumentally.

> The only time we really give consideration to a girl doing a motor-vehicle job, or whatever, is because it is useful publicity. Really. Whenever we're looking for publicity as we are at the moment, we're looking for the out-of-the-ordinary. Not the Joe who's going through the training as a mechanic and is doing a good job. Because that doesn't draw attention. It's the girl mechanic or coal miner [sic] or whatever, that does.

A Programme Manager said, yes, they would act fast against any instance of actual discrimination. What they could not do was 'social engineering'. He said of his LPAs, 'I know what they'll say. They'll say "It's not going to be *me* that forces a young girl to be one of the pioneers" '.

The issue of course is not *really* whether young people should be 'forced' to do something 'they don't want to do.' It is a question of recognising that the circumstances of the school-to-work transition in which YTS plays such a big part today make young people's choices less than genuine and free. To do more than they were doing, however, the officers and Board members of this London area would have to step across the line from equality of opportunity to positive action. This was simply not on the agenda in the 1985/6 Scheme as designed by MSC. That there were no voices at local level protesting the lack of positive action was because of the popular analysis of the causes of the sexual division of labour. These were seen as lying entirely outside YTS and therefore beyond the reach of the influence of the Scheme. It was 'biological', it was 'historical' it was 'parents', 'teachers', 'employers' and above all it was 'the kids themselves'. Consequently, 'I don't think it is (high priority for us) and honestly I don't feel it should be, given there are only so many hours in the day and that would not rate particularly high,' said one officer. And the YTS Manager confirmed that dealing with sex-segregation could not be:

> my top priority, from a purely operational point of view. From a personal point of view of course it's different. I've come up through a school in which it is accepted that it is important to be supportive, to say the very least, to women... But here and now my priorities are, first, to get a two-year YTS programme off the ground. And second, to do something about the appalling underrepresentation of black people on YTS in the area. Girls are not really under-represented here. We are in a buoyant female labour market... in the area. So it has to be third priority.

1986: a shift of gear

It is doing MSC no injustice to say that during the first three years of the Youth Training Scheme action for young women as a 'special group' was at the level of tokenism. However during the third year there were beginning to be glimmerings of recognition in Sheffield that YTS could and should be a site of positive action for young women. In late 1985 a change had begun to be felt in the climate of opinion in the Manpower Services Commission. Bryan Nicholson replaced David Young as the Manpower Services Commission's chairman in late 1984. He showed a more supportive inclination than his predecessor to positive action for women. The departure the following year of Peter Morrison, who had been the Minister responsible for the Commission's affairs since YTS began, was also hailed by outside observers as creating a more favourable atmosphere for positive interventions on the problem of sex-segregation.

YP-3 had submitted to the Youth Training Board, at its July 1985 meeting, a paper reporting on the position of young women in YTS during 1984/5 (Manpower Services Commission, 1985a). The main point to emerge from that paper was that young women were concentrated in three 'occupational training families': the traditionally 'female' office, sales and caring roles which we have already noted. The chairman invited officials to report back to the Board with proposals to encourage young women to pursue a wider range of training opportunities. With the extended two-year Scheme due for introduction the following April, which as we have seen was deemed by the Department of Employment's lawyers to make positive discrimination in YTS legal, YP-3 now felt able to respond with a proposal for some experimental positive action measures. First, encouragement of some single-sex schemes for young women in non-traditional areas of work – six were expected in the first year, nationwide. Second, encouragement to some male-dominated schemes to reserve places for young women: ten schemes up and down the country in 1986/7. Third, encouragement of job-sampling or 'tasting', especially in employer-led schemes which until now lagged behind Mode B in this respect (Manpower Services Commission, 1985b).

Unfortunately this new philosophy was not backed by much money. There would be £120 000 in the first year to be spent mainly on publicity, a national conference and monitoring. A press release was issued in December 1985 but there the matter rested until introduced at a Regional Directors' meeting in the spring of 1986. Slowly the news penetrated downwards to Area Offices where it met with a mixed response. In the London Area Office some felt 'it's a laudable aim'. Some that 'it might do more harm than good'. There was an uncomfortable feeling that 'positive action' meant 'positive discrimination' which in turn meant replacing one evil by another. But the YTS Manager took the challenge seriously and set about finding schemes in the area to participate.

The positive action measures of 1986 were bound to be welcomed by feminists inside and outside YTS. Throughout the country there had only been two girls-only YTS schemes – an operator scheme in engineering and a short-lived project for the conversion of a play-bus, using manual skills. Though they had had approval from the Secretary of State for Employment, they must have been – if the Department of Employment's legal opinion was correct – technically outside the law.

Documents emerging from Moorfoot in connection with the new-look two-year YTS bore the mark of the new thinking. The report that prefigured the expanded Scheme, published in July 1985, contained the statement 'We shall redouble our efforts to break away from sex-stereotyping', though it gave the MSC a let-out with the addendum 'this problem is particularly intractable since stereotyped views are held by so many of the parties involved, not least many of the young people themselves' (Manpower Services Commission, 1985c).

The new *Managing Agents Handbook* also followed up the usual genuflection to 'equal opportunities' with the following:

'Positive action' training can be made available when a particular racial group – or a single sex – can be shown to be underrepresented in a certain skill or occupation. Now that YTS has a greater vocational focus it is likely that you will find it easier to satisfy the requirements of the Sex Discrimination Act 1975 and the Race Relations Act 1976 which relate to the provision of positive action training (Manpower Services Commission, 1986c).

The new 'training proposal forms' supplied for YTS-2 also had a new clause on 'equal opportunity' (Manpower Services Commission, 1986a). And the favourable climate for positive action was evident in the guidance issued to managing agents preparing to apply for the status of 'Approved Training Organisations'. ATOs would be 'expected to demonstrate such positive steps not only in their recruitment procedures, but also in the allocation of trainees to the various training programmes run by an individual organisation' (Manpower Services Commission, 1985d).

We saw in Chapter 1 that the new two-year version of YTS launched in 1986 puts more market pressure on schemes, marks the end of the 'Mode B' concept, and reduces the already inadequate extent of monitoring by MSC. In this context, a small positive-action programme for young women could be seen, as one LPA called it, as 'pissing in the wind'. Something will nonetheless be attempted now by some schemes in some Areas. It therefore becomes even more important than before to consider the kind of action most likely to be acceptable to young people. The following chapters will demonstrate the strength of the relationship between the culture of gender and the experience of work. Measures to break down occupational segregation by sex, it will become clear, have to be widespread rather than piecemeal; they have to consider the actions and reactions of young men as well as young women; they have to engage both with YTS and with careers guidance and the job market; and they have to take account of gender relations, in particular the interaction between the job market and the actively sexual relations in which teenagers are caught up.

Notes

1. The Youth Training Scheme was not originally covered by the Sex Discrimination Act 1975. For purposes of recruitment, it was brought within the scope of the Act on 21 July 1983, but trainees once in training still do not have the same protection under the law as employees. It should be noted however that the requirement on 'designation' under Section 47 was removed by the Sex Discrimination Act of November 1986.
2. A reorganisation later took place which increased the number of Regions and Areas and converted training Division into the 'Vocational Education and Training Group'.
3. The Manpower Services Commission is male-dominated, like any government department, quango or indeed any large institution. In Moorfoot, MSC's headquarters, in March 1986 there were only two women above the grade of Principal; women were only 7 per cent of principals; 11 per cent of senior executive officers; 25 per cent of higher executive officers; and 40 per cent of executive officers. Women began to predominate only among secretaries, clerks and other support staff. A not dissimilar pattern was evident in Training Division field organisation where only three out of fifty-five Area managers were women.
4. The figures here omit trainees placed with large national firms that run their own in-company Youth Training Scheme. Though one MSC Programme Manager at local level is responsible for local monitoring of these schemes, they are administered nationally by Moorfoot's 'Large Companies Unit' (LCU) based in London. LCU trainees are not included in local statistics.
5. In April 1987 the Greater London area was to be reorganised into six, rather than four, MSC administrative zones.
6. MSC at this time were using four racial categories in their statistics:

white, Afro-Caribbean, Asian and 'other'. See Chapter 1, note 2. Since 'other' was often used by managing agents as a residual category for white trainees from other countries than Britain and for uncertain cases I have excluded it from the count of 'black' trainees which consists of Afro-Caribbean and Asian.

7. This should be distinguished from the provision known as 'additionality', as envisaged in the Manpower Services Commission's original plan for YTS. MSC had proposed that for every three YTS trainees taken on by an employer as supernumeraries the employer might convert two of his/her normal under-18 employees to the status of YTS trainee. While the 'additional' trainees would continue to earn their full pay, the employer would receive the training allowance. This concept appears quickly to have fallen into disuse and was not commonly understood or practised in the area in which I was working. It should also be noted that the 'employee-status' places in my area were employee-status from the start of the YTS year. In addition to this some YTS trainees would be 'taken on' to the firm's payroll during the course of their YTS year.

5

Typing: 'A Really Funny Bloke'

I wanted to do typing at school, and they wouldn't let me. They said to me, when I put down typing as an option – they tried to have a little joke. 'You can't do typing, it's all women. You'll have to change it.' The head of my year, for instance, he tried to persuade me out of it. Sort of. Not saying, like, that it's a girl's thing, but saying 'I can give you something much better, why not try this?' So I changed it. And I think that happens to a hell of a lot of boys. They want to do it and are persuaded out of it. *Kevin*

I think it's a hangover from the nancy image. 'It's a woman's job.' You say 'secretary', you say 'woman'. If you say 'secretary' and say 'bloke', it would be a really funny bloke. It's not like that, but that's the way of the world isn't it. *Tony*

When Kevin's teacher told him 'I can give you something much better' he seems to have spoken, almost self-consciously, as a representative of the patriarchy. Businessmen and their office managers, men who have the power to hire and fire, to train and promote, do indeed give their better opportunities to their own sex. Such jobs lead to more responsibility and to higher pay than the jobs women get. To be 'better' however a man's job need not even promise these things. Some men's jobs are dangerous, uncomfortable, unskilled and low-paid. Some women's jobs, especially 'temp. typing' in The City, are relatively well-paid, besides involving a skill. The truth is, a man's job is seen as 'better' simply because women do not do it.

In this chapter I will look at secretarial and typing work in the context of the Youth Training Scheme, where it is an important subcategory of the 'occupational training family' known as *OTF-1: administration, clerical and office services occupations*. Apart from the question 'why don't young men do it?' discussed by Kevin and Tony above, there will be other questions. Why do young *women* do it? What does the choice mean to them? Is it appropriate to see it as a 'choice' at all? What will the outcome be? And could we or should we try to change things within the context of YTS?

Becoming an office trainee

Bridgebuilders Youth Training Scheme was a 100-place Mode A scheme. The managing agency was a Christian voluntary organisation, working among the unemployed of its local community. The YTS project was a one-man show. The coordinator, overworked, highly committed to his young trainees, was a Mr Mayhew. He had recently been made redundant after a lifetime in business. Bridgebuilders was an umbrella scheme, operating from the business centre of a suburban area on the fringe of London, and placing young people for a year's training with a cluster of relatively small local firms. Among the employers were butchers' shops, chemists, health-food stores and builders' merchants. There were professional practices including solicitors, accountants and dentists. But the greater part of the YTS clientele were commercial offices: insurance brokers and estate agents, shipping agents and publishers.

None of the sixty-six trainees who were on the scheme at the time of my case-study of Bridgebuilders were breaking any gender stereotypes: none were taking training remotely non-traditional for their sex. No young women were attempting building work, garage mechanics or photography. On the shop side young men worked in builder's merchants, young women in florists. The distribution of Bridgebuilders' trainees into OTF-1 was itself gender-skewed, with three-quarters of the young women being found within it, but only a quarter of the young men. And though on the face of it the office placements seemed innocently unisex, a closer look showed that within OTF-1, too, there was sex-segregation.

The young people themselves were similar in most respects. They had the same kind and quality of school-leaving exams (or rather the same lack of them), the same desire for 'a good job'. They were apparently undifferentiated material, the raw recruits of YTS. They were almost uniformly white. While black people were 11 per cent of this borough's population, only 6 per cent of the trainees enrolled at Bridgebuilders during the year were black: two Afro-Caribbean and three Asian young people. Among the twenty-one office trainees available for me to interview only one was black – an Afro-Caribbean young woman. Apart from this the only way in which the office trainees varied significantly was by sex. But as we will see this had been enough to ensure that YTS would be a different experience for each group, and would lead in different directions and close off different pathways.

The great majority of trainees had found their way onto the Bridgebuilders scheme through the Careers Office. It was quite normal for employers to advertise their YTS places as though they were normal jobs and for trainees to be placed straight into the workplace. Only later would Mr Mayhew come round and make contact with them, and invite all the newcomers to an 'induction day' at Bridgebuilders' office.

Off-the-job training

The first distinction I noticed was in the way the work placements filled respectively by young men and young women were designated in Bridgebuilders' records. Half the young women were in places called simply 'office', 'clerical' or 'clerical/typist'. Only one out of twelve of the young men was in such an unspecified clerical traineeship. The remaining eleven were in places that, though clerical, were also specified by a substantive interest. They were called, for instance, 'insurance clerk', 'forwarding clerk', 'salaries clerk', 'trainee programmer' or 'trainee contracts coordinator'. Mr Mayhew himself stressed that this was fortuitous: nothing was to be read into it. It was however a distinguishing factor between male and female that increased in significance when read along with a difference in the off-the-job training received by young women and young men, one day a week at the local technical college. Two courses had been selected as appropriate for OTF-1 trainees. One was Secretarial Skills and the other Business Studies. The first was designed to lead to typing 'speeds' and office-practice certification by Pitmans and the Royal Society of Arts. The second led to the Business and Technical Education Council's General Business Studies Certificate.

Of the twenty-one women in office places who were attending a course or had been attending a course, sixteen were on Secretarial Skills, and only five on Business Studies. Of the twelve young men, none at all were on the secretarial course. Nine were or had been on Business Studies. One was doing the more advanced BTEC National. Another had started on a Mechanical Engineering technical certificate because he was a trainee salesman in an engineering firm. A third was doing the Association of Accounts Technicians preliminary course. Of the young women whose placement was specified by some substantive involvement in addition to 'clerking', only half had been placed on the business course, the other half going onto Secretarial Skills. Thus, although the overall figures were small, there was an unmistakeable tendency for females to find themselves learning typing and office practice while young men learned about business or professional subjects more generally. This is not surprising of course. Perhaps it is more surprising that *any* young women had evaded the secretarial course. In YTS, both within my area and elsewhere, there exist entire secretarial schemes run by private training agencies, such as *Sight and Sound* with its 4000-place scheme, where the 'battery hen' trainees in their cubicles are 100 per cent females and expected to be so. I chose to look at Bridgebuilders not because it showed an

Secretarial skills, a safe option

extreme of sex-typing but precisely because it did not. There were some young men here in the office sector who could be studied in relation to their female counterparts.

The Secretarial Skills course attended by Bridgebuilders trainees was offered by the technical college's Faculty of Secretarial Studies which ran a range of other further education courses, the overall emphasis being on 'office skills and techniques', including preparation 'for posts as secretaries, personal assistants, shorthand-, copy- and audio-typists'. Double sessions in the YTS course were committed to typing and to such matters as filing, use of office equipment, photocopying, handling mail and answering the telephone appropriately. The Business Studies course on the other hand was provided by the Faculty of Business and Professional Studies, which offered courses in 'professional subjects, management studies and ancillary skills'. The YTS Business Studies course was designed 'to equip young people with a broad base of business skills'. For their double sessions the trainees chose a specialism from one of three options: accounts, information processing or keyboarding. The keyboarding was of course typing, but its modernised name was clearly intended to associate it with electronic equipment.

Both heads of department at the college were enthusiastic about YTS and committed to making their contribution to it work well. The Scheme had brought them headaches however, with little in the way of compensatory resourses. 'New courses, no help, no time to plan. It's very *ad hoc*. Everything could be improved with more time to discuss and review, especially YTS. It's a lot of extra work and there's no history to rely on and no definitive authority to ask.' Apart from the time-consuming liaison involved with YTS managing agents and the Manpower Services Commission, the Scheme had introduced to the college a new kind of 'problem student'. By definition, those who become YTS trainees have rejected school. They are of a lower academic level than most FE students and poorly motivated for college training. 'They're not really interested in getting further qualification' said the head of Secretarial Skills, sadly. 'If they have a job they're content.' Certainly the trainees I interviewed had their own reasons for being dismissive of education. College they found tedious. Their dreams were of a 'real job'.

Most of the teachers on these courses had worked in the business world at some time in the past and shared its values. They welcomed the closer liaison with industry and commerce, the 'new realism' that YTS heralded. In particular the head of Business Studies was keen to tell me, at the outset 'You're talking to a businessman.' He said 'YTS has influenced our method of teaching. We don't do so much lecturing. We involve the student more. Do more workshop-style teaching. We've equipped a model shop with cash tills.' There were new possibilities of purpose-designed training for the big firms operating in the area. Such firms are invited to specify their training needs and 'We'll tell you if we can teach it'. The aim on the YTS courses is to link with sponsoring employers so as to provide the trainee with realistic 'work-based assignments' during her or his time in college. Many teachers have been sharply critical of MSC's incursions into 'non-advanced further education' (NAFE). The 1984 White Paper 'Training for Jobs' extended MSC's purchasing power in the NAFE sector from £90m to £200m, to 25 per cent of total provision (HMSO, 1984). The Business Studies Department here however felt itself in harmony with the 'new vocationalism' fostered by the MSC.

Secretarial Studies too were intent on making their course appropriate to the new kind of trainee. The head was encouraging staff in the development of new student-centred methods: 'profiling' and 'negotiation sessions' at intervals with each trainee and her managing agent, talking through the student's achievements, failures and aims. She said 'I see YTS as accepting the trainee at the level at which they come to us, helping them to the best of our ability to achieve the highest level they can in the time we have'.

The sex-composition of the two departments was in sharp contrast. The head and a majority of the staff of Business Studies were male and among their students there were two males to every one female. The head and most staff in Secretarial Skills were female and with very rare exceptions all the students were female too. In fact the staff could only remember ever having had one male student in the past. There were however two young men at present. They had turned up among the current batch of YTS trainees, not from Bridgebuilders but from another managing agency with whom Bridgebuilders shared its college courses. These two young men were 'remedial' cases, 'almost educationally subnormal', who had been lumped in with the young women in Secretarial Skills because it was felt 'there would be less writing than in business studies'. They were considered by all to be an anomaly. They had not chosen to be there. They did not want to be secretaries, and their work placements were not in fact in secretarial but in storage and despatch work.

While the staff of neither department wished to impute a status difference between the two courses, it was modestly suggested in Business Studies that their course 'takes a slightly more academic approach perhaps'. Although there was no formal admission requirement to Business Studies I did find that the YTS trainees on this course had slightly better school-leaving exam results than those on Secretarial Skills. BTEC General is, besides, the first step in a training ladder of nationally recognised qualifications that can lead (theoretically) to management jobs. The head of Secretarial Studies believed strongly that the practical skills her department taught were both demanding to learn and worth acquiring. There was no real difference in the levels of the two YTS courses. Yet 'maybe the secretarial course, being all girls, has a lower status in the eye of the beholder'.

Divergent routes

How was it that the young women on the Secretarial Skills course had come to be there? None of them, it turned out during my interviews, even knew that some Bridgebuilders office trainees were on a Business Studies course. They had not chosen between the two courses. It was generally believed that the managing agent had chosen the course for them. Employers to whom I spoke also said the managing agent chose the appropriate course. The managing agent, for his part, said that he followed indications from the employer at the time of devising the 'training plan' for the placement. The process of selecting a course had, unconsciously and in a way that seemed natural to everyone, been different for female and for male trainees. A lot hinged on the job definition. The main criterion had been 'Does the job involve typing?' If it did involve typing the employer tacitly assumed the trainee would be female. In any case, only a trainee who could type or wanted to learn to type would be put in that placement and this would invariably be a young woman, since a high proportion of them had already done some typing at school. Boys avoid typing at school: a lad like Kevin is a rarity. The female trainee in the typing placement would then be sent, with relentless logic, to the Secretarial Skills course. The way the few young women on the Business Studies course had got *there* was either by requesting a placement with 'definitely *no* typing please', or by positively opting for one involving 'accounts'. For this was the second criterion: Business Studies was chosen, whatever the sex of trainee, when the placement involved figure work.

Mr Mayhew pointed out that few young women felt confident at maths. In his experience they shied away from accounts and towards typing.

The process for male trainees had been implicitly different. It was taken for granted that the Secretarial Skills course would be inappropriate for them, if for no other reason than that it was assumed that their job placement would not be a secretarial one. If a young man was in a placement with out-of-the-run demands, and if his talents were adequate, he might be sent to a higher level or more specialised course. If he was clearly not up to the standard needed to benefit from Business Studies, he need not slip into Secretarial. There existed a lower level course for him: Vocational Preparation. There was no similar fall-back course in use for less competent young women, who would be put with the rest in Secretarial Skills.

Mr Mayhew was emphatic that he did not engage in sex-discrimination in any way. But somehow the combination of what young women and young men said they wanted, what school had prepared them for, what employers' expected, and finally what Mr Mayhew himself deemed suitable, was producing distinctly different outcomes for male and female.

Out at work: filing and typing

Of all Bridgebuilders trainees enrolled in the YTS year 1984/5, an extraordinarily high percentage (66 per cent) had been placed in 'employee status' work placements. That is to say, by the combined efforts of the managing agent and the Careers Officers, in two-thirds of cases employers had been prevailed on to pay the trainee a 'proper' wage of between £40 and £60 a week. The training allowance was paid not to the trainee but to the employer to offset the wage. The employer also gave an assurance that if the trainee proved satisfactory the placement would continue as a permanent job at the end of the YTS year. Young men outnumbered young women in Bridgebuilders by three to two, and slightly more of the young men had the more desirable employee-status places.[1] This did not apply within OTF-1 however. In administrative, clerical and office placements the girls performed as well as the boys, with two-thirds of both sexes getting employee-status places. Here then we are looking at a privileged form of YTS, barely known in Inner London or indeed elsewhere in the country.

There was no observable difference between the sexes either in the matter of job satisfaction. Two-thirds felt they were being enabled to get some genuine training on the job, while one-third felt they were not. All were sure however that they were just doing a job like any other junior employee in their firm. 'I don't do anything different from the other employees because I'm on YTS. I do exactly the same as everyone else.' The only concession to 'training' seemed to be their absence at college for one day a week. To many of them this was a doubtful favour, as it happened. Most would rather have been free of the requirement to attend classes and simply earn a decent wage instead. Employers too confirmed that the YTS places were not the additional places that MSC had aimed to create through the Scheme. The manager of Seaforth Shipping, for instance, was clearly using YTS for his normal youth recruitment to the firm. The year on the Scheme amounted to a protracted job interview – for his were strictly 'trainee' places and most trainees could expect to be laid off at the year end. The firm treated the training allowance as a government subsidy of the pay-roll. Mr Mayhew was a convenient filter, sifting the labour market for them. 'We tried advertising in local papers and got a poor response. We tried the Jobcentre, but that is more or less a self-service system now. (Jobcentre) candidates are not vetted before they are sent to us for interview and they are useless.' So he had turned to Bridgebuilders as a source of youngsters, which, besides, was 'cheaper than an employment bureau'. YTS has become the actual youth labour market in this area. A second employer confirmed 'You have to have the need in the first place' before going recruiting a YTS trainee. 'When YTS came along we couldn't believe our luck really... Let's face it, we're in business. We have to have a reason to employ someone. So we wouldn't take on two or three more just because it's the start of a new YTS scheme.'

The trainee, then, in those four days a week spent in the workplace, is getting a feel of what it is like to be at the bottom of the office work-pile. Some were happy, enjoying being out of school at last, feeling their way into a new identity. But others now found themselves subject to a bossy, petty regime and a boredom that was hard to bear. One 'secretarial skills' young woman, Louise, described her dogsbodying 'office junior' job like this:

All I do is I sit at the desk and I get a file and I write on it who it's gone to, on a card. And I just file it in a cabinet. And when the person doing the post does it, I have to write, make a form out, write the number on the form, fold it up and put it in an envelope. And I have to do that for every letter to go out. And that takes a lot of time. And then I get someone coming down from upstairs, saying 'Put that in the filing cabinet, will you?' and it's right next to them! They could just as easily do it themself. He (the boss) had a go at me the other day because three people asked me to do something urgent and I couldn't do it all at the same time. The boss had a go at me and said I should be able to. I just can't be bothered with work now. It's getting me down. All right, it's good there. I mean it's better this last week. I don't make so much coffee, because I said the boy (the other YTS trainee) had to take turns which he didn't want to do. But I still have to go up to the shops when it's raining, to buy food and that. Half the time it's all right. You can get on with people. But they can be a bit snappy when they feel like it. The thing is I'm just doing the same thing every day, and it just gets boring. I don't usually smoke, but I smoke myself to death in there. I get so bored.

Louise, it so happened, was not typing. The reality of 'office practice' for most young woman trainees includes a lot of slogging at the keyboard. While Bridgebuilders trainees were monitored by Mr Mayhew to avoid the employer simply putting them to typing all day long, many employers want to use youngsters, as they are accustomed to, for this kind of repetitive work. One firm, the head office of a chain of high-street shops, had taken three young women from Bridgebuilders for its forty-strong clerical department, where quite a lot of typing was involved. They too attended the Secretarial Skills course one day a week. The personnel manager, Mrs Binley, described what she was looking for in 'her girls'. What she needed was 'a brightness about them, some sort of sparkle if you know what I mean. And a nice appearance of course. We wouldn't want anyone with green hair and yellow tights.' She made it clear that what the firm wanted out of YTS was *production*. 'I'm interested if they'll sit there and *work* all day. That is difficult to ascertain at interview.' It was worrisome of course when it came to filling in the trainee's log book, which was intended to testify to different things taught and learned month by month. 'It's a pain in the neck, because (the work) is repetitive. It's difficult to say anything new each month' said Mrs Binley.

Typing and secretarial jobs are notoriously limited in the promotion and career development that is available to those who do them. Mrs Binley said of her 'girls', there was 'frankly *very* little possibility of promotion. It's up to £80 a week and there you stick.' She said that even when women left to go to other firms, they tended to move sideways, to other comparable jobs, without gaining more responsibility or pay. The same story was told in other firms. A second employer emphasised that in his firm typists and secretaries on the one hand and clerical employees on the other came into the firm differently classified. It was unusual thereafter for typist/secretaries to escape from that classification. Was there no promotion possibility for them at all? I asked. He smiled knowingly. 'No, really. No.' He mentioned however one secretary who had worked hard and studied in evening classes, eventually obtaining membership of a professional institution and professional status within the firm. He added however that though she had started out as a typist, she had converted to being a general clerical employee before beginning her climb: from typist there is nowhere to go.

Employers were clearly sex-typing their secretarial and typing placements as female. This however did no more than reflect a uniformly traditional sexual division of labour within all the firms I visited. Mrs Binley was engagingly frank. Her pool had always been women. It started before computerisation when they were mainly NCR punch card operators and 'I don't suppose men would have stuck it.' Now they would be unlikely to consider a man in the job: it would upset the social relations between the women. The women were accustomed, she said, to engage in conversation most unsuitable for men's ears. 'It makes my hair curl sometimes and I'm an old woman' she said. Here was a curious inversion of the normal problem of men's 'dirty talk'. To clinch matters, Mrs Binley explained that there was no 'gent's toilet' in the building except for that of the directors.

Out at work: clerical snakes and ladders

If secretarial and typing work is clearly sex-typed female, clerical work is not: it is unisex. So too, at the junior level, is administration. Though individual firms may sex-type individual departments, areas or functions, in the economy overall there are openings for both women and men. This is what has brought some young men into OTF-1 and given some young women access to work that has seen

them placed on the Business Studies course, in contrast to Secretarial
Skills. Of course, the day-to-day reality of such jobs, especially when
you have just begun and are on the bottom rung, can be every bit as
boring as being the typist or the office junior. The three young women
I interviewed from Business Studies were, as it happened, not
altogether enchanted with their working lives. On the other hand they
felt that the 'secretaries' had it worse. The only black young women I
interviewed (one of the few black trainees with Bridgebuilders) was an
accounts clerk with Seaforth Shipping. She said 'We give secretaries
the work to do. Secretaries get pushed to hurry all the time. I wouldn't
like to do their job.'

Though the door is more open, clerical recruits are not necessarily
seen as potential developers, and new technology is tending to make
these roles increasingly peripheral and expendable. In fact when I
asked the manager of Seaforth 'Are your clerical jobs the ones that
will in the long run be wiped out by computerisation?', his reply was
'Not in the long run. By next year, we'd hope.' The practice of some
firms, however, like Irwin's Insurance, was, as the manager put it, 'to
grow our own' administrators. 'It's good to recruit them young and
indoctrinate them in our ways.' The clerical recruit was seen as raw
material from which a few would be selected for promotion. Some of
the male Business Studies trainees were clearly preparing for a better
future. One young man had entered his uncle's firm and saw himself
as a management trainee, soon to 'run the office'. 'This course is training me for work in an office. How jobs are made up, different limited
companies, communications, all different things that intertwine with
office work.' Another was in a freight-forwarding firm, 'the sort of
business where you never know it all'. And a third, Tony, was
delighted with his job as a trainee computer-programmer. He said:

I spent the weeks after leaving school visiting the four local
Jobcentres every day. I went to bureaus, got my name down on
books, but it was a total waste of time. There's a lot of people in the
computer field and they've got a good choice. I wanted ideally a
programmer's job but that was perhaps aiming too high. I didn't
want to do operating because I know that's a dead-end job. And I
was getting nowhere towards a career job, anything. Eventually it
was the Careers Office that came up with a vacancy. I didn't know
at first it was YTS, they said it was a programmer's job in a small
company. There was stars in my eyes, because it was precisely

what I wanted. There's only two directors, and you are good friends besides. You respect them because of their position, but they are friendly.

These young men, however, are in the main working-class. They may be male and thus have a male's advantage over women. They may be making a bid for work in the commercial and business world, glossier and more prestigious in reputation than some working-class men's jobs. They may be white – and a white man is three times as likely as an Afro-Caribbean man to get office work.[2] But they will not easily escape a class position. They are entering the lower and more humdrum jobs in the male-dominated hierarchy. As they aim for promotion they will find that middle-class young men, university-educated, with more polish and more pull, are favoured for the managerial openings. But almost always there will be more chance for the working-class young man than for the working-class young woman to climb. More senior men will have in mind the expectation of their male employees supporting a family. And there will be others, female, black – and both – to form the lower strata on and over which men may climb.

In summary, then, there is a clearly female environment, in typing and secretarial work. There is also a clearly male and white environment, in the upper echelons and in the specialisms such as computing, accounts and the substantive concerns of firms: insurance, property agency, publishing. The few men who might in their schoolboy innocence have fancied 'typing' will be persuaded along a more manly route, away from the female ghetto. There is always a 'better job' for them to aspire to. Some women do aspire to these better jobs too – and by wit or by chance get into the less sex-typed areas of clerical and administrative work from which the exit door is ajar. Being on a Business Studies course helps but does not assure this. Being defined as a secretary does not rule it out – one or two young women were hoping to learn the substantive side of the business and were making it their own project to do so. But being on a Secretarial Skills course certainly did not help this. It made it less likely that they would be taken seriously, or take themselves seriously.

Contradictory terms: the male secretary

During the weeks I spent with Bridgebuilders I interviewed nine adults and twenty-three young people (this included the two 'secretarial' boys) and I sat in on lessons and review sessions, spent time in the staff-room and canteen. In interview I asked the trainees about their work placements, four of which I visited.

Most of the young women had noticed a traditional sexual division of labour around them in their workplace. You could hardly miss it. 'All the women at our place do the same work. It's fifteen or twenty of us, checking invoices, filing, typing. There are no men there. The men are in the warehouse. And there's men upstairs, you know, directors.' Young men noticed it too. 'It's men doing this type of job and women doing that type of job, sort of stuck in channels and they never get out.' One young man generalised about it, expansively and with satisfaction: 'A woman does all the typing and the man, he takes all the risks. Typing is just the same thing all the time. Governors, they have changed tasks, they vary.'

I questioned the twenty-one Bridgebuilders trainees on two topics, to draw out their ideas and feelings on gender and work. First I asked them why secretarial work was nearly always done by women. Could men make good secretaries? Most young women were generous about this. They asserted that men *could* make good secretaries. One said candidly 'Most boys I should think could be a better secretary than I am, because I'm not that great!' And another said, 'Yes, they can actually. One answered the phone to me the other day. He was all polite and everything like that.' This was the worry expressed by some young women: would men be pliant enough to play the social role of a secretary? The appropriate manner, they were in no doubt, involved a soft voice, a gentle ministering tone, attractive clothes.

The real reason why men 'aren't secretaries' however was clearly not felt by the young women to be prejudice against them. It was, rather, they way men felt about themselves and about women. One young woman supposed that 'boys would like more active jobs', 'to be a man, do heavy work'. A second young women said of secretarial work, with a laugh, 'I don't know, I suppose they think it's poofy'. And another, 'They are too frightened to [do it]. You very rarely see men looking after the baby while the women go out to work. They are frightened of what their friends will say.' 'Probably blokes they think it's a sissy job, blokes they won't want to be sitting at a typewriter, you know. They'll do the man's work.' 'I think it's the thought of talking to their mates and saying "I'm a secretary".' They'd be ashamed.

Young men simply affirmed, 'It's classed as a woman's job', and that was enough to explain why they wouldn't consider it. They are averse, as men, from learning efficient touch-typing. Speaking about one of the 'remedial' young men in the secretarial class, a young woman said, 'In typing he just *sits* there, doing it with one finger, poke, poke.' And she demonstrated. One of the Business Studies young men said of himself that *he* didn't need typing skills. 'Well, perhaps on telex. It's quite important that a person does *know* the keyboard. But perhaps not a typist *as such*.' I met this over and again in the three projects I saw that included typing or keyboarding. Young men would only tolerate instruction in the keyboard if it was associated with computing. And they asserted their distance from 'typing' by refusing to use the officially-designated fingering, sometimes tapping quite fast but only with index fingers. I asked one young man 'Wouldn't you like to be an efficient typist, using all your fingers? He answered, 'It doesn't really matter, because the things I type are just short telexes or filling out forms. Anything long or complicated, we put it across to the typists to type. We have fully qualified typists there, women.'

It was interesting to hear the young women's views about the two 'remedial' young men in their Secretarial Skills class. It was recognised, as we've seen, that David and Paul were youngsters of low ability who were working in rough jobs and had got onto the Secretarial Skills course more or less by mistake. They should have been in Vocational Preparation. One, said Samantha, was 'a bit of a dumbo.' The other, too, was 'a bit weird. He works in despatch and he wants to be a lorry driver, so he doesn't need typing and office practice. He thought he was going to be on another course. He says this one is no good for him.'

I interviewed one young woman, Donna, when David was present. She said, 'I don't think they are getting *anything* out of it. I don't think they will get jobs as secretaries.' David giggled. She turned to him. 'David do *you* find it easy, typing?' She answered her own question. 'No. There! [Triumphantly] He *hates* it. He can't pick it up. Nor can Paul.' David said, defensively, 'I never turned up for half the classes'. That proved Donna's point. She went on relentlessly 'That's what I mean. So you don't like the course.' David admitted, 'No I don't. 'I mean they don't feel in place being with all us girls' she said to me. 'David, *he* don't mind so much because he knows us all. But Paul, he feels so embarrassed. It's horrible for him. I mean I can never see Paul being a secretary.' She and David both laughed at this thought. But David looked uneasy, unsure whether this was a slur or a compliment to a man. 'I'm not taking the micky' finished Donna kindly. 'That's the way it is.'

One of the teachers summed up the relationship between the young women on the course and these two young men. 'Some of the girls are very sophisticated and the two boys aren't very bright. They'd eat them for breakfast, sort of thing.' She also wondered how best to address her class. Should it be 'Girls, David and Paul'? 'I don't like to *ignore* them' she said. But clearly she felt her role with the boys was less to teach than to baby-sit.

Woman as boss

The second question I explored with the trainees was 'Do women make good business managers?' This opened up many subsidiary matters, on the one hand to do with ability, ambition and staying power, on the other with domestic life and responsibilities.

Young women on the whole were positive about the idea of women as managers. 'Yes. They'd probably be better at all the paper work than men. All my boss does is sit there with his tape-recorder, recording letters. That's all *he* does.' They foresaw problems for the woman manager however. 'I think if you're strong-headed – I think you'd need a strong head and that. It all depends on the firm, too, it depends a lot on the workplace. If you had a whole force of it, like, men – they might not accept a woman telling them what to do.' Women they felt could only make good managers by exceptional effort. 'If they're prepared to work and work and *work*. They do make it eventually' said Louise, the young woman who was 'smoking herself to death', in her boring job. And she added, shrewdly, 'Where I'm working now, looking at everybody, you know the people who are going to stay in the odd-jobs for ever and ever, and you know the ones that aren't.' So why don't we see more women managers? Louise's friend Pauline said, 'It's always thought that a man is the strong person of the two. So if there's stress and strain it's thought that a man can deal with it better. No other reason. No matter what the qualification there's always going to be sexual prejudice.' Would you like to be a manager? I asked Pauline. 'Oh yes.' But she hadn't mentioned this of her own accord, I pointed out. 'No. Because I doubt if I will. But it's a nice thought – having people underneath *me*.'

Though some of the young men were fairly positive towards the idea of women as managers, three were negative. For instance, 'I suppose they can't handle the job properly'. And 'I think men tend to be harder working and better educated'. Two of the young women too thought that men would make better managers than women. 'I've always got the impression that men are better than woman at that. That sort of thing. They just seem to play the part. It's like reception, women being better than men. They fit the part more. Men are more better at meetings than women I think.' And 'You find most men, they can talk their way into things and also talk their way out of it. It's the gift of the gab. It's confidence. I mean, I couldn't do what they do.' One young man, however, felt very differently from most of his peers about this. He is Kevin, the young man who had wanted to type while at school. Of women, Kevin said:

I think they've got more of it, like. More of the gab. More of the intelligence. In our exam results, my exams didn't value *nothing* to what some of those girls had.

So why don't they make it in business?

Male chauvinist pigs, isn't it? Yes, that's what it is. I reckon it is. I reckon it's got nothing to do with women. The men *think* they can't do it. It's men not giving them the opportunity.

What was happening here was that business management was being associated with power, initiative and will. These qualities were identified with masculinity – and only the exceptional young man claimed them for women. Some young women felt that they personally wouldn't want the responsibility and the competitive hassle of being a manager. Most however believed women could have the necessary qualities: only men stood in the way. In contrast to secretarial work, this field was protected by its 'owners'. Garry for instance felt there was something wrong about having a women in an area otherwise male. 'I really think it's better if men are all together you see. If it's all men, all of them can speak frankly and express their feelings. If there's a woman there, you know, it can be different... I think it's best if all boys do something that boys should be doing.'

On the other hand everyone knew today that the law allowed women free access to the work of their choice. Besides, there is a sense of fair play in many young people that pulls against and contradicts the self-interest of men as a sex. Tony for instance said, 'No, I think it's much better for everyone if it does change. A woman deserves that respect. You can't say, "You're a woman. You do that." The more you respect other people, the better it will be.'

Life as it is

We've seen that employers have their own ideas about the sex of the person they are seeking to recruit to their particular job openings. Discrimination is rife. At the same time, young people themselves are undeniably playing into the sex distinction. It is obviously in young men's interests, by and large, to do so. But why the young women? Why do they aspire to what any unbiased assessment would have to characterise as the subservient roles and the dead-ends among office jobs? Many young men – often with wild unrealism – think of themselves as potential managers and bosses. Why not young women?

One factor is what young women anticipate their future lives to hold. I met no-one of either sex who appeared to anticipate anything other than the most conventional division of labour in domestic life. The men would continue working, trying to earn enough to 'keep' a family. Women would marry, and though they would hope to keep some association with the world of work, they anticipated that it would be interrupted by the need to look after children. Roslyn was one of the few young women who had begun to look further. 'I've been thinking about it' she said, 'And I think when I'm a lot older I want to be somewhere at the top of a company.' She paused, and then went on. 'But I can't *say* that, can I. Because I'm bound to get married. So there'd be a sort of break in it.' And she paused again, and added hopefully, 'But women do still make it to the top, sort of thing'.

It has been suggested that middle-class girls on leaving school aspire more wholeheartedly to 'work' and to 'careers' than do working-class girls (Sherratt, 1983). Bridgebuilders young women, however, working-class though they were, were unmistakeably work-oriented. Nearly all, when asked 'What do you expect to be doing in five years' time?' mentioned some occupation they expected to be pursuing. Only one said nothing more than 'being married'. On the other hand, many mentioned a family as well as work. No boys did this.

The young women were pragmatic. They wanted marriage and children in due course. They were aware that the pattern of their working lives would be obliged to respond to that clearly chosen by the young men of their class and generation: a totally inflexible commitment to full-time uninterrupted earning. Committing yourself to training for a career in management, especially with a demoralising school record, did not seem feasible. On the other hand young working-class women today also fear unemployment and know that earning on their own account will always be important in a world they see as increasingly uncertain. Secretarial skills and typing make very good sense in such a context.

A second factor may have been even more important. Marriage and children still seemed far away to some of these 16- and 17-year-olds. What was much closer was undoubtedly having a good time and in particular meeting young men. The workplace is the site of a job market, but it is also the site of that second 'market' we've seen young women operate within. Employment is clearly somewhere to pursue romance, a place to look your best, to move in a social world:

> Pressures to get a man influenced young women's entry to the job market: office work was seen as a particularly 'good job for a girl' because it was expected to offer young working class women the chance to meet eligible men in high-status white-collar jobs (Griffin, 1985, p.189).

Seen in this light the fact that offices have clear-cut masculine and feminine roles makes them positively attractive to heterosexual young women. The job of secretary is no neutrally-defined occupation waiting for a neuter person to fill it. It is gendered. It has been forged in gendered practices and it confers its gender on the person who does it. The archetype of the secretary has many of the qualities of the 'ideal woman': supportive, sensitive, diligent, compliant, competent but retiring, neat and yet attractive. *Of course* male bosses want the secretarial job inflexibly gendered. Their own job after all has been forged in a complementary gendering process. They get some of their own gender-power from it. *Of course* young men scrupulously avoid typing or secretarial skills. They can be nothing but a source of contamination and emasculation. And for young women, struggling in their mid-teens to achieve a workable gender-identity, a job that is unambiguously feminine, safe from competition by men, and bestows a little extra femininity on you, is a secure place to be. Kelly Girl and Brook Street employment agency advertisements play on this theme to great effect.

Norma Sherratt has suggested that the notion of 'glamour' leads young women into certain kinds of work. She found that middle-class girls, dropping out of college courses for semi-professional occupations and 'settling for office work', explained it to themselves and others in terms of leaving a 'boring' world of college – even though it could lead to semi-professional jobs – for more 'interesting, exciting and different' possibilities. If office work offers this to middle-class girls with their wider opportunities, how much more will it attract working-class girls for whom the alternative is serving in fast-food chains, being on the till at Tesco's or sitting at a sewing machine in a sweatshop? As Norma Sherratt pointed out, 'the girls' definition of dead-end differed from more conventional definitions'. Glamour was what made that difference (Sherratt, 1983, p.56).

It is important not to marginalise those young women who are lesbians and do not seek to join in the heterosexual romance market. They are reduced to silence, as it is, by the aggressiveness of heterosexual culture. But there was no mistaking the commitment to a heterosexual identity of the majority of Bridgebuilders trainees. The young women were knowing, self-possessed and clearly gave a lot of attention to their make-up and clothes. 'Being a secretary' was only an aspiration as yet. The reality as a new YTS recruit to office work was using the franking machine, hammering away at the oldest typewriter and answering the telephone when the boss's secretary was at lunch. Nonetheless it was easy to see how aspiring to be a secretary could seem to fit the short-term needs of a Roslyn, a Pauline or a Donna. The job was associated with style. It involved a set of relationships, romanticised in girls' magazines, in novels, films and on television. It could lead up the Underground line to a job in the City. 'Well, everybody does have a go up there' said Donna, 'and I want to as well.'

Finally, of course, a good reason for choosing the secretarial route is that Donna and others like her still do stand a good chance of getting such work, the inroads of technological redundancy notwithstanding. While jobs were vanishing in manufacturing, construction and transport during the 1970s, 100 000 new jobs were being created in banking, finance and business services. By 1981 typing and clerical work in offices accounted for nearly 40 per cent of the paid work of women in London (Greater London Council, 1986, pp.74, 97). The very fact that men and women go different ways within office work, to different kinds of offices and different slots within offices, creates

Office trainee – hammering away on the oldest typewriter

protected ghettoes for women. The effect that men in clerical work earn £4.10 an hour on average, while women earn only £3.36, is a misfortune. But on the positive side is that women have only to compete with other women for these jobs. So today in the London area there is nearly always work for a good fast typist or a smart secretary. Such skills have even more immediate pulling power than a 'BTEC General'. Whether you liked typing or not it was, as the mothers of these young women said 'something to get behind you'. But Roslyn said she felt trapped. 'There isn't that many jobs about.'

No positive action here

It is no use therefore complaining of these young women: 'They have no ambition. They only want to be secretaries.' They are doing the best they can with the possibilities they have inherited. The question surely is not how should they, at a vulnerable 16 years of age, adapt and change and swim against the tide? It is, how should the world change to allow them to have *all* of what they want and need? It is, after all, not so very much.

What the Manpower Services Commission, Bridgebuilders, the Careers Service, the college and the employers were engaged in here was at worst traditional sexist practices, and at best a wishful *laissez faire*. None of the adults involved with these young people's training had a concept of positive action, of active intervention to *change the circumstances and the nature of the training to make possible a similarity of experience and achievement for young women and young men on the Scheme*. For example, they were not using the period of recruitment and induction to the Youth Training Scheme to explore and open up possibilities for each sex. They were not using these early days, when the trainee first became their responsibility, to slow down the moment of decision and to open up horizons. They were not explaining the nature of the world of commerce, the careers it offered and to whom, nor those it thwarted; they did not ask the trainees to reassess their initial choice of an occupation. They were not even discussing the two kinds of off-the-job training currently on offer. The managing agent and the Careers Service had perhaps allowed their perculiarly 'progressive' relationship to the Scheme, in which the trainee placements were ideally viewed as 'real jobs', offering employee status, to inhibit them from challenging firms, many of whom had dubious employment practices. They were not taking issue with the way the employers defined their trainee placements, the different way many of them tended to relate to female and male recruits. Some were being allowed to get away with clearly discriminatory recruitment. None were being told: if you want free youth labour, compliments of the MSC, you must commit yourselves progressively to change the internal structure of your firm from the bottom upwards.

Bridgebuilders and other managing agents in the area had the power of the purse when it came to commissioning off-the-job training courses from the local college. Yet it had not occurred to them, nor had it occurred to the college administration, simply to *stop offering* two separate and unequal courses to office trainees. Why did Secretarial Skills and Business Studies exist as distinct courses at all, if not to replicate existing divisions? How much better and how relatively simple it would have been to offer a single course for young women and young men starting work in offices. It could have been called Business Skills, perhaps. It could have afforded all trainees useful and worthwhile skills, like keyboarding; storing and retrieving information both manually and electronically; handling communications by telephone, telex or fax. But it could also have explored more extensively the world of business as it is: profit and loss, information handling and finance. Such a course could explore alternative forms of running businesses: self-employment, cooperatives, projects. It could explore different forms of decision-making. It could have involved the 'white-collar' trade unions in teaching about the rights and hazards of office workers, about problems of sexual harassment, about pay and conditions, and the values of belonging to a trade union. It could have been a course that helped young people of either sex to develop *similar*, not different, expectations and ambitions. As they carried those out into work, that itself might have begun to change the workplace.

In spite of the best efforts of some of the Careers Officers, few consciousnesses were being 'raised', it seemed, concerning sex equality. It is pleasant to imagine a conference among all the adult participants of this scheme – something that only a new enterprise like the Youth Training Scheme could have prompted, something that would indeed justify its existence – in which the parameters of office work and gendering were discussed anew from first principles. (And why just adults? Trainees too could contribute.) The head of Secretarial Studies was a far-sighted woman who already felt she would like to see the traditional secretarial role redefined. 'Because secretaries have tended to be submissive. It's not necessary'. The head of Business Studies was already aware that the computer might be a means of breaking down young men's resistance to typing, and that in fact 'men might have the ability to break those barriers that exist that prevent secretaries from climbing higher.' The managing agent, Mr Mayhew, had himself worked under a woman manager and was an advocate of such opportunities for women. Of course, many snags would be encountered in the course of such a discussion. Would young women lose out if men were to take seriously to entering and changing secretarial jobs? Would employers boycott the scheme if pressed to reform their practices? Would the domestic division of labour always be a stumbling-block, or are men amenable to change on this front too? Could young men and young women, given an innovative and supportive environment, feel safe enough to relax their feverish grip on stereotyped relations to each other and to employment?

This is fruitless invention, however, for no such conference was taking place. The possibilities and the problems were being skirted, not confronted. And meanwhile a new annual intake of YTS trainees were going their sex-determined ways, she to the typewriter and he to the desk.

Notes

1. Three out of five Asian and Afro-Caribbean trainees had employee-status places.
2. The Labour Force Survey, 1981, categorises non-manual employment into 'professionals, employers and managers', and 'other non-manual'. In this 'other non-manual' group, which includes the lower ranks of office work, are found 25 per cent of all Asian employed men, 56 per cent of Asian women; 8 per cent of Afro-Caribbean men and 51 per cent of Afro-Caribbean women; 23 per cent of all other men and 60 per cent of all other women – including white European (Greater London Council, 1986, p.109).

6

The Manly Trades: No Soft Touch

I don't think I ever thought about metal work. I never thought I
could do it or nothing. To see it – you've never done it before, you
think 'Let me have a go at that!' *Angie*.

If Bridgebuilders was a somewhat quality scheme, it was typical of
Mode A in one respect: it was failing to get young women opportunities in male manual trades. Market forces prevailed, and the
untrammelled market has only stereotyped openings for women. If
gender innovation was occurring at all in YTS it was likely to be in the
more sheltered environment of Mode B's community projects and
training workshops. To see what was happening I spent a month with
a fairly typical B1 scheme, Pond Close Training Workshop. Its name,
a relic from London's rustic past, had a ring of irony in these leafless
inner-city streets.

Pond Close was set up in April 1983 by the local borough council
to train forty-five unemployed school-leavers in seven trades: light
engineering, carpentry, upholstery, bicycle-maintenance, catering,
fashion-and-furnishing and office skills. The council therefore
became one of MSC's managing agents. Its Finance Department had
a contract with the Manpower Services Commission to supply this
YTS provision. The contract served as a benchmark when the Training
Division Area Office sent round its Local Programme Assessors on
their occasional monitoring missions. The responsibility for day-to-
day running of the Workshop was delegated by the Borough
Employoment Officer to a resident manager. Tom Stimson, as it
happened, was a former MSC officer, 'gamekeeper turned poacher'
as he put it, now committed to working at first-hand with young people
and making Pond Close a success. Wages of staff were paid by the
MSC but were topped up by the council, who felt they would other-

wise be inadequate to attract sufficiently experienced people. Tom sent in wages sheets to the Finance Department monthly, and had authority to sign orders for materials and to draw cash to cover day-to-day expenses. He made his monthly returns to the council on trainees joining and leaving the scheme. The council in turn reported to the MSC. On the whole the Workshop was left to its own devices, however. 'We are an oddity. The council don't have anything else like us, so we've been able to create our own environment to work in' said Tom Stimson.

The Workshop was involved in a network of relationships – not only with the MSC and the council but also in out-reach work with Careers Service, Jobcentres, local schools, youth clubs, parents and social services. It was in the nature of the area in which it was situated that many of Pond Close's trainees were living in relative poverty. 'They aren't different from other people' said the training officer, 'just less lucky.' The Workshop was very open in its recruitment. Young people simply had to be 16 or 17 (MSC rules). Because there were no facilities for language teaching they had to be able to read and write English to a very basic level. Beyond this, however, anyone was welcome. 'Unless they have a well-publicised record of grievous bodily harm. Then we might think twice.' The goal was to draw 25 per cent of the intake from among physically, mentally or socially disadvantaged young people. There was no policy governing intake by race or sex however. In this respect 'we simply take who comes' they said. When I visited Pond Close in 1984/5 there were currently forty trainees, of whom around 50 per cent were Afro-Caribbean, Asian or Middle Eastern. This proportion was well over the odds for the borough, in which 17 per cent of the population was Afro-Caribbean or Asian. 60 per cent of the trainees were male. While women were thus unequally represented, this was not due to 'discrimination' but simply to the unimpeded operation of the outside world's sex-stereotyping. The statistics were a function of the subjects in which training was offered. It was because male-stereotyped sections (carpentry, engineering, bicycle-maintenance and upholstery) out-numbered female sections that young men predominated as they did. It was because fashion and furnishing and office skills were offered that women were present at all. Catering alone drew both female and male. In terms of trainee-weeks over the eighteen months Pond Close had been in operation, if we exclude catering, the incidence of gender-innovation in choice of section amounted to precisely 5 per cent.

Imitating life

The regime at the Training Workshop appeared strict, partly because of Tom Stimson's own preference and style. Work began at 8 a.m. Trainees clocked in and out. The training allowance, the bare £26.25 of the 1984/5 Scheme, was docked without hesitation in the case of lateness or absenteeism. Fighting or damage to property were met with instant dismissal. Poor attendance or bad behaviour were dealt with by spoken, then written, warnings and finally by dismissal. Seven trainees had been expelled in eighteen months of operation.

The intention was to imitate factory life. The scheme took young people who on the whole had not had successful school careers and tried to make them basically employable in as few months as possible. The various sections actually produced goods and services to the value of £16 000 per year, each one a little business with its own suppliers, products and clients. The upholstery section repaired council furniture. The engineering section made security gates on contract and garden furniture for sale. The catering section ran the Workshop canteen and the office-skills section ran the office. The idea was to give the trainees a taste of what waged work is really like. Of course the Workshop came up against a contradiction here. Most work for unqualified school-leavers is repetitive and boring, with hardly any learning potential in it. Tom and the staff wanted to prepare their youngsters for this harsh reality, yet at the same time they wanted to give them a happy and constructive time, involving a variety of work and friendly relationships. So while the aim was '50 per cent work, 50 per cent training', in practice the contradiction was not so easily resolved. 'Where we fall down is that, however hard we try, we are a sheltered environment. You could never get this variety of work in any workplace.' And though a masculine authoritarianism prevailed, this was partly a front. It hid a degree of understanding and tolerance not characteristic of employment.

On arrival at Pond Close each trainee was given a week's 'induction' period, during which she or he spent half a day in each section on a little project that would produce some finished result: a sewn bag, a metal pot-holder. It was not a question of testing the trainee's aptitude for the section, rather 'we are advertising ourselves to them', said a supervisor. At the end of the week the trainee sat down with the training officer to talk about the induction experience and make a decision on which section to settle in. Once the trainee had made the choice, the supervisor of that section was consulted. Provided a vacancy existed there would normally be no impediment to a trainee getting her or his choice. 'We give trainees an opportunity to do what they want to do. After a period of time, if that doesn't work out, we ask the trainee to choose again.'

The 'off-the-job' element of training at the Workshop was not carried out in college, since most of these trainees had 'had enough of school'. 'We'd lose them on the walk to college', said Tom. Instead, a 'life and social skills' teacher came in one day a week from a local FE college. Even four hours of her – well below the MSC minimum of thirteen weeks a year – was too much for most trainees. Visits outside the Workshop, to exhibitions for instance, also counted as off-the-job training, and the Workshop staff were racking their brains for a way of building in an element of computer studies as required by MSC. Perhaps the carpenters and engineers could use the office computer to keep their stock records?

The trainees were sent out on work-placements as soon as they were felt to be ready – 'ready' meaning having developed a little practical skill and the 'right attitude'. Placements were for two to four weeks, and a trainee might get two or three such opportunities in a year. Contacts were continually being formed and nurtured with local employers. The Workshop found that many firms were cooperative and willing to help young people. Employers, however, were no sooner found than lost, either because a trainee messed things up and alienated the employer, or because she or he performed well and was taken on permanently. That was the real aim. 'We are *meant* to get jobs' said one trainee. Generally the feeling among them was 'Any job's worth leaving YTS for. You're getting paid, aren't you?' And Tom confirmed, 'Yes, if they are offered a job we would say "They are better off".' There was no point, he felt, in YTS for YTS's sake.

Tom felt that it was due to the efforts of his team and to the high standards of the council, where a left-wing Labour group was currently in office, rather than to either the MSC's intention or its somewhat perfunctory monitoring, that Pond Close was a 'good scheme'. The supervisors for their part recognised a certain cynicism in the government's intention in YTS – laundering the employment statistics – but nonetheless they said 'It's the only scheme we have.'

Somewhere to go

Besides simply spending time in the Workshop, being in the canteen
at coffee-break, eating dinner with trainees, hanging round the office
and joining them in work sessions, I also interviewed all those who
were available. Some of course were out on placement, some were off
sick. I also excluded the bicycle-maintenance trainees, who were in a
separate unit some miles from Pond Close. This way I saw twenty-
four in all, twelve of each sex. Nine were Afro-Caribbean, two Asian,
and thirteen were white. One had a physical impairment and was also
deaf. Several others had educational or social problems. How they
differed from Bridgebuilders' trainees has been described in Chapter
2. In general they had few school-leaving exams, many difficulties in
their home lives, and little chance of getting a good job.

Pond Close trainees were certainly not there for love of the Youth
Training Scheme. Many had decided at school to steer clear of both
dole and YTS if humanly possible. 'I heard about it before but I didn't
think I'd go on one of *those* [government schemes]. I used to think it
was a mug's game. I still do. But... as long as it's bringing in some
money I'd rather be doing that than at school.' Boredom and having
nothing else to do, were sufficient reasons for being at the Workshop.
But more positively some people said 'I wanted to train'. Even if the
money was bad, 'it might help you get a job'. One frail young man who
had known a good deal of ill-health and unhappiness said 'The
Careers Officer told me the Youth Training Scheme could build up
your hopes. It's built up my hopes quite a bit now. I got more
confidence now.' In fact, to some of the trainees the Workshop was
not really what they'd imagined YTS to be. One young woman had
only found out after enrolling that it was a YTS place:

> I didn't know this was a YTS scheme. I didn't want anything to do
> with these slave-labour schemes. Doing proper work and not
> getting paid for it. I didn't realise till I got here, when they gave me
> this sticker to put on my folder saying 'YTS'. But then I thought –
> I'd just got so bored, doing nothing. I thought at least I'll be doing
> something constructive.

Most of the trainees had known which section they wanted to train
in before they started at the Workshop. First choices were almost
universally sex-stereotyped. But they had been required to do an

induction day in each section anyway, and had been asked to give second and third choices too. The aim was to have an experience of at least one other section before the end of the year. I was interested to see if subjects tended to be clustered in people's preferences, and this was indeed the case. Young men showed a strong preference for staying within the three main 'male' craft sections. There was less clustering of preferences among young women. Although they almost all put down office, fashion or catering as first choices, they were more likely to mention a 'male' manual trade as a second or third choice than boys were to mention a 'female' skill section. An interesting exception to the universal sex-typing was catering which, as at school, was popular with everyone at the Workshop and was seen as a kind of 'fun' option. The trainees enjoyed being the centre of attention at meals, even if the food was greeted with colourful insults. Eveyone knows that in the food business are found male 'chefs' as well as female 'cooks'. The facts that the women often stick at the lowly level of catering assistant and that there is more scope for males as kitchen porters than masters of *haute cuisine* after their stint on YTS did not discourage them. Besides many young people in London have by now had a part-time job in the unisex uniforms of the fast-food chains. Catering was popular with Pond Close trainees partly because it provided an environment where the sexes could be together (involving both fun and tension) without either sex feeling themselves to be on wrongly-gendered ground.

People on the whole were enthusiastic about the subjects they were learning. The light engineers said 'I enjoy making things, seeing finished products, learning a skill.' 'It's kind of easy. It knackers you, though, in a way. Keeping a straight line is difficult.' 'It was like a challenge. It seemed hard. I was surprised when I found I could do it.' I asked, 'Isn't engineering difficult?' 'Well,' said one young man, 'that in a way is why I done it. Because, you see, when you learn how to do it it's not as hard as you think. If you want to learn about the stuff you ask the supervisor. He'll explain what it's made out of, what you can do with it, all that. I often ask.' The carpenters said, 'We make nice things. It's quite easy if you concentrate and use your mind.' One young man said he had chosen it because it seemed to promise real work. He was 'thinking of the future', he said. And down in the office the young women were saying – an echo of Bridgebuilders – 'Office skills, it's something you can always fall back on'. Some of them 'just liked typing', and others were there because they 'liked meeting and talking to people in reception and on the phone'. Trainees were sharply divided, though, into those who positively wanted office work and those who couldn't tolerate the idea. Many of the young men in manual trades sections declared office work 'boring' at best, and at worst something to be despised.

With few exceptions, the trainees seemed to be enjoying each other's company and that of the staff. 'It's a nice place. The people, they're cheery. It's got a good atmosphere. Most of them are good supervisors. And altogether I reckon I'd recommend it to anyone who can't get a job or go to college.' A college place, of course, was something these school-leavers were likely neither to get nor to want. 'I've had enough' several said. 'You'd have to write.' 'It's really for *higher* jobs.'

Gender politics

Questions of gender, of sex inequalities and occupational sex-stereotyping were issues that individual members of staff at Pond Close sometimes worried about. They had not, however, been consciously defined as a management problem. They were not on anyone's agenda as a problem actively seeking solution. The borough council – the managing agency – was exceptionally keen to promote equal opportunities on the dimension of both race and sex. The ethos at the Workshop was one of fairness. Tom said, 'You've come to the right place if you're interested in equal opportunities.' And a supervisor added 'I can genuinely say there's no prejudice in this place at all.' The staff themselves however were in sex-typed posts. The manager, the assistant manager and the training officer were male. The supervisors of carpentry, engineering, upholstery and the bicycle-maintenance shop were male; those of office and fashion were female. Catering had one of each sex. The administrative assistant was a woman. But all this was taken to be the way of the world. 'We don't get many applications for supervisors to work in non-traditional areas', explained Tom, reasonably. As we've seen, the aim of Pond Close management was to replicate the actually existing world as closely as possible. The contradiction was apparent in Tom's words. 'We don't see it as our role to promote necessarily a difference to what happens in the real world. But we also want to give them all equal opportunities. The real world isn't actually equal. So to that extent we don't reflect it.' That is to say, the Workshop was already out of step with the world in being *more* equal than is normal. So although Tom would have liked to do more because he thought the world was changing and they should reflect those changes too, it was unlikely that the Workshop would see its mission as running ahead of social change. Breaking down sex-segregation was 'certainly not my main concern', he said. It was reasonable, on this reckoning, that the leaflets and posters put out by the Workshop reflected the real world fairly accurately: the majority of photos showed young women and men in conventional roles.

Perhaps even more important in the minds of the staff however was responding to young peoples' expressed needs. If the trainees wanted to innovate, fine. If they did not they should not be pushed. 'I don't see mileage in pressing people to do things they don't want to do. There's enough compulsion in their lives already.' 'I wouldn't call us trail-blazers... I don't think we are doing anything special to create an environment to break down traditional barriers.'

In the course of my interviews with staff we discussed at length both the current and past instances of gender innovation at Pond Close. There were John in office skills, and Andrew in fashion and furnishing. Also, as we'll see, there were Sarah, trying out carpentry, and Angie and Karen who had recently chosen to try engineering. In general I encountered enthusiasm for young people to 'have a go'. 'Often those who take non-traditional options know better than the others what they want to do.' Some however admitted that they found it easier to teach single-sex groups, 'fewer distractions'. One male supervisor said he felt it wise to keep a circumspect physical distance between himself and female trainees when instructing them in the use of tools, for fear of mischievous interpretations. But others said it made no difference to them at all whether their group was single-sex or mixed. All pointed to the strong gender-identifications with which most trainees arrived and the gendered culture they proceeded to generate in the various sections. They referred to the 'macho mafia in the basement' where carpentry and engineering were housed.

At Pond Close I was specially interested in the experience of young women in male manual trades. It was one of few YTS schemes in my MSC area that could afford an opportunity of seeing such situations. 'We aren't stereotyping anyone' said the training officer. 'If we see a girl or a lady is going into (engineering or carpentry) we say to ourselves "okay, we're going to get her a job in that." We aren't saying that because she's a girl she's not going to make it.' On the other hand most of the staff had observations to make about little differences they felt existed between female and male. 'Girls are more organised. Boys jump in quicker.' 'Girls start very keen but when they get into the work they lose keenness.' 'In general, boys want everything to happen immediately. The girls do it perhaps to start with but quickly become more realistic and recognise their limitations.'

There is a tendency in each of the manual trades to look for things that 'girls could do' in working-life within the trade, things that would take them out of the run of direct competition with males. In engineering it is 'wrought-iron work'. In upholstery it is 'restoring antiques'. In carpentry it is 'making toys'. 'They don't *have* to work on a building site, hunking great heavy bits of timber about. They can work at a bench. They can do these little craft things. It's all carpentry, whichever way it falls.' In one sense these ideas are encouraging, helping the young women to see a way into a male trade for themselves. It is kindly, foreseeing a means of steering them clear of hard, heavy or dirty work, and perhaps also clear of trouble with men. But in another sense it is saying to them 'You are different. You will never be a *real* carpenter or a *real* engineering technician.'

The craftsmen teaching male manual skills (all men and all white) clearly represented this masculine 'real world'. They had all had to drop their craft standards on coming to the Workshop. This itself was hard enough. Reinforcing defence of the craft tradition was the feeling that the government's New Training Initiative was a destructive attack on craft control and one that called for resistance. They were trying seriously however to unlearn craft-attitudes in so far as they were understood to disadvantage women and black people. Some were being more successful in this contradictory reorientation than others. 'When I worked with apprentices they were boys. I never had a girl apprentice. You can't see beyond the end of your nose. Whereas now in the last few years it's opened out. I'm still learning, same as they are.'

The job situation in industry was of course discouraging gender innovation. The progressive 'employment orientation' at the Workshop was therefore pushing ever so gently and, in a sense, inadvertently, against young people trying something that might be a false start, and in which it might be impossible to get a job. In this borough manufacturing employment fell by more than 50 per cent in the ten years 1971 to 1981 (Greater London Council, 1986). Skilled manual jobs were hard enough for young men to come by, let alone young women. Management attitudes are known to be particularly adverse to introducing young women to skilled areas of work in the face of stubborn opposition from male workers and often their unions too (Hunt, 1975). The Workshop had had little experience as yet in trying to place young women in non-traditional work-placements: few had stayed long enough. The manager had come across employers prejudiced against taking on black trainees. He had not yet had occasion to encounter sex-prejudice.

The trainees themselves seemed happy with their sections, regardless of the current gender mix, or lack of it. On the whole there was much less preference for single-sex working than is common among adult women and men. Nearly all thought that catering, with a more or less even mix, was ideal. Only one young man out of the twenty-four said he felt 'there'd be too much messing about' and a young women said 'I prefer mainly girls'.

I used the current 'gender innovators' as instances to start a discussion in interview. What did they feel about John in office skills? Or Angie and Karen in engineering? It is curious that, in spite of being so unwilling to innovate themselves, they were universally supportive of others who were. 'It's up to them' was the characteristic response. The right to choose was consistently emphasised. John, a young loner who liked to tease, was routinely teased in his turn as a 'poofter' or 'wanker'. But in principle they supported him in his choice. It was made easier to do so by pointing to his interest in computers and the fact that, as his supervisor put it, he 'played the little manager'.

To summarise, then, the Pond Close Training Workshop was providing a helpfully open situation free of actual discrimination. Any prejudices held by staff or trainees were not openly expressed and probably, where they existed, were unconscious. Induction was encouraging people into unaccustomed activities. And a small number of trainees were choosing non-traditional sections. Though they did not normally stay in them long, the fact that they began at all proved there were no impediments being put in their way and indeed that there do exist young people wanting to do something different from the run of their sex. As at Bridgebuilders however it was too readily assumed that women now had a fair deal. In reality all they had was equality of opportunity – an absence of closed doors. It was not held to be anyone's responsibility to secure actual equality, let alone similarity, of *outcomes* for young women and young men. In default of positive action, it is interesting to see what was happening to individual 'innovating' young women.

Sarah: carpentry

Sarah was a new trainee at the time of my visit to the Workshop. She was a young white woman, mature for her 17 years, brought up by a mother and three older brothers. The brothers had developed in her a strong sense of politics: pacifism, anti-racism and self-respect. ('I was really shocked when I learned that once women hadn't had the vote', she said.) Sarah had been alerted to yet more things about the world by a spell in FE college. They were 'the best months of my life'. 'They were tutors there, not teachers. You called them by their first names. And like, if someone was a racialist you had to sit down and discuss it and work it out.' She was an extrovert, a drum majorette, and she defined herself as a rebel. At school, sewing had been a bore, cooking a drag. The best thing about school had been the fun of bunking off. She was at ease with men. 'Most of my friends, the closest, have been boys. I used to know all the girls, but I didn't really go around with them. I get on well with girls if I don't get to know them. But if I do get to know them, I don't really like their company.'

Sarah knew she wouldn't ever 'work in a factory or a supermarket, or any dull situation like that. Anything humdrum.' That included office work. 'You're sitting there talking all the time. I'd feel like an old woman.' She dismissed YTS as a slave labour scheme in which you might find yourself 'putting someone else out of a job' which she felt was a horrible idea. Her aim, she said, half humorously, half seriously, was 'to be a millionaire, an actor'. Meanwhile, however, here she was. Her black boy-friend joined the Workshop at the same time as Sarah and together, after their induction week they settled for carpentry. 'I thought it was a bit of a challenge. I always thrive on a challenge. And the kids in there, they aren't so silly as some of the others' said Sarah. 'And I liked the supervisor. He's an easy person to get on with. None of them looked on you as a girl.' The visiting Careers Officer had been discouraging. 'You can't keep changing, you know, if you don't like it' and 'the only thing you'll be able to do in carpentry is reconditioning antiques'. Sarah said, 'I felt labelled'. But she stuck to her choice.

She got on well in carpentry at first and stayed for three months.

Young women make good carpenters

She found the supervisor fair and 'very sensitive towards teaching. He is still learning himself and he's not ashamed to admit he goes to college. Some teachers won't let on they don't know.' She felt she was 'treated as an individual, not as a woman'. For instance:

> I was messing about down in carpentry and when I couldn't do something I said 'I'm too feeble for this'. I didn't really mean it that way. I wasn't putting myself down, I just came out with it. Because I was sawing away and not getting anywhere. But the supervisor said right away, 'Don't kid yourself'. You know, he was more encouraging about me than I was.

Sarah thought she would like to have a go at actually working in carpentry. But she realised it would not be so sheltered as here at the Workshop. 'I've never seen a carpenter before, come to think of it,' she admitted. 'A woman or any other, come to that. But if I really, really wanted to, I would. I wouldn't take any other job, even if it took years, if that's what I wanted to do.'

Nonetheless, Sarah gave up carpentry after three months. She began to get restless, got across the supervisor, decided to try something else. She'd give upholstery a go. Soon she left the Workshop and I lost track of her. It seemed likely that, although she would not find work as a carpenter or upholsterer, her confidence had in no way been diminished. She had been confirmed in her promise to herself not to accept a woman's predetermined lot in life.

Angie and Karen: light engineering

I arrived at Pond Close just as a new batch of trainees enrolled. Among them were two young women: Angie (Afro-Caribbean) and Karen (white). After their induction week they settled for light engineering. 'Oh no' I heard one of the lads say, 'What do you want – to make us trouble?' But he was 'only joking', and did no more than provoke Angie and Karen to reassert their choice. They were both 16 and, in comparison with Sarah, still little more than schoolchildren.

Angie was a tough nut. She said of herself:

> When I was very young, just a kid, I was like a boy, that's what they used to say to me. I was like a boy. I was rough, scruffy, never combed my hair nor nothing. I just used to climb trees and jump the ditches. I was terrible. I was really stubborn. I used to tell my mum I wanted to be a bus conductor, and I told my nan I wanted to be a boxer. All stupid things.

She'd first thought of working with children. But that option did not exist at the Workshop. Of light engineering she said 'This is more exciting. I can do child-minding later. I can go on to college you know, and take it up again there. I'd rather be learning something I don't know anything about now. So I'd have a second interest.' She added, 'What I hate is working in an office. I've got a friend who does typing. And seeing as she doesn't like metalwork she can say "Ugh!" to me and I don't like typing so I can say "Ugh!" to her.' In comparison, engineering 'it's different. It's fun. You learn how to use all those electric guns and things.' It was not that she seriously intended to take up an engineering job. She'd just got a taste of metal-work during induction week and 'It's for the interest. For something to know in case I might need it, if I was really, really down suddenly and a metal-work job came along, I'd be able to say "I could do that".'

After a week or two in engineering she told me she found the boys 'all right'. But:

> sometimes they get annoyed with you. Like, if we jam up the machine once too often they say 'Oh, you girls you can't do anything right, can you'. And we just say 'Nor can you boys', you know. But Pete, he's getting used to us and he helps us all the time now. He didn't use to. He just gave us dirty looks. But now he's all right. But Vince and Ali they can get angry. If I call Vince he says 'God, hold on a minute, will yer?' Or he says he's tired and he's really had enough of us.

There was a bit of tomfoolery:

> Vince, he's so stupid really. I'm telling you. Today he had this thing and he was putting it on everyone's heads and if you didn't like it he says, 'Girls can't take jokes. They haven't got the same sense of humour as boys'. He's stupid. Even Pete says he's stupid.

As to the engineering supervisor, Ken, however, 'He's all right. He's a nice man, he is.' Does he treat you the same as the boys? 'Yeah, he does. That's what I like about him.' Even though Karen was there, Angie missed girls' company in some ways, she said. 'Girls can have a laugh between them. Because downstairs the boys have got their man-chat, right, and when we walk over they say "Scuse *me*, this is a man's chat", you know. When me and Karen walk away, they know we don't want to know.'

Karen was Angie's partner in the engineering experiment. She was a follower rather than a leader. She was a calmer young woman and approached engineering more equally than Angie. 'They just do their work and we do our work' she said of the young men. 'They don't really interfere with us.' 'If you call them over they'll say "Oh, no, look!"' (putting on a grumbly tone). But they're only saying it for a joke. They're only mucking about.'

The supervisor, Ken, was quite matter-of-fact about the arrival of Karen and Angie in his section. He was clear in his own mind that they were there for what he called 'the wrong reasons': their main interest was boys. He was waiting for these real motives to reveal themselves. Initially he let the two stay close to each other, working together, to build up confidence. But when he found they were chatting too much he split them up and set them to separate tasks. He ensured that they were not allowed to avoid heavy jobs like carrying metal supplies, and that they did not slip away to the washroom at the end of the day when the time came to sweep up. Ken had doubts about where Angie and Karen would fit into engineering in the long run however. 'I think women can be fine in *light* engineering. It's obvious, isn't it? There are certain jobs we get, it's heavy work. Physically heavy. The only thing that really gets them eventually, unless they're very keen, is the dirt aspect.'

The young men in light engineering were rather bemused by the arrival of Angie and Karen, the first girls to try such a thing. One said 'I don't mind them being here. It's what they want to do. They're allowed to do it, there's no problem. If they don't want to be stuck doing things that they're supposed to be doing, like dressmaking and cooking and they want to try something different, you know... It hasn't changed since they've been in here. We use the same language and everything. They've fitted in well.' Another said, 'I think girls *should* do it. Because its always been men. Look... at first I thought that girls couldn't do it. But they've made a bench and a table and it's just as good as what we've done. You can't really call them rubbish can you?' And later he said, 'These days women are just like men. They're just like men now really.'

Others in the Workshop, young men and young women alike, were on the whole supportive of Angie and Karen's efforts. 'I think it's up to them if they want to do that sort of work' said one of the young women. 'They shouldn't let the boys worry them. Because it's up to them. Some boys say "This is a boy's job".' And another said 'I hope they'll pass an' all.' 'They are trying to do something – they are trying to do something like *men* are supposed to do. And they could handle it. I think it's a good thing.' Angie and Karen did need *explaining*, however. Some said 'They're tomboys really. They like doing men's things.' As for themselves, the other young women hadn't even considered it. 'I wouldn't like doing it. I'd get dirty and I don't like getting dirty. I like wearing nice clothes an' that. But I think it's okay. Because when I was younger I wanted to be a truck driver. I stopped when I was about fourteen.'

After two or three weeks in light engineering, however, Karen went absent and did not return. There were various opinions about the reason. The manager, Tom, blamed her mother who, he said, had been against metal-work for Karen from the start. Angie reported that Karen had a job as a packer now, boring, but real money. Then I bumped into Karen herself who said she was working in a hair-dresser's. Besides, she wanted to go to college, or 'do studio graphics' she said – hiding what she knew was a lack of realism under a cool confidence. Any or none of these things could have been true.

Ken was philosophical. He had known from the start that the experiment would not last long. Soon after, Angie, clearly finding life impossible in engineering without Karen's support, started to show an interest in catering. When she brought in an application form for a job in a fast-food shop, Ken helped her to fill it in, without attempting to dissuade her. She in fact moved into the Workshop's catering section soon after, and that was that.

Tom said of Angie and Karen's attempt, 'I think it was worthwhile that they tried. But I think their motives weren't quite right.' He was confident that if they had stayed he would have been able to find them work-placements, but: 'Angie was too lazy to do it, basically. She was just making her statement. And Karen, I think she went into it because Angie did, or perhaps because there were boys working there.' In my perception the reasons for Angie and Karen's failure to stay with engineering lay elsewhere: in the social relations of the Training Workshop. The interaction between male and female built a wall between male and female spheres and policed this boundary continually.

Interactions

During the time I was at Pond Close I did an 'induction week' with a batch of new trainees, among whom were Angie and Karen. We learned a little carpentry and metal-work together, as well as having a go on the computer and in the bicycle-maintenance workshop. I was able to watch the interaction between trainees, and between trainees and staff in these first few crucial days. The following series of obser-vations may throw some light on the subtlety of the relations between young women and young men on the issue of occupation and skill. They show, I think, that though the sexes want to work in mixed-sex situations and, in the case of young women, to try out unconventional occupations, in practice existing gender relations and expectations make it all but impossible for them.

There is a perceived status-ranking of the sections at Pond Close, in the eyes of both sexes. The female sections – office and fashion – rank lower than the male sections like carpentry and engineering. This ranking combines with certain realities of the labour-market and job-market to produce a lopsided effect. Young men can step across (and down) to female occupations but, being male, they carry some potential status with them and have a chance of pulling themselves upwards above the women in the group. John was not going to become a typist or receptionist as the young women were. He in fact soon left to take up a job in general office work for a meat wholesaler. Andrew was not going to become a sewing-machinist, like his female counterparts. He left to do a job as a cloth-cutter, a traditional male craft-occupation in the clothing industry. In the case of young women, like Angie, Karen and Sarah, to step across into men's occupations is to step upwards. But they take their lower female status with them, and there is little likelihood of them being seen as performing better or even as well as their male colleagues. Unless they do so however they will be treated as amateur. One way of proving oneself as a serious contender would be simply to survive, to stay on. But everything conspires to make this unlikely.

A number of things can be seen in the interactions. One is the prior knowledge about tools and equipment that young men bring to the situation. Second, there is a live heterosexuality in the situations, a need to be handling both 'romance' and training, two very demanding situations, at the same time. In this situation what is represented as 'harmless fun' can, when continually sustained, become a kind of harassment. And third, young women and young men both show a need to maintain self-respect and, in the case of both sexes, the respect of *men*.

In the bicycle maintenance section

Carol and John (the John of office skills) are part of a group being given a morning's introduction to bicycle maintenance. They are both put to unscrewing the spokes of a wheel. Before Carol is one-third of the way round her wheel, John has finished his. 'Come on' he says. She resists help. But after a while he ignores this, and starts in on the other side of her wheel, while she continues with the first side. When this is finished, the next job is to remove the spokes from the hub. One of Carol's gets stuck. 'I can't get it out', she complains to the world at large. 'Here, give it me. I'll do it' says John, happily. *'There* you go!' He hands it back to her, done. He tells us he has a ten-speed bike at home, now out of commission. He describes the various possibilities of a BMX.

In the office skills section

Angie, Bill and some others are having induction to office skills. Angie and Bill have grabbed first go at the keyboards and screens of the word-processors. They sit side by side, fingering the keys. Bill then leans over and types his name on Angie's keyboard, so making it appear on the screen. He has colonised her space. The training officer says sharply, 'which machine is yours, Bill? Then stay on it.' The office-skills supervisor has only one floppy disc for the typing programme. She puts it in Bill's machine. Angie has to copy type instead, from a card. She plods away. Bill says to everyone, 'I'm not used to this machine. It's not like my Commie.' He has a Commodore at home, purchased with his own money. From time to time Angie asks for advice. Bill leans over and taps a key for her. I ask Bill, 'Would you do this for a job?' 'I couldn't bear to work in an office all day. Tap, tap, tap,' he says. He is above seeming to learn to type. He says it is not necessary to type to use the computer. He prefers to use his own method. He chats to the computer as though it's a person. 'Wot you done that for? Stop arguing!' He is relaxed and having fun. He is now cheating on the typing programme and altering his typing-error scores by overtyping them. He is cleverly defeating the object of the programme. Angie is tapping on. Soon Bill discards the typing programme and obtains a musical one. He makes the machine play the theme from *Chariots of Fire*, so having an impact on the entire room. Angie is getting bored. She is glad when it is tea-break.

In the canteen

At each break time the ribaldry about Angie and Karen opting for light-engineering section escalates a little higher. There is some sexual ambivalence being acted out between Karen and Pete, one of the lads from engineering. 'What is it?' I ask Pete 'Will the girls mess it up for you going in there?' 'They won't mess up *nothing*' he says defiantly, but (scornfully) '*She* thinks she can paint. [They have to spray paint the metal work.] Have you seen *my* artistic work?' Then Angie says, almost going over the top with this, 'Pete fancies Karen, and he doesn't want her to do metal-work. Because he doesn't want his missis doing the same thing as him. He wants her to be in catering, so's he'll get a good meal cooked.' Howls of disapproval, approval, disavowal from all concerned. Pete runs out of the canteen shouting challenges to Karen, who rises to it and chases him out of the door.

In the carpentry section

Six of us are getting an introduction to carpentry. The group includes Angie and Karen. One of the more experienced trainees is taking the class, in the absence of the supervisor. He is an Asian lad called Azar. He has set out for each of us, two bits of hardwood, cut to 8-inch lengths, a ruler, square and pencil. Karen picks up the square and points it like a pistol. 'How do you use this saw?' she asks the room at large. Azar starts off, without telling us what we are doing or what we are making or what in general the tools are for. He expects us to learn by copying. Angie however does not catch on to the fact that you must have one edge of the square flat against the side of the wood in order to make a right angle. She has hers waving about.

The boys are riding on the girls' questions. Angie and Karen continually ask Azar what they should be doing. The young men do not reveal their ignorance. They do not need to. The girls show themselves up, the boys learn from it. In any case, the boys appear to have used these tools before. Angie hears some music on the radio and starts a little twirl. 'Anyone know how to do this dance? Want me to teach you?' (Here is something she can show them.)

Azar, the stand-in instructor, shows Angie that she has drawn her lines wrong. There will be a gap left between her two pieces of wood. 'I *want* a gap' she says, stubbornly. She has nothing invested in getting this right. Meanwhile Karen is getting fretful. She passes her square and wood to Bill. 'Do mine for me' she says. He complies readily.

At last Azar realises that it may help if he shows us what we are making. He fetches over an example. 'It's a half-joint lap' he says. That means nothing to Angie and Karen. Even if he had said it right, it would still mean nothing. Now we get to the sawing part. Little saws, used for dovetailing, are distributed. Angie picks hers up appraisingly. 'My grandfather had one of these'.

After tea-break the supervisor returns and takes things in hand. The two duffers are moved to a separate table. He concentrates his attention on them, but it is too late. Angie is now putting her efforts into grassing up all and sundry to cover for her poor performance with the tools. She circles nearer and nearer the transistor. The young men are grouped with Azar now, making good progress with their task and talking interactively.

Tomorrow is decision day. Angie and Karen have to confirm their decision to opt for light engineering. From the surrounding conversation it is clear that this has become a project of some bravado for them both. 'I'm not coming in tomorrow. I've got to get my gold tooth', says Karen. 'I'm not coming in tomorrow. I'm sleeping', says Angie. But they both turn up.

In the light engineering section:

First day in engineering for Angie and Karen. They are put to work sawing box-section steel for the legs of a park bench. The metal is in a vice, set on a table 34" high. The work height is therefore 44", too high for Angie and Karen to saw. It is up under their armpits. They soldier on, however, subdued and serious. Their eyes are everywhere at once, wary, dealing with the metal always in its social context. Catching Pete looking at her Angie shouts 'Wot *you* lookin' at, man?' She breaks two hacksaw blades in quick succession. This is not surprising, because she has to saw while looking from beneath her eyebrows round the room to be sure that no-one is taking the micky. The supervisor, Ken, is not angry about the breakages, but Angie is shaken, nonetheless. She gives over to Karen. 'Hey, Karen, you do it with this sword.'

Ken had told me he thought that Angie and Karen were doing engineering because of their sexual interest in the boys. I am beginning to disagree with this diagnosis. The engineering workshop – where everyone must wear dirty overalls, sensible shoes and a competitive mien – is the last place for a girl to work if she wants to be desirable to men. Angie and Karen are doing it because they have character and self-regard. There is a sexual undercurrent, but it is mixed up with rivalry. What the two of them are trying to do is to grab a bit of the action from under the noses of the men – action the other young women have not the nerve to join. Sexuality, however, keeps intruding.

Pete extends a length of steel rod through the vice and has it aimed at Ken's rear. 'Cheap thrills' he calls, loud enough for everyone but Ken to hear. Next minute he is waving the same rod over Karen's head, from behind, unseen. Ken grabs him firmly by the nape and shakes him gently. Another lad, Afro-Caribbean, walks in, late. He is Mr Cool. He saunters over to the young women's bench. 'Wot's this *messy* bench?' he asks, expressionless, fingering the tools. He turns on his heel and walks away.

Meanwhile, Karen has got out a picture of a short hairstyle with a flick fringe. Angie takes it over to Pete and whispers in his ear. 'Her?' He pulls a face. 'Anyway, she's going to get it' says Angie. Vince overhears. '*Get* it?' he smirks. 'Aren't you, Karen?' says Angie, ignoring the innuendo. 'Oh, get a *hair-do!*'

Escaping the gender straightjacket

Of Angie and Karen the other young women were saying in effect 'they want to *be* boys'. There is nothing of course that boys like less than this. One young man in YTS in printing said to me of a young woman trainee on his course, with a truly unpleasant snarl, 'Thinks she's a boy – right little bruiser'. The staff at Pond Close were saying, on the other hand, 'they want to be *with* boys', or 'they want to *get* boys'. This seems to be a common belief among adults. Chris Griffin, in her study of young women in the Midlands, found that 'female students who took "boy's subjects" were either presumed to be interested solely in flirting with boys, or discounted as unique exceptions' (Griffin, 1985, p.79). It seemed to me that there was something different involved here for Angie, Karen and Sarah. They simply wanted to escape from predetermined feminine roles: office work or sewing. They wanted to be out of feminine cultural environments, that were all girls together. They wanted a challenge, to learn something demanding and perhaps a little dangerous. They wanted to be respected by their peers and by the male supervisors. They did not particularly want to be in a section where there were only young men for company, or even necessarily to be doing 'a man's job'. It happened however that the interesting things to do had been cornered at Pond Close, as in the outside world, by men. They could only be won by challenging a male monopoly and by running the gauntlet of men.

There may well have been other young women who would have liked these things too, but they could not see beyond the cultural barrier erected by the males at the Workshop and elsewhere. They were not prepared to run into trouble. It does help to be not too bothered about forming immediate sexual relationships: Sarah's own quiet 'steady' was a beginner in carpentry like her. It also helps to have female company: neither Angie nor Karen would have had the nerve to tackle engineering alone. But these two cared 'too much' what the boys thought of them, both as engineers and as 'girls'. They did not have time to develop the work motivation that could have pulled them through the first difficult months. On the other hand, by maintaining a demonstrable interest in the boys they had evaded the slur of 'lezzie'. The distaste shown by boys for girls that do 'men's work' was illustrated by a group of male computer trainees to whom I

Strength and skill, can that be a woman?

showed the photographs prepared for this book. They admired the young women in the hairdressing salon and asked (nudge, nudge) 'Where's that, miss? Is it near here?' When I showed them the young women in an engineering workshop by contrast the reaction was 'Ugh!', 'Men!' 'Turn over the page quickly.'

These findings are by no means unique. By now many research studies of women in male manual trades have been published which show that the difficulties faced by Karen, Sarah and Angie are common-place (See for instance Walshok, 1981; Newton and Brocklesby, 1983). Anne Stafford's study in an Edinburgh training workshop under the Youth Opportunities Programme is particularly relevant here. The young men were in painting and decorating, and joinery; the young women in knitwear. An attempt by a young woman to break into the male paint-shop involved very much the same painful and delicate negotiation of the contradiction between gendered sexual relations and gender-contrary work relations that was apparent in the case of Angie and Karen. But Anne Stafford's study showed above all how young men most of all want an adult male's skilled-craft-identity while young women, for whom a real skilled status is not an option, are forced into making their priority the impossible goal of a genuinely mutual love relationship with a young man. The young men, for their part, desire, abuse and despise the girls (Stafford, 1986).

Young women, it seems, want two things and they want them both: choice of a full range of worthwhile and rewarding kinds of employment, and viable sexual relationships with young men – or perhaps with women. This should not be too much to ask, but as gender-relations are at present constructed it apparently is. That is no reason however why a training scheme should not set about making the first a possibility without foreclosing on the second. It is interesting to consider what principles might have guided a restructuring of the Pond Close Workshop to have brought this about.

Take staffing. The supervisors in the male sections were traditional craftsmen who, although they were trying to change their attitudes, still gave the impression that the old days ruled on. What a difference it would have made to the perceptions of female and male trainees alike to have introduced women supervisors in carpentry, engineering and upholstery. In principle the manager said he would have considered employing women in these roles, but the absence of such women in the labour market had been taken as given.

Would it have been possible to create more female space within the

Workshop? In adult training it has been found beneficial to provide women-only courses in the male manual trades. Centres offering training in both old and new technologies exclusively to women have been over-subscribed. Women, it is now abundantly clear, thrive and perform well in technology when it is lifted out of the gendered relations in which it is normally embedded. As we have seen, even MSC is now recommending single-sex courses and schemes for young women in non-traditional occupations. Pond Close would be an ideal site for the provision of women-only workshops in carpentry, engineering and upholstery. At the very least the opportunity could from the outset have been taken to use the workshops and tools to give all young women, in addition to their chosen subject, a general basic training in useful skills such as electric wiring, plumbing, carpentry and maintenance of equipment and vehicles. Many young women came and went from the Workshop having spent no more than a day or two, on induction, using all those resources: they might as well not have existed as far as they were concerned.

The women who attend adult single-sex training schemes are often over 25 years old and may already have children. They have normally experienced a number of dead-end 'women's jobs' before feeling themselves desperate or determined enough to break into a 'male' trade. At 16, as we have seen, YTS trainees are still adolescent, acutely aware of their gender-identity and of gender-expectations. While some would welcome women-only situations, others might reject them. Indeed, Sarah, Angie and Karen were all trying to avoid just this. Their needs point us in the direction of a more significant challenge: changing the attitudes and behaviour of men to make it possible for women to train alongside them without disadvantage. As things are it is only the bravest pioneer that can survive. Manual trades in a mixed-sex environment should be a viable option for the *average* young woman. What is more, her choice of occupation should not need to incur a penalty in terms of sexual relations.

A prerequisite for mixed-sex groups in technical training is that they should be balanced. At least one Mode B workshop similar to Pond Close in London has introduced 'quotas', holding half its places open, in all sections, for either sex. Beyond this, however, a purposeful programme of consciousness-raising is needed – an exploration of attitudes, bringing prejudices to light, opening minds to new ideas about masculinity and femininity, new forms of relationship between men and women. It would have been quite appropriate here for classes in 'life and social skills' to have included anti-sexism work with young men, assertiveness training and self-defence for young women. At a quite material level the technologies and their applications need rethinking by women. Employment possibilities for women, following training, need opening up and testing. The almost military regime in many Mode B workshops, deliberately imitative of the masculine world of apprenticeship and craft, needs reshaping if women are to feel at home there. All these things would have taken more staff-time and money than Pond Close Workshop had available, yet it was not out of the question to have sought additional funding.

The contrast between Bridgebuilders and Pond Close – an employer-based Scheme and a workshop scheme – in the immediate possibilities they offered for the de-segregation of the sexes in the various occupational groups will by now be apparent. A survey of YTS in London found that far more workshop-style schemes than employer-based schemes had independently initiated consciousness-raising and positive action for girls (Edmond, 1986).

The staff of Pond Close were much more closely in control of the environment and relations of training; change was far more readily imaginable. Yet it is precisely schemes like Pond Close that are penalised by the provisions of the new two-year YTS. Many are closing as the emphasis shifts yet further to employer-based provision. Even when a trainee spends the first year in a workshop it is intended that the second year should be in a work-placement. An opportunity to work systematically and developmentally at changing the gendered relations of technical training is being thrown away before it has been used.

7

Computers: Hands On, Hands Off

While some young women are beginning to push their way into the acquisition of male craft-skills like wood- and metal-working, we are being warned that these forms of technology are quickly losing their earning power. Though skills like this are still vital to all women, to give them a grip on their world and open up more choice of work, in career terms they are today offering less than the skills associated with the new technology: electronics.

Training in these subjects within YTS is mainly handled through a network of specialist Information Technology Centres (ITeCs). These are (or were) Mode B1 provision, in which the training is mainly on the Centre's own premises and with its own equipment. A survey in 1984 covered 108 out of 175 ITeCs. Of these 96 per cent had male managers; 97 per cent had a majority of male staff; and 99 per cent had a majority of male trainees. For every one female trainee learning computing skills in an ITeC there were six males. For every one young woman in electronics there were eighteen young men. Something here was very seriously wrong. I decided to look in closer detail at one particular ITeC, not far from Pond Close Training Workshop and within the same borough and the same Manpower Services Commission administrative area.

The ITeC on City Street was opened in 1985, again on the initiative of the borough council, with seven full-time staff and places for thirty trainees in four subjects: electronics, computer applications, computer programming and office technology. It is governed by a board that has representatives of the council, the local Chamber of Commerce, the trades unions, the education authority and the voluntary sector. Financial support comes from four sources. The main contribution of the Manpower Services Commission is to personnel costs and trainees' allowances. The Department of

Environment's Urban Programme subsidises the council's contribution. The council helps with accommodation and tops up the wages. Finally the Department of Trade and Industry made an initial grant of £75 000 for purchase of equipment. This is what was obtained: first, the office-technology section had a fully networked LSI Octopus system with eight units consisting of keyboard, monitor, disk and processor, together with a daisy-wheel and a dot-matrix printer, mainly for use as word-processors. This section also of course had ancillary equipment such as photocopiers, dictaphones, franking machine, calculators and a telephone switchboard, so that it simulated a real office. The computing sections had a set of BBC/ Torch computers, again fully networked, some with colour monitors. In addition to the normal printers these sections used a graphics plotter. The electronics workshop was equipped with additional hardware including an oscilloscope, function generators, logic analysers, multimeters, global logic probes and micro-processors.

From the start the recruitment policy of the ITeC had been one of 'open access'. The philosophy was that there would be found among the school-leavers of the local community young people who had failed at school, or whom the school system itself had failed, who might nonetheless thrive in the ITeC environment and find in themselves possibilities they had not till now had a chance to develop. The Careers Service was the main source of school-leavers. The main limiting criterion in accepting trainees was: can they physically handle the equipment. For instance, some items of hardware were being adapted for the use of a young man with impaired sight. Beyond this the only other criterion was: are they keen to come? At first the trainees were given a practical aptitude test, not to 'pass' or 'fail' them but to help to guide them to an appropriate section. When the test was found to be intimidating to some recruits, it was dropped. From then on all that was required was that the trainees each fill in a one-page form about themselves, have a chat with the assistant manager or training officer, and a tour of the premises. Then, if they wanted to join the ITeC and there was a vacancy they did so.

New technology, old gender patterns

When I spent a month making a case-study of City Street ITeC in late 1985 there were twenty-eight trainees on the register. As we have seen, this borough council had a strong commitment to equal opportunity, and the ITeC tried to reflect this in its recruitment. More than two-thirds of the trainees who were at or had been at the ITeC since its formation earlier in the year were black. In late 1985, there were ten Afro-Caribbean, four Asian and fourteen white trainees. This ethnic distribution was something of which the staff were justifiably proud. On the other hand, of the twenty-eight trainees only seven, (a quarter), were female. Apart from the low overall presence of young women in the City Street ITeC, they were strikingly segregated. All but one were majoring in Office Technology, the one exceptional young woman being in Programming. All the young men were either in Electronics, Computer Applications or Computer Programming, with the exception of a lone boy whose main subject was Office Technology. He wanted to type because he had ambitions to be a writer.

We should look more closely at what this choice of section implied. Electronics was at the hardware end of the spectrum of opportunities in the ITeC. It offered a broad range of skills applicable to trainees wanting to go into such work as assembling, servicing, maintaining or testing electronic equipment. It could also perhaps give a trainee the knowledge needed to get a start as a junior member of a sales team, or as an equipment demonstrator. The course covered the recognition of various components and their uses; building and designing circuits; fault-finding and repair of microcomputers, radios, televisions and video-recorders. It also covered aspects of basic electrical work. The electronics trainees were also given some teaching in maths and algebra as a basis for their practical engineering work.

In the course on Computer Applications trainees were given practical experience of commonly-used computer hardware and software. The section offered skills to equip them to operate computers in a business context. The software packages in use in the section included a word-processing programme (Wordstar with Mailmerge); a database programme (D-Base II); a spread-sheet programme for preparation of accounts (Supercalc-2); together with Lotus 1-2-3, Graphox Plus, the Psion Xchange suite and the Perfect Software suite. The work of the section involved some background theory in hardware, operating systems, networks, communications, problem-solving and documentation.

In the Computer Programming section the trainee, coming in without any prior knowledge, could hope to leave with a reasonable competence in 'BBC Basic Z80'. More able trainees might move on to 'Pascal' and 'C' programming languages. The programming was taught within a context of computer systems analysis and there was some overlap in this respect with Computer Applications section so that the trainee could learn to use as well as to design and adapt programmes.

The Office Technology section, using similar computer terminals to the other sections, trained its recruits mainly on word-processing and touch-typing training programmes. The ITeC hoped to turn them out at the end of the year as speedy and accurate touch-typists, reasonably competent with the word processor. But trainees also learned about office organisation, telephone and reception technique, filing and keeping records, photocopying, dealing with mail, handling petty cash and writing invoices. The aim was to equip them for work as office juniors, though it was believed that the more competent might enter work as typists or secretaries.

The system at the ITeC was that trainees would choose one of these sections as their 'major' training situation. They also chose two sections in which to 'minor'. They would take their minor subjects in total, for one quarter of their time. The trainee therefore had to drop out of one section completely. This choice too was significant. *All* the current young women trainees had dropped Electronics. Almost half the males had rejected Office Technology. If we see the Office Technology section as stereotyped female, and the other three as male, the extent of gender-innovation in 'major' subjects during the first nine months of operation of the City Street ITeC amounted to only 1 per cent of trainee/weeks.

In the time I spent at the ITeC I attended the introductory sessions with three new trainees – a young Afro-Caribbean woman, Lisa, and two young men, one white, one Afro-Caribbean. I joined in some of their induction lessons in each of the four sections, and was there when they discussed their choices with the training officer. I sat in on 'life and social skills' lessons too, and had the chance to interview thirteen trainees, including the three newcomers, and all the staff.

The trainees seemed to enjoy their two weeks induction period:

I thought they'd just put you down and work. A lot of people thought that. That they'd say 'What you want to do?' and then you'd do it. But it wasn't like that. You got a chance to experience the different things. Say you chose electronics, and you got there and found you didn't like it. You'd have had to stick with it for a whole year. So it was quite good.

One striking fact about induction however was that, though half the trainees to whom I talked said they had found they quite liked subjects which they would previously have dismissed as 'not for them', none of them in fact had acted on this by joining the newly-discovered occupation. Two young women for instance enjoyed Electronics, but they did not opt for it, even as a minor subject: they chose Office Technology.

The sex of the individual members of staff at the ITeC, as in the Training Workshop, tended to reinforce traditional sex stereotypes. The manager was a white male, as was the training officer. The instructors in the three technical sections were men of whom one was Afro-Caribbean. Only the assistant manager's post, unusually for the ITeC world, was filled by a (white) woman. The senior staff and the board had been aware that it would have helped matters if they had been able to recruit women instructors for the 'male' sections and perhaps even a man for Office Technology. They had scrutinised all the job applications carefully with this in mind and had interviewed one or two 'non-traditionals'. But all, they said, had been 'hopeless'. The extreme difficulty of recruiting staff of either sex with the right skill and teaching qualifications for these jobs was such that it simply proved in their minds the impossibility of giving priority to the gender question.

I asked the adults what they thought characterised their particular bunch of young trainees. They said, 'they are fairly typical kids.' 'They're all different, they don't fit into a category.' 'They aren't backward. They just got nothing from the educational machinery.' 'Quite a lot of them have ability which they haven't used at school. They've ended up with only two or three CSEs, not really doing themselves justice.' What did they think the trainees wanted out of their year at the ITeC? The training officer said, 'Well, they prioritise a job, strongly. But they do also want something interesting to do to spend the time. They want to meet other young people, they want some kind of structure to spend their time in. An opportunity to actually grow up and develop.' They saw themselves as being there to help them gain the skills, practical and social, which would get what the trainees themselves wanted so much: a job. This was impeded by the trainees' complete lack of background in computer technology. School encoun-

ters with computers had given them nothing – particularly the girls.
But anyway, as one instructor said 'What they are doing here is they
are being given some time between school and work to mature. That,
in addition to the skills they are learning.'

The three male instructors said they had no preference for teaching
single-sex rather than mixed-sex groups. Indeed, there were some
advantages to having young women in otherwise all-male sections.
Girls could be an aid in controlling boys. 'A lot of boys do have a
strong male ego and they see that the girls are able to achieve things
and it spurs them on to try.' 'I think the boys come to attention quicker
if the girls are there.' The woman instructor in Office Technology had
another point of view. Although boys were still seen as the control
problem, her circumstances were different:

> It's easier when it's all girls. I don't know why that is. I think
> perhaps the interaction between them is more calm. When there's a
> boy around it's different, the atmosphere. More bantering going on
> between them. It's not so conducive to work.

Sometimes, the instructors said, they had to treat the sexes a little
differently. The Electronics and Applications instructors for instance
found a slight modification of their usual approach was helpful when
dealing with girls. (These girls were of course only 'minoring' in
these subjects.)

> You have to voice things differently. Express them differently. For
> example you usually get the best response from a boy if you simply
> tell him straight 'Right, this is what you have to do, so do it'.
> Whereas with a girl you tend to get their back up a bit and they feel a
> bit put upon if you just tell them to do things. I tend to put it a bit
> more gently and say 'I'd like you to do this'. Then they mostly go
> ahead and do it.

The Office Technology instructor felt she was obliged to teach a boy
more as an individual, whereas girls were willing to accept instruction
as a group.

Everyone was quite clear about one thing. All were convinced that
young women could do as well, and probably better than, young men
in all the ITeC subjects. Even in Electronics 'the girls on the whole on
the induction taster have performed very, very much better than the

Nothing uni-sex about computers

boys.' One young woman who had been in the section for a couple of months as a minor subject had done so well that the instructor had taken photocopies of her notes to use as a standard for his boys. The experience of the Programming instructor was that neither sex outshone the other, and that of the Applications instructor was that the girls 'are more motivated and practical than the boys.'

Being equally *competent*, however, did not necessarily always mean the girls actually *achieved* as well as the boys. Their lack of informal experience of technology could impede them. Young women 'tend to be more wary of the whole subject. Boys seem less scared to plonk a few keys... Girls don't get to do subjects that involve manual activities, bikes and video games and what have you. In arcades it tends to be boys playing, girls standing watching.' It is an established fact that young women get less hands-on time than their male peers on school computers, and fewer have their own computers at home. 'School computer clubs are attended predominantly by boys' point out Anne Lloyd and Liz Newell. 'When girls do attend, they are rarely able to compete with the boys for access to the limited number of keyboards available. The attitude of many computing teachers is also disturbing: they constantly refer to their pupils as "the boys" – as if it is accepted that there will be no girls in their classes' (Lloyd and

Newell, 1985, p.243). A survey by Acorn Computers of twenty primary and secondary schools found that boys are thirteen times more likely to be using home computers than girls (Thorpe, 1986).

Odd woman out

For many young women the time at the ITeC on City Street was proving no different. Office Technology, the section in which all but one were training, was really barely technological at all. They might use a word processor instead of a typewriter, but the aim was still to produce an office worker, not a technical cadre. A closer look at the interactions in the ITeC made it easy to understand why.

Lisa: to programme or not?

Lisa was the young Afro-Caribbean woman who came new to the ITeC on the day that I began my research there. There were two slightly conflicting perceptions of Lisa's hopes and intentions in coming to City Street. She herself believed that she had told the training officer at her initial interview that she wanted to go into the Programming section. He believed she had said Office Technology. On that basis he had reserved a place for her in that section. In fact, had he understood her to ask for Programming, he would have been obliged to ask her to go on a waiting-list, because Programming was currently full.

When Lisa came to the ITeC and began her fortnight's induction she did say, both in a group session and in interview with me, that she had a spontaneous feeling against doing what all the other girls were doing: Office Technology. 'I do want to be different' she said. This had also been the case at school, where she had had the choice of doing office skills as a subject option but had said to herself that she would not follow the lead of all the other girls but do something else instead. Lisa had a healthy respect for herself and her own potential and, in general, a confidence in women's abilities. 'Women can do anything, I reckon.' She felt that women, in contrast to men, were good all-rounders: 'Jobs like engineer and plumber and that, I think women could do it.'

Lisa completed her fortnight's induction, getting a try in each section. She had good reports from all the instructors including the Programming instructor. Which section would she now choose? During her session with the training officer she explored the choice. They rehearsed together her long-term hopes: she said she wanted one day to have a business of her own. They considered her short-term aim: to go to college like her older sister to get a business (BTEC) qualification. During the review two points emerged and became the ones that eventually clinched the decision. One was that there existed no immediate vacancy in Programming. There did however exist a space in Office Technology – which had indeed been reserved for her. Second, Office Technology might be the better grounding, in the opinion of the training officer, for eventually doing a Business Studies course in FE college. (This is not necessarily so; BTEC General affords specialisation in Information Processing as well as in Keyboarding, for instance.) Listening to these arguments, therefore, Lisa agreed, somewhat regretfully, to go into the waiting opening in Office Technology. It would of course always be possible for her to ask to be moved into Programming later, as and when a space occurred, and if she still wanted it.

What Lisa was feeling when I interviewed her later was a kind of impotent frustration. It was not frustration with the ITeC or her advisers there so much as with the exigencies of life. She felt she was doing the practical and sensible thing. She would probably not now move to Programming, even if given the chance, she said. But Office Technology just did not inspire her. 'It's all right, I suppose, I can just about bear it. The thing is, I just want to know how to type. That's all I'm interested in there.' She regretted missing out on the challenge of Programming, the theoretical work it would have involved. It would have been something unexpected and demanding. 'It's a nice subject, a nice thing to know.' She was also annoyed to find herself after all in the feminine culture of the rest of the 'girls', when she had determined to get away from it.

Lisa is perhaps an example of a young woman who had the confidence, the ability and the will to step out of sex-segregation. She was held into it by some obscure forces. There was certainly a far-reaching pressure from the job-market, mediated both by her own perception of reality and that of the training officer. There was perhaps a prior expectation in the mind of the training officer when he thought he heard her say 'Office Technology' in that first interview... though he was upset to think, later, that he might have misunderstood her. There was a lack of will to fight her way out, perhaps because of conditioning at home and at school. In a way Lisa is more interesting than the young women who do manage to enter the male technologies, because while they are, in today's circumstances, pioneers and therefore exceptionally strong and determined, Lisa is just normal. Any system we develop to enable more women to break out of the female ghetto will have to be designed to help women like her. The incident raises questions. Is it worth while, is it right or wrong, to push young women towards computer skills if they show an inkling of interest? Would the ITeC have served her better if all young women had been obliged to learn Programming? Would she have survived in an all-male Programming section?

Salima: go ahead and do it

Salima was an open, chatty young Asian woman, the only female in any of the three masculine sections at the City Street ITeC, the only one who had chosen to major in any subject other than Office Technology. Why was she there? She was relatively bright, within the context of the ITeC, having CSE passes in English, maths and computer studies. Her Moslem Indian family were business people and her father an accounts manager. He was keen, and so was Salima herself, for her to follow in his footsteps and train to be an accounts technician with a view to going into business herself. At home she had been encouraged by her father to do many things that girls normally would not attempt:

> I sometimes do DIY at home, fixing plugs and that. So it was okay. Being the only girl in the family, I did women's things and men's things as well. I just go into it, I don't care what anybody says. And my father says 'If you want to do this thing, just go ahead and do it'. Like if the car breaks down I usually go and have a look. Or mend the shelves or do something of the sort. Say I'm going to live on my own, I'm going to need to be capable of doing all sorts of things. When I did electronics in the induction week the first thing we had to do was fit a plug. And Arnold [the instructor] was very surprised I knew how to do it. You see what I mean? 'Oh, gosh, it's a woman, can she do this? Can she do that?' That sort of question mark.

Salima felt that other young women of her age were not doing such things because they lacked ambition. 'Many girls I know tend to think office work is how far they can go. They don't want to go any higher.' She felt she could easily enough pick up office skills later in life, if she should prove to need them. It was something more technical and demanding she felt she wanted to get out of the ITeC now: that was why she had chosen Programming.

She also believed that girls were often pressured out of making unusual choices by the social expectations they encountered:

> People might criticise them. I remember when I was under the bonnet of my father's car one day and my brother's friend walked by, and he goes to me 'God, you trying to fix a *car*?' and I says 'Yes, well what about it?' [defiantly]. So he looks at me. Because I was a bit annoyed at the time. And he goes 'Oh, nothing, nothing', and walks off. Another time I was cutting the hedge and a next-door neighbour walks by, and I smiles and he smiles back at me, thinking. It's that look. You could tell what he's thinking.

It was men in particular and men's opinions of women that steered women away from such choices, in Salima's view. 'It's because of the male population you know. They say a woman should stop at home. If men think a woman's place is at home and this kind of sexist remark, they aren't thinking about equality.'

Salima was encountering a bit of teasing in Programming section, but it was fairly light-hearted, she said, and not hurtful. She gave as good as she got. But the price she paid for being there was being obliged always to make a positive effort to be and to seem invulnerable. 'See, I have a rule that I've gone by for a long while. If I come in and feel a bit low or down the boys can sense there's something wrong, because I will start criticising them when I come in the door. I try very hard not to bring my problems in.' How would it be for a shy person? I asked her. 'It depends on how the others react. If she was willing to get to know them and become one of the boys. They treat me as one of the lads. You have to go along with them, and they'll go along with you. But [intake of breath] – there you are!' A less confident, adaptable young woman might not have found it so easy. Would it be nice to have another young woman as companion in Programming? 'Yes. But beggars can't be choosers so – you just treat everyone as normal. Not say "Oh, he's a boy, grrr!" People have to be treated as equal. That's it.'

Salima came across as bright and brave. She was more, not less, able than the average male Programming trainee. She was consciously tackling the whole issue of women and technology. It was not by chance that she was in the Programming section, without other female company. The others recognised this, and encouraged her. 'Women can do anything I reckon' they said about her, 'if they work really hard at it, as hard as the boys.' 'As far as I'm concerned, what a male can do a female can do as well. I don't see why you should put a female lower than a male.'

The absent woman: electronics

The Electronics section in the original ITeC conception had been intended to train its trainees in the maintenance and repair of computer systems, similar to those whose use was being learned in the other three sections. This had proved too ambitious an idea to work in practice. The trainees had not been up to it. What the section had turned into instead was 'basic electronic engineering', learning about components and how to put them together on circuit boards to achieve certain simple purposes. In recent months it had gone even further from its original purpose and taken on basic electrical training too. In this way it had moved away from the other three sections, which were now seen as more of a logical cluster of subjects, fitting well together. Electronics was the odd one out.

Socially, too, it was the aberrant section. Partly because its instructor, Arnold, was the only black member of staff (and male), the section had come to appeal strongly to Afro-Caribbean young men, and among them, to the least academic, least work-prone and most disruptive. A happy sound of music emanated from the Electronics workshop, because Arnold allowed them to work at repairing their own sound systems. In the view of other instructors, discipline was too relaxed. Electronics was very popular with the fun element at the ITeC.

All new trainees, young women included, were obliged to do their half-week induction in Electronics, as in other sections. Some found they enjoyed the work more than they expected and, as we saw, Arnold said in his experience the girls were by far the more promising trainees. However, only one young woman had ever chosen Electronics as a major subject. A quiet, shy person of Spanish origin she had only stayed a week, and had then left the ITeC to go to college. Another two young women had taken Electronics as a minor subject. They had stayed a couple of months and again, one had left to take a job in another field, and the second had gone on to further education. The fact that Electronics had become the odd-ball among the four sections meant that young women were less likely to do it. To do Electronics, in a sense, was to reject Office Technology, and this is what the Afro-Caribbean lads were doing: they would go anywhere but that room.

The mixture of social and practical reasons for women to steer clear of Electronics will be clear. Socially the Electronics section looked and felt totally impenetrable to the average young woman. I sat in with this group of young men in one of their 'life and social skills' sessions. They were playing a game, prompted by my conversations with the training officer, to provoke discussion about 'men's jobs and women's jobs'. The subject was treated with both annoyance and hilarity. The dominant view had it that nappy-changing and flower arrangement were for women only; being a jet pilot, a judge or a refuse collector were for men. 'Women should drink martinis' one of them stated. 'It's unfeminine if you see a woman picking up a mug of beer. It looks like they're saying "I'm one of the lads".' And then, reluctantly, after protest from the teacher, 'It might be okay if they drank *halves.*' Arranging cut flowers was universally condemned as unmanly. A concession was negotiated for the watering of green pot-plants.

The solidarity on this issue was unexpectedly shattered, however, by one of the number: Stephen. He stubbornly piled up all his activity slips in one pile and insisted that all jobs could as a matter of principle be done by either men or women. He defended his decision. 'People have said all the time that men should do this and women should do that', he said. 'And that's how it's become. But people can do anything. These jobs that you need to be strong for – it's not really that, is it? It's common sense. You would get help if you couldn't do it.' There was a surprised silence. It was clear that Stephen had shown an unexpected liberality: he never spoke this way in the male brotherhood of Electronics lessons. His best friend was clearly taken aback, annoyed and hurt to hear him expressing ideas he never knew he had. It was no longer just a game.

I asked this group of young men how they would feel about having a woman instructor. 'No way', said one promptly. Another made a routine salacious remark. But Stephen stepped out of line again, exasperating his colleagues. 'A man shows more authority. But if she was able to impose her authority she'd be all right. It's not physical strength. After all, she's not paid to *wrestle* with us.' The truth of course is that she would have to wrestle with them, if she were to attempt to change the gendered nature of the section. Her own woman's presence would be pitted not only against the trainee culture but a solid substructure, the masculine associations of the subject, electronic engineering.

Masculinity and technology

The staff of the City Street ITeC were very committed to their youngsters. Some were rather short on experience – either of the subject they were teaching, or the practice of teaching itself. The manager saw staffing as his main problem. But all were trying hard to learn the skills they needed as they went along. The training officer was well qualified in teaching, counselling and careers guidance. He was creating an atmosphere in which trainees could explore and express their feelings. Together they had created a supportive environment for any young woman (or young man) who showed signs of wanting to train in a non-traditional area. They were however waiting for the individual recruit to make the first move. The trouble was, few individual young women were showing signs of wishing to be pioneers: Salima the Brave was a hard act to follow.

The resulting inequality at the ITeC was serious. City Street justly prided itself on serving the various ethnic groups of its community well. But what was meant by ethnic groups? Men only? The ITeC was doing far less for young women, black or white, than for young men. Only a quarter of its opportunities were going to girls. Even those opportunities were inferior to the ones boys were getting. It was males who were acquiring the technical manual skills in electronics. It was males who were learning to control the computer by the techniques of programming. It was males who were learning to use the computer for management purposes. To have named the office section 'Office *Technology*' had been misleading. The young women were destined to work as typists and office juniors, albeit on glossy new equipment. There were no signs that this imbalance was a passing phenomenon. Indeed it was built into the very structure of the place.

The ITeC was effectively reproducing the world outside. The unequal position of women in relation to computers and computing skills is well attested. Anne Game and Rosemary Pringle, who made a study of male/female interaction in six industries, concluded 'computing is the most ruthlessly cut-throat. It is synonymously the most macho.' They describe the division of labour in the industry. Women predominate in unskilled data entry, where they form virtually 100 per cent of the workforce. Operating is defined as male and paid much better:

> Programming is supposed to be uni-sex but men predominate and women tend to be concentrated in the lower ranks of the coders. Relatively few women move into systems analysis and fewer still into management. They do however appear in demonstrating, teaching and consulting work, jobs that are held to be consistent with 'femininity' in that they draw on interpersonal skills and are less directly competitive.

Women's role in computing and information processing therefore is almost entirely limited to the initial keyboarding of data. 'In computing, the gulf between the key-punch women and other computer workers has been treated as so natural that half the labour force has been effectively removed from consideration... not even regarded as part of the same industry.' They conclude 'computing is no more uni-sex than Playboy' (Game and Pringle, 1983, pp.81–2).[1]

In previous work I have shown how the introduction of electronic technology in various kinds of workplaces has transformed the kinds of jobs and shaken up the relation between them. But when the dust clears the traditional pattern can be seen to have fallen back into place: women are found as unskilled and semi-skilled operators of the various new kinds of electronic equipment, and as assembler-wirers in its manufacture. It is almost universally men, on the other hand, who hold the posts that call for, and develop, electronic engineering skills, computer skills and systems knowledge. The old technologies were always associated culturally with masculinity, but even these new ones, cleaner, lighter and safer, men have been able to appropriate for masculinity (Cockburn, 1985).

Something of the way men's power operates *culturally* can be seen in Anne Lloyd and Liz Newell's study of women and computing:

Women who work in computing do so on terms which have been laid down by men. Because men generally hold the positions of power in the industry it is they who define what is desirable and acceptable. The personal qualities required are those usually associated with men – hard-headedness, single-mindedness, ambition, toughness – attributes employers demand in many other areas of (male) work (Lloyd and Newell, 1985, p.247).

Were it not that men set the terms, computing skills might just as well be associated with qualities seen as feminine: carefulness, say, and sensitivity; expressiveness and diligence. In fact of course computing does not need to be linked with any particular set of qualities, nor does a woman or a man. The gendering of people and the gendering of jobs is not really necessary to the competence of the one or the performance of the other.

Opening up space for women

It is not only in ITeCs that computer skills are being taught in YTS. The Manpower Services Commission prescribe them as part of the core content of training for all trainees. Research has shown a shameful male bias in this aspect of course content, with the effect that 'women and girls were being relegated to a secondary and essentially marginal role within new technology' (Thorpe, 1986). From this finding and my own one might think perhaps that there was little to be done, that the ground-rules of YTS and the nature of ITeCs together were quite immobilising. Yet another ITeC I visited, in the North of England, had started with a more positive policy and had produced better results for women.

This ITeC had appointed a woman manager. From the outset a 'quota' had been established, whereby 50 per cent of the staff and 50 per cent of the trainees would be female. Places were held open for three months from the beginning of the year – and this had been sufficient, given some energetic outreach work, to bring in the required proportion of young women trainees. (In the light of MSC's legal opinion on the scope for positive discrimination in favour of women in YTS in its one-year form such activities had been technically illegal. But there are times when it is better to avoid talking to lawyers.) The subdivision of training at this ITeC was thought out carefully in advance, with the problem of sex-typing in mind. They had decided on three sections, in contrast to City Street's four. These were: electronics; computing; and electronic office. In the latter, 'office skills' were played down. Instead, word-processing was combined with use of the computer for data base work and spread-sheets. If boys did not choose electronic office here they would really miss out on some valuable computer skills. For a year, a women-only electronics stream was offered. The ITeC's provision was advertised as a broad-based course on information technology skills. There was less specialism than in the City Street ITeC. Everybody trained in all subjects for at least three months of the year. The induction period was a full month. The staff and board used the sex discrimination law itself discriminatingly. Since they could not advertise specifically for women trainees, they simply designed leaflets to appeal to young women, used the women's movement network to reach them, and developed inventive approaches to outreach such as a caravan in the shopping precinct, a jingle on the local radio station. Further to tip the balance of numbers in the Centre and create a more positively female presence they arranged for the local council to pay for some additional trainees – particularly women of the 18–25 age group, some of whom had children.

Many difficulties were encountered of course. The step from ITeC to job at year-end still saw women tending to look for sex-stereotyped occupations. They feared 'Yes, but if I go there I'll be the only woman', 'It is one thing doing it here, but not outside'. The rigid, centrally-determined framework in which the Youth Training Scheme is set and which ITeCs must observe limits what is possible. The woman manager of this highly unusual ITeC explained:

Responsibility for implementing equal opportunity here rests with the staff and it is in the face of the dominant way of doing things. It is costly. And no extra time or staff are allowed. The need is for additional resources. We need additional strategies and funding for them. We need to allocate time for these purposes. In 1986/7 under Two-Year YTS it will be worse. We will have to say in advance how many places for what level and what age. We won't be paid for places that are temporarily empty, which we are holding open for girls. It will be much more difficult.

Indeed, a question mark hung over the future of ITeCs under the new two-year scheme. Proposals from the government were being awaited. But it was feared that they would be expected to exist on considerably reduced funds and to supplement their income by revenue generated by productive work by trainees in all sections. Even 'open access' was now being questioned. An ITeC was to become a business.

The experience of this north-country ITeC could, however, have been a starting-point for City Street and others. There were two key factors recognised there that City Street's approach to new technology training had overlooked. The first was the significance of gender culture: individuals cannot change it piecemeal by crossing one at a time on to the territory of the opposite sex. A large-scale feminisation was needed *as policy* if an environment was to be created in which young women could make really free choices. What was altogether lacking in the City Street ITeC was women's 'technological space'. What could such space have meant? At the simplest, it could have involved a basic electrics session once a week for young women. Better still, single-sex streaming in some or all sessions. Would it be out of the question to consider an experimental woman-only ITeC sponsored by some progressive local authority?

More space for women could also be developed within a mixed-sex context. Despite the recognised difficulties of working with young men, not all young women want to be trained separately. They need supportive training policies however. Women teachers in technical subjects could help. So could intensive work with young men on sexism.

The second neglected factor was the significance of the specification of occupations, the separation of different areas of work and training. In certain ways the City Street ITeC was *more* sex-stereotyped than the world at large. Even on sophisticated equipment, a year on YTS cannot train relatively low-achieving school-leavers to anything more than a modest level. It may be that the Electronics section cannot expect in twelve months to train its YTS trainees to much more than the level of an adult assembler-wirer in an electronics factory, or the Applications section to go much beyond data preparation and input. These relatively lowly new-technology jobs, outside the ITeC in the world of work, are overwhelmingly done by women. Yet in the ITeC these were male-stereotyped sections. This leads one to believe that their male image in the ITeC resulted simply from the presence of female and male in a situation where there were separate sections to choose from. Males tend to create and preserve their own spheres of expertise, their own cultural space. They elevate its status. Women respond by creating their own safe places, and take the level of technology as the cue. The existence of an 'office skills' or 'typing' option is certainly one such cue. Three sections here had become male, by following these cues, one had become female. If the skills on offer had been, say, hair-brushing and tooth-brushing – the latter by battery-operated toothbrush – it is certain that the thrust to male separatism and the minimal cues would have been sufficient to gender the former female and the latter male. The fragmentation and ranking of occupations, then, itself aids sex-segregation and the more jobs can be unified the fewer places men have to escape to.

These issues, fundamental to the current failure of the ITeC to attract women trainees and give them technical skills, were seldom discussed among the staff however. Nor were they discussed between staff and trainees. The staff might worry individually, but their worries did not change their approach to ITeC policy. Of course, sex-typing, 'Yes, in a very general way it matters', but 'I don't see it as the role of the ITeC to break down sex-segregation.' Besides, 'I'm not active in that field and I don't know how one would go about it.' 'I'm not here, I'm not being paid to break down society's stereotypes. I'm here to look after the development of these trainees.' The manager said:

Personally, I feel that the world would be a far better place if there were more women in positions of authority and fewer men making decisions. No war has ever been started by a bunch of women. I think that women have every right to earn the same salary as a man does... But that is way beyond the issues here at the ITeC.'

Notes

1. Women's subordinate position in computing is a world-wide phenomenon. The example quoted comes from Australia. It is confirmed however by G. L. Simons who writes of the British computer industry:

    a demeaning or patronising view of women is conveyed in technical computing journals and books, reflecting attitudes of the broader culture. And the lower the grade in a computing organisation the higher the proportion of women tends to be: for example, there is a relatively high proportion of female key-punch operators but female data-processing managers are rare (Simons, 1981).

Research from the USA adds to the picture:

> Software work is barely 40 years old. It does not carry the burden of a
> tradition of discrimination against women. Indeed, modern computer
> programming began as an all-female occupation. Yet women in
> software today... although relatively better off, are still confined to the
> least responsible, most routine, worst-paying (and probably dead-end)
> jobs. For whatever reason, software work has replicated the sexual
> (and racial) divisions that characterise older occupations (Kraft and
> Dubnoff, 1984).

8

Caring Work: 'You Can't Make Friends with a Car'

Accounts of women's attempts to get a foothold in masculine occupations, their successes and failures, the rewards and disincentives, are now no longer a rarity. The foregoing chapters have added a few more to the genre. We have explored the problems of young women in relation to administration and management, in relation to male craft occupations and in relation to new technology. In passing, we have glimpsed a very few young men moving in the opposite direction, mainly into typing and office skills.

It is clear that there is always an asymmetry, an imbalance, in the experiences of young women and young men 'gender innovators' when they are put in the balance alongside one another. Young women are responding to what they and others see as a *challenge*. They tend to see themselves and to be represented by their friends as being exceptionally daring or exceptionally resourceful. In the Youth Training Scheme, as we have seen, such women are rare. They were sprinkled thinly among the hundred or more schemes in my MSC London area, as garage mechanics, in building trades or in print. One of the Mode A schemes I investigated was in fact operating in the printing industry and there I found that, though young women trainees were in a small minority, they were not entirely absent. Indeed YTS managing agents – ironically, by defying trade union demarcation and 'closed shop' practices and using non-unionised firms – had helped young women to get into the potentially skilled print jobs from which females have historically been excluded. One of the young women print trainees, Catherine, afforded a good example of someone typical of the successful 'woman in non-traditional trades' in the sociological literature: a trifle careless of what men thought of her, independent in style, rebellious and combative – above all, committed to the occupation and skill in question more than to the quality of social relations in work. Innovating young women can see a world to gain and are prepared to pay the price to gain it.

For young men it is very different. Because the stratum of occupations known as 'women's work' involves a step down in status for men, their presence has to be explained in other terms. Young men training in 'office skills' sections of the three schemes examined in Chapters 5, 6 and 7 were of two kinds. Either they were failures, judged by the rigorous and unkindly standards of masculinity. Or they were in the ascendant over their female peers, aiming to by-pass the female employment ghetto, taking what they wanted from office skills training in order to become managers, computer specialists or writers. However unrealistic these aims for a working-class lad on YTS they explained to his own satisfaction his presence among women. In the first instance the young men were in the female environment as a kind of refuge. In the second they were exploiting it for their own purposes. The two explanations of course can and perhaps often do coexist. A young man moving horizontally into office skills training because he feels safer away from the abrasive culture of other lads may explain his choice to himself and others by citing a perceived advantage in the pursuit of positions vertically superior to those of the majority in the female-stereotyped occupation: chef among catering assistants, proprietor among hairdressers, cutter or designer among sewing-machinists.

The asymmetry in the experience of young women and young men is logical enough: it arises from an imbalance of power. Gender complementarity is not a meshing of two identical halves of a whole. It is top heavy. Masculinity has some of the authority of the template, the matrix or the mould. Femininity has the compliance of the material that is formed to its image and outline. Men have the initiative in the cultural construction of gender as they do in the economic sphere of paid employment, in institutions, in physique. This is why women sometimes feel that as feminists we ought not to concern ourselves with occupational gender innovation for men. It is our business to help women into male work, they would argue. If we help men into women's work (besides, what men need our help? they are only too good at looking after their own interests), we will simply give them a leg up that will assist them in climbing into positions of authority over us. Better, they would argue, put our efforts into boosting the value ascribed to women's work and women's skills and making sure we are better rewarded for them.

While the truth in this has to be respected, there is another point of view to be considered. We say that women's skills are undervalued and we are right. Men's skills are overrated. This does not stop us saying, quite correctly, that women should have access to the skills known today as men's. Even more to the point, however, we need to recognise that the wellbeing of society depends on all human beings having women's skills.

I would argue that we should make a special case for positive action to involve men in more work of the kind that develops nurturing and tending skills. If gender is a social construct as we believe, it is formed and changed only by lived experience. The only way we can work for an association of men with caring and affect, a dissociation of men from hardness, aggression and violence, is by changing the experiences that men have. This means changing the upbringing of little boys, the schooling of older boys, the experience of training and work and the pattern of adult domestic relationships and roles. Men learning the skills and doing the work involved in child care, or nursing the old and disabled, brings changes at more than one level. It develops the boy or man himself as a different kind of adult; it relaxes the sex-stereotypes in the minds of the adults who are tended by such men and in the world at large; and it changes the upbringing pattern of the children who are nurtured by them. It is arguable that making possible new and better experiences for men in our society, though it involves a short-term risk for women, is one we have to take in the interests of a longer-term future for everyone. At the very least we have to give careful consideration to what happens, in practice, when men set out to learn women's skills and take on those feelings and ideas we often represent as 'women's values'.

86 per cent female

It was with this in mind that I looked around in the Youth Training Scheme for some instances of male trainees in *OTF-10: community and health care*. We saw in Chapter 1 that this occupational group has a greater sex imbalance in YTS than any other, with 86 per cent female and only 14 per cent male trainees. In my area I found around sixteen schemes that had offered OTF-10 places in the years 1984/5 and 1985/6. Typically they were in nursery nursing, playgroup work, schools or homes for the disabled and elderly, and in youth and community work. It was impossible to locate for interview more than one current male trainee however. A second scheme that had two young men refused me access to them. The coordinator replied in a peremptory manner that he 'had difficulty with the concept of non-traditional occupations' and evaded further questions with 'I'm reluctant to go down that track'. Half of the remainder of the schemes had never had a boy trainee. But eight schemes had, at some time in the past, had one or two male trainees in OTF-10 places. I decided to break with my research formula which involved interviewing exclusively current trainees and to look up some of these schemes and their ex-trainees to find out what their experience had been.

Of the eight schemes that had experience of young men in OTF-10, five were Mode B schemes, characteristically Community Projects. The three Mode As were local council, local health authority or chamber of commerce. In total there had been perhaps a score of boys, of whom at least half had left after a spell of only a few months or weeks. I talked to the coordinators of three of the schemes. They all confirmed a dearth of male applications. 'There aren't many boys coming through.' One Community Project YTS had had forty-two trainees over two or three years, only three of whom had been young men. It was not for want of trying. The (male) coordinator told me, 'In the early days we went round the Careers Offices saying "We want blokes on this scheme. Where are they?" We contacted local schools. We made a point of sending our leaflet to boys' schools and in some cases talking to head masters.' This project had even changed its title from 'Community Care and Health' to 'Community Work', in order to appeal more to young men:

> We developed a whole range of placements, moving consciously away from the model of pre-school playgroups and nursery schools to include community centres, urban farms, pressure groups, detached community work and so on. Things it was felt would appear less feminine, with a small 'f', and that therefore would seem more attractive to boys. We tried to change it from the submissive feminine attributes. To acknowledge that that is there, but emphasise also the social and political responsibilities of young people working in the community.

In this way they had reluctantly felt obliged to reinforce a division already noticeable in the Youth Service, whereby women tend to be located in part-time jobs working with younger children, men in full-time professional career posts working with older youth – mainly male. Aware of this, they had at the same time tried to sell the idea of boy trainees to local pre-school playgroups. 'We had the help of supervisors. Some were quite keen in fact. I could have got more placements for boys. We were able to create the environment. The problem was, we couldn't get the young men. That was our singular failure.' When the initial steps failed, energies tended to fail with them. 'I couldn't put my hand on my heart and say that now we are taking active steps to break the mould.'

A second Community Project YTS had tried adapting the recruitment process to open young people's minds to new possibilities. 'We always talk about equal opportunity and during interview we always ask them if they would like to consider other things.' They had tried to keep places open for young women in male sections. 'But we found we couldn't really do that in community care for the boys because boys just weren't coming forward wanting to do it. The Careers Officers have often said to us, "The boys just don't seem to see it as being for them." ' This scheme too had a plentiful supply of nurseries and playgroups eager to have male trainees, conscious of the lack of men in nurturing and tending roles as role models for children. When boys did show interest, however, parents often emerged as a problem. A father would say 'No way. That's sissies' work'. A mother would phone saying they did not want their son to do that because 'he'd never get a job at the end of it.' They no doubt also had in mind the very low pay and status in these 'women's jobs'.

Curiously, one scheme was intent on discouraging trainees of either sex from taking up their OTF-10 places, which were mainly in child care:

> We tend to steer them away from community and health care because the health authority here won't employ anyone without Nursery Nursing Examinations Board qualification. Our youth trainees tend to be low achievers who are not likely to get onto an NNEB course. Most aren't up to the educational standard. Without it there is no long-term career prospect for them. There are very few openings and too many qualified people they'll be competing with. Besides, the YTS placements aren't that great. A lot of employers will use YTS trainees to 'help out', 'do the cleaning' and not give much training.

Rather than lead kids on to what she saw as a dead-end this co-ordinator was blunt: 'Low achievers are better going into small office jobs with clerical and typing skills and a decent wage.'

A second scheme followed this same discouraging line with young women for the same reasons but nonetheless actively encouraged young men to take up OTF-10 places because the coordinator believed that they had better employment prospects 'because of the shortage of males within that area'. Local authority nurseries and playgroups in particular were on the look-out for young men, and as we will see, one young man after his year on YTS working in playgroups was indeed 'snapped up' by an NNEB course which 'fell over backward to take him', although he had very poor literacy and lacked the required school-leaving exams. A further reason for discouraging young women, in the view of this coordinator, was that 'working with children tends to be a refuge for 16-year-old girls who've got experience with younger brothers and sisters. It's safe. It isn't challenging. For that reason we make them do a package of placements here, including not just child care but also the elderly and mental handicap work too.' With boys, in contrast to girls, nurturing work could be seen as stretching.

Those schemes that had had experience with young men in OTF-10 summarised it as follows. First, they had encountered 'massive resistance' from young men to considering anything more feminine than working in a youth club, looking after animals on an 'urban farm', or getting involved in 'community action'. Of those few that did want to train for nurturing or tending occupations a substantial proportion were themselves in special need of a supportive situation. 'They tend to be unusually subdued gentle boys who never try to compete with other boys. Maybe they have come out of care themselves. The mental handicap places attract trainees who are in need of that particular kind of help.' Another coordinator confirmed this:

> The reasons they came were not mould-breaking reasons. Two had been in care and had a history of contact with caring institutions. One was perhaps modelling himself on the social workers he had had contact with in his own life. The second had counselling and emotional problems that it was felt the scheme could help with.

These needy boys however did not represent the entire male intake to OTF-10. There was a second type identified by the scheme

organisers – an outgoing and daring type, 'the pioneer who is confident enough not to feel his macho threatened. There's a common
character, a degree of bloody-mindedness, doesn't care what people
say. Someone who is going to go in and change things.' If they stayed
with their occupational choice long enough, some from the first group
might mature and grow in confidence and ability to become adequate
nurturers themselves. But the chances were weighted toward that
maturing process leading them to compete with and join 'the real
men'. Likewise some of the second group would eventually succumb
to teasing from other boys – and from girls. One young man who took
up nursery nursing 'got so much flak from the girls he couldn't take it.
"What you doing working with children? That's women's work."
Snidey comments. He lasted two days and then disappeared.' Others
might be more philosophical, ride the harassment and come to
identify with the work. For every young man that was held into a
career in this kind of work by the experience of YTS, however, many
more were drawn back into a man's world. Of two young men who
worked with animals, one in an urban farm and the other in a play

You have not to care what people say

park, the first became a security guard, the second went to agriculture college. 'You could say', the coordinator commented wrily of the latter, 'We made a man of him.'

Three young men

To illustrate not only the difficulties faced by young men who step out of gender tradition, but also what they lose when they step back again, I will describe three trainees and their experience on the Youth Training Scheme. All three are white European.

Nick

The first is Nick, a fair-haired young man of slight straight build, whose mother was a school cook and father an electrician. Nick had attended a mixed-sex comprehensive where he had chosen cookery as an option in his fourth year.

> I got on really well with it. Apart from the fact that the teachers didn't like it, because I was the only boy in the class. They set up a special class called 'home maintenance' for all the kids that weren't exactly manageable in the school. They put them in one group to go round and do building work. And they put me into that instead of cookery. It was just a joke, because it was all the baddies in the school so nothing ever got done.

I asked him why he thought they had moved him:

> It might have been the teacher herself. We didn't get on that well. Could be that. I don't know. I was just asked to go into that class. And I got on better with the teachers by doing that. I think I would have had a lot of trouble if I'd stayed on in the cookery class.

When the time came for Nick to leave school he went to the Careers Office and said he would like a job in archaeology because he liked history at school and was interested in old things. They asked him what other subjects he had done at school. When he listed them, they picked straight away on 'home maintenance' and, taking their cue from this, gave him a list of building firms in the area to apply to for a job. 'They didn't listen to what I wanted. They only gave me the same as they gave every other guy in the class.' In this Kafka-esque manner, Nick was first hijacked into a male manual trades class and then assumed to have chosen it. There seemed no escape. Fortunately he had a voluntary job with a Catholic priest at a community centre, who put him in touch with the YTS Community Project. Having done youth work at the centre, he now asked to go into a placement doing similar club work. He was sent straight out for work experience to a club for 8–12-year-olds, run by a wife-and-husband team.

Nick stayed at the club six months. 'We played games, pool and badminton. You would be keeping an eye open for anything else – if a child got hurt. Otherwise you just joined in and played with them.' One afternoon a week he went for his 'off-the-job' training to a Pre-school Playgroups Association course where a woman taught Nick and a number of young women techniques for nursery work with small children.

> Like finger painting and things. Some of the time it was quite good. But most of the time she used to ask us to do things that got everybody embarrassed. It was a bit of a joke. She even talked to us as if we were little children. So we just started to act like it. We was just messing about.

After six months the club's circumstances changed. It couldn't keep him and he was placed instead in a nursery for 3–5-year-olds, where he was the only male. 'At first I didn't think it would be that good or anything. And then after the first couple of days I got over the embarrassment and just mucked in and it was great.' I asked what the embarrassment had been about. 'I think it's that you've got to come down to the child's level. I mean you've got to talk to them and everything. And at first it seems a bit silly, when you've got other adults there watching you. Ladies. You feel a bit embarrassed. But after a bit I just used to do it naturally.' He thought he was not the only one to be embarrassed. Girls were too 'if men or boys are around. Say when I was around. In front of me. I don't think they would have if it was just all ladies.' The difficulty, it seemed, was in acting out the adult female part in front of the opposite sex, whichever sex you were yourself.

When he left YTS Nick continued working with children, moving to a scheme with disabled infants from six months to five years. Here:

the different classrooms was for children with special problems. Some was dependent on drugs. And then we had a unit like a hospital where the disabled children were. Where I was. And with the disabled children there was one girl, she'd been knocked over, but she could speak really well and everything. She used to be quite attached to me. And the children in the other room whenever I walked past them they'd shout my name and come running out. And the other nurses would have to run after them. I think a lot of that was – a lot of them used to call me 'dad', because they'd never had a dad – I was the only bloke in the place, otherwise it was all women. And a lot of them saw me as a father figure.

Nick had learned to be very conscious about sexism:

I remember times when a little boy was playing with a pram and another little boy said 'You can't push that, it's a girl's pram'. And I used to teach them it doesn't matter if it's a girls' pram. If he wants to do that he can do it. I used to try and do that.

I asked, 'Did you used to tend them physically, if they needed it or were hurt?'

Yes. If in the unit a little boy had messed himself for instance, I'd go and change him. But the nursery nurses in there would say 'Oh, I'll do it'. They'd think because I'm a boy I couldn't do it. Well, they knew I *could* do it, but it was still automatic for them to take the child. But I used to do it anyway. I'd say 'No, it's all right. I'll do it.'

If kids were upset or hurt and crying, they came to Nick just as to the women:

The others used to call me Speedy. Because we used to let them do roughly what they wanted and there was quite a few accidents. And I used to see them and run to grab the child before it fell. I used to be there before them, because I could run fast. But sometimes a child would fall over. And I'd run over and they'd put their arms out to me. I think it's about the same [as for a woman].

Nick felt that during those months he'd learned a real skill. 'I had the attitude basically. But I've learned things as I went along.

Different ways of going about teaching children. Every child is different and you've got to use different tactics. I think you have to learn it.' His male friends accepted what he had chosen to do, mainly because he already had a reputation for going his own way. He was aware, though, of being the odd one out. 'A lot of people I know, they wouldn't do it. It's all this macho stuff and everything.' Nick felt it had been easier for him because he had had two little brothers whom he had always looked after a good deal. Besides, his sister was a nursery nurse. And at school he had learned to ignore gendered expectations:

> I hate football. So I used to refuse to play it. When I played it I used to mess the game up by kicking the ball into my own goal, things like that. So they threw me out of boys' games and put me in with the girls. Which was ideal for me, because they used to do gymnastics, trampolining, things I enjoyed. So that didn't bother me at all.

Nick liked individual sports. His hobbies were climbing, canoeing, swimming. He hated men's team games. 'But they give you no choice at school. They should ask the boys "Do you want to do gym or trampolining?" But no. It's just football and cross-country you are expected to do. And boys like that grow up macho, and they aren't going to think about doing child care.' I asked Nick, 'Do you think if more men went into child-care work, the macho ones, it might change the nature of nurseries so that they became less caring places?' 'I dunno. No. I don't think just any boy *could* go into it actually. They'd have to actually care about it, otherwise they wouldn't last. Because the children can sense it just like that.'

Nick's experiment was about to end however. After he had been at the disabled unit five weeks a friend offered him the chance to come into partnership in a little self-generated business. And so he left. 'The way I looked at it, there's more money in it than I'd ever earn in child care', said Nick, 'and better prospects for me, to have my own firm.' What was the business? He looked shamefaced and laughed, recognising the incongruity. 'We instal burglar alarms.' He went on:

> the advantage mainly is that you can get on, you know. If you've got your own business you can get bigger. The disadvantage is, it's not so rewarding. It's good to go in and do the job and get it done and think 'That's a good job, it's neat'. But when you work with the kids,

I mean every day's an achievement. Like, you can teach them different colours. And when you hear them say 'That's blue', 'That's red', you know, it makes you feel good. Because you think, 'I taught them how to do that'.

The pleasures of child care however had not been able to outweigh economics. 'I think I would have kept it up if I knew I was going to get somewhere. But it just seemed I weren't going to get any promotions or get any further.' The future was a business in property protection.

Andy

Andy was a strikingly good-looking young man, with cropped fair hair, a scarred and flattened nose and an ear-ring. He was athletic and muscular, but gentle in his movements and manner. He was the oldest of eight children. The father was a profoundly violent man who frequently attacked his wife and children. Not surprisingly Andy's mother was in a nervous condition and Andy lost a lot of school through staying at home to look after his younger brothers and sisters. Eventually his mother left home. All the young ones were taken into care. Andy was left at home with his father:

But then he started taking it out on me, just me being at home. And one day I walked into Social Services and told them I couldn't take it. I asked to be put into care with my brothers and sisters. I was very, very lucky because I was put into the same place as them. I hadn't seen them for months.

In the home, Andy looked after 'his family' as though he were their parent.

So it had been little children all the way along and when Andy was 'released home' at 16 it was not surprising that he should look for work with children. Like Nick, however, he had to outface the careers advisers who told him that, being male, he would not stand a chance of working with children. 'All they thought of was shop work, factory work and all that.' Andy heard of a local YTS scheme that offered a year's training in child care. He went along and was immediately welcomed and sent out on a placement in a nursery for 3–5-year-olds. The other workers were all women. The way he saw his work it was:

keeping the children active, making sure they're not bored, that they're all right. Not being picked on, not sitting there moping. I'd play games with them – all kinds. Sitting-at-the-table kind of games. Or football. One game was a parachute – I used to enjoy that myself. Making puppets, making ear-rings, I liked doing that. But one of the girls would sit down and do sewing with them. They never asked me to do that. I wasn't bothered, there was always something else to do. At meal time I put out the knives and forks, put the food on their plates, made sure they weren't spilling it everywhere. Sometimes I'd get a spoon and feed one of them. I'd clear up afterwards. I'd take the little boys to the toilet – not the girls. The women used to do that.

The things Andy liked best were 'making them laugh, really. Or teaching them something what I'd learned in school, drawing or something, and they'd pick it up and make a picture of their own. They might want to take it home. Things like that.' He had his special friends there:

There was one little Indian boy, his mum was very young and his dad too but his dad had died of cancer. And he always used to come to me. There was some other little girl in there too, she never had a dad and because of me being a male she used to come to me for comfort sometimes.

It could get frustrating:

I mean there's a lot in the nurseries I worked in, boys and girls, that can't understand English. And that's frustrating because you've got to make signs to them. There are some English little kids too, you tell them to do something and they just say 'Ner', and you have to say 'Come on now', and you feel like, grrr – throwing them over there. But you don't. You don't do that.

He reckoned he had learned patience doing the job. It could get boring, sometimes, too:

At times the time would go slow. Because they didn't tell me what to do. I had to do it myself, think 'What shall I do now?' Because sometimes all the kids would be busy. You can't be involved with them all the time, they are doing their own thing. You just walk round the tables.

At these times the staff would just chat: 'Sit around talking to each other, about 'man problems',' he laughed. Sometimes he felt left out. 'But they would change the subject if I came and sat down. We'd talk about what we done the day before, what happened last night. Or about some little kid that's done something.'

Andy worked in a number of different nurseries during his time on YTS. Once there was another male trainee for a while. Otherwise it was always women he worked with. But they all welcomed him. 'I was sort of the pet really. I showed them I could do it. They was really overboard. They was always going, "Oh, you should go on, you should do this or do that." No-one ever said to me, "Andy, you should give up." Nothing like that.'

I asked him what quality it was you needed, what you would look for in a young man good at that kind of work? 'Friendship with children', he said. 'Know how to be friends with little children, how to talk to them, how to be gentle with them. That's the main thing, I think. It's for the children, not the staff. That's what we're there for. It's to make *them* happy.' Nobody outside had supported or encouraged him in taking up the work. He had taken the step all alone.

> I was told I was stupid. My mates laughed at me. Told me I was a poof, doing child care, looking after children. Especially being only 16 at the time. You're still young, you know. If you want to do it and you haven't done anything like that before, you don't know what to expect. Especially from the other people you're going to be with. Especially because they'll be all girls.

And it had felt strange at first. The year as a whole, however, had been such a positive time for Andy that he decided to stay in this kind of work. When he applied for jobs they told him he had to have his NNEB. The coordinator of his YTS scheme put him in touch with a college. 'I got on the course straight away. I didn't even have to have an interview. Being a man they just said come along. They'd never had a boy doing that work. And some newspaper come down and they put it in the paper.'

Andy did not stay at college long however. 'I felt so uncomfortable.

The fact of being the only bloke in thirty-five girls, I felt so embarrassed. I'm a very shy person anyway so I was frightened to open my mouth or anything.' It wasn't that they picked on him. 'Just funny remarks really. And at first, when I started, I had to walk up in front of the class and try this apron thing on, girl's thing, and I felt so embarrassed. The teacher said "This won't do, we'll have to get you a male's one. We'll send off for a special one for you". And everyone started laughing.' After a few weeks he left the college. Now he had a part-time job as a gardener. He felt nervous of factory work, the only full-time openings he had seen. 'I don't know nothing about mechanics, electrics. I've got no skills at all' he said – overlooking the very real skills he had already gained. But:

> what's at the back of my mind is, it's going to be difficult to walk into a job and mix with men now. (Laugh) I'm so used to mixing with girls, it'll be difficult mixing with men. I've *never* done that before. I think they're more outgoing than what girls are, more talkative. Because I like to get on and do my work. And there's a lot of swearing, a lot of boasting, all that kind of thing. I don't like sitting there boasting and swearing. If you don't feel part of it, if you don't feel they can accept you, it's going to be awkward.

It sounds, I said to him, as though the way you experience it there's a very big divide between women and men. 'Yeah', he said. 'I think there is. It shouldn't be like that. We should be all together.' Sometimes, even now, he thought of trying to get back into working with children. 'I should have kept it up. But never mind.' The money, he knew, would have been terrible.

William

When I met William he was a trainee care assistant in an old people's home, now in his tenth month on the Scheme. He was a gentle-looking lad with a square-shaped, pale face. His voice was breaking and shifted unreliably up and down in pitch. He had soft brown hair cut neatly but rather long, just an inch or two longer than you expect in a young man today. But for the trousers he wore, in this skirt-uniformed place, he could easily have been taken for a young woman. He was a quiet kind of person whose hobbies were listening to music, and walking the dog. He came from a church-going family and had one sister and a mentally handicapped brother. All the family had been practically involved in tending this brother:

> I always used to help him out, help my mum. I enjoyed teaching him things. I thought at first I'd work with the handicapped. That's what I asked for first. But they couldn't find anything. So they said 'Would you mind old people or children?' So I said no, I wouldn't mind. And now I think I prefer the elderly because handicapped would be a bit more tiring.

Like Nick and Andy, William had a depressing tale to tell of the Careers Service. 'I told her I wanted to do care work' he said of his Careers Officer, 'But she sent me off places, interviews for post work, to be a postman. I just went along to satisfy her. She said "This is better than nothing, isn't it?" ' He had found the YTS place without her help.

The institution in which William worked afforded sheltered residential care to sixty old people. It had a staff of twenty-two, all women but for the caretaker and kitchen porter. The matron said:

> We've never had a male care assistant. And William is the first boy we've had on YTS.' She said about William, 'He's just an ordinary lad. He is – he's *tender*. He's more tender than the hard nuts, but I imagine that's the way he's been brought up. He did get a little bit of teasing here but it soon wore off and he was, well, one of the girls. He fits in so well. He even came out with us one night, the only fellow with twenty women. I thought it was very good. And he enjoyed himself. He doesn't stick out like a sore thumb, he blends in.

His ideals, she said, were the same as those of the rest of the staff: 'The residents come first.'

The matron described William's work:

> First thing in the morning it's getting everybody up, emptying commodes, going round making sure the residents are clean and washed, that they look presentable and haven't got their dresses on inside out or their shirts buttoned up wrong. Then he'll serve breakfast. And after that toileting, bathing, making beds, general everyday needs of the residents.

What William told me added to this account:

> After baths, you take their washing down and do it and dry it and
> take it back to their room. You sit down and talk to them. Ask them
> if they need anything. We serve lunch, put the gravy on the plates
> and that. When the afternoon staff come in, you tell them what's
> been going on during the day. In the afternoon we sometimes take
> one of the residents out shopping, or go to the chemist for prescrip-
> tions or to the library. Or to get their pension. Some of them can
> walk, but some are in a wheelchair. And some can't go to the toilet
> on their own.

At first William had been limited in some of the things he could
do:

> Like going to their rooms without asking them, taking their keys,
> going through their drawers. You have to, because some of them are
> a bit 'gone' and can't manage themselves. You have to tidy things
> up for them. At first I had to have someone with me, because there
> was some money stolen. But now I can do it. And one day they let
> me have the bleep they use for if someone wants help urgently. I
> was shocked when they asked me, but they said 'You have to get
> used to it.'

His favourite times were 'talking to them, sitting down and talking.
There's so much work, we don't have much time for that. But just
being around is nice.' He found the early and late shifts and the
weekend-cover tiring. 'And sometimes I say to myself, "Why did I
pick this?" you know. Because some of them put it on a lot of the time.
They lean on you. And you say to yourself "Why did I choose it?" '
His worst time had been

> walking into a room when someone's wanted the toilet – that was a
> bit shocking at first. I'm used to it now. And bathing people. At first
> they wouldn't let me bath people, just the men. But now I can bath
> the women too, the ones that don't mind. I always ask them.
> Because matron may tell you to do it, but I ask them if *they* mind,
> because if it's uncomfortable for them, it's uncomfortable for me.
> It's their right, isn't it?

William felt cautious about making very close friends among the old people because there were frequent deaths, and he found that upsetting:

> There was one old man – I used to sit with him. We used to have jokes and that. Being the only boy we used to have jokes. He would say 'I can't laugh and joke with the women like I can with you', you know. He liked me to give him his bath. He said 'You're much better than the women.' And I said 'Why?' and he said 'You've got firmer hands.'

William laughed, remembering this. But one day he was looking after him and 'the next day I was going to be off duty and I said to him, "I'll be back. Keep on fighting." But he died, and when I came back they told me he had died. And I felt, like, I wished I'd been there. But at the same time I was glad I wasn't, really.'

I asked William, if an old person were in pain or frightened, and might need comforting, would he be able to do that as well as a woman? 'I think so' he said. 'Perhaps with a man I would – I might pat him on the back or something. But with a lady I'd put my arm round them.' Women are supposed to show feelings more than men, he felt. So while they might play the role of a daughter to the old people, he saw himself playing the role of a son.

Matron was encouraging William to go to college to study nursing. 'For a man, it would be better for him, he would have more qualifications at the end of it, and he could still come back into residential care. But with a nursing qualification it would be better for the rest of his life.' To be fair to the matron, she had also recommended this course of action to a young woman care assistant: 'Everyone needs qualifications.' She would have liked to see other young men following William's example:

> There have to be more eventually. Because there are more elderly men living longer today. The numbers are going up, and there's a need. The majority of men coming into residential care, all right, yes, they've been married and had a wife to fuss round them. And they still like a 'wife'. But also they do love a man to relate to. They don't want to be surrounded by a load of women.

She felt most boys never even considered such work,

because they think it's sissy. That's it. That's their idea. Even my sons when I told them about William said 'A boy doing that, mum? Bathing people?' And I said 'Yes, why not. Just sit back and think about it. Why shouldn't a boy bath someone? If it was me bathing a man, you wouldn't look at it oddly. And if he baths a woman, what difference does it make? For either of them?' And he said, 'Oh, I suppose so, but it's not really a man's job.' And I said 'Things do change. The world is changing. We've got to change with it.' And he said 'Oh, I suppose it's all right.' William may get a lot of stick outside. But I would say he is very, very lucky. Because he's able to show his feelings. Boys have such difficulty in expressing their feelings.

I asked William, 'Did you ever think of doing jobs like garage mechanic, engineer, things like that?' He said, 'No, never interested me. I like to do something more than a job. Working with a car you can't, you know, get involved. Not as much as working with a person, seeing them getting well, seeing them progressing and that. And making friends. You can't make friends with a car.' Low pay and poor promotion prospects did not worry William. He planned to remain a care assistant for the rest of his life, if necessary.

Preparation for parenting

The staff at the old people's home used to say to William, 'You'll make a good dad one day.' He and Nick told me that they would like to marry and have children. Nick added, 'when I'm 27 or 28, you know, when you've grown out of your teenage life and are more of an adult and have some money behind you.' Both of them also said they would want to spend more time than most men looking after their own children. 'Having money behind you', however, is the barbed point here. The domestic division of labour whereby women are expected to stay home with children and men are expected to earn enough to keep them there, drives women towards this kind of low-paid flexible 'appropriate' job and drives men away from it. Yet doing the job gives you the skills you need for parenting. Nick said 'A lot of my friends lose their patience with kids straight away.'

The coordinators of YTS Community Projects told me of many young women trainees who had been pregnant while on their schemes. Some had come to the scheme already mothers. 'Some trainees think they want a nursery placement so they can take their child there with them. That's not on. But I do allow a late start and I work with their social workers. *We* should have a nursery here, really.' But young men too become prospective parents while on YTS. The coordinators had been aware of several instances though they said 'we don't always get to find out'. 'Sean, Danny, they come back here and talk about their children now.' Soon after Andy came out of care at 16, his girl-friend became pregnant by him, and by the time I met him he was a father. Though problems with the mother meant he did not see the child, he was currently living with another young woman, older than himself, with two children of her own, who now called Andy 'father' and whom he actively fathered.[1]

Such experiences cannot be unique in YTS, and two-year YTS of course doubles the scale of the phenomenon. A scheme that is providing for more than half a million 16- and 17-year-olds up and down the country is undoubtedly dealing with thousands, possibly tens of thousands, of pregnant young women and expectant young men, whether managing agents and the MSC recognise it or not. If we reckon that the fact of being pregnant keeps thousands of the YTS age-group of young women off the Scheme altogether, we can suppose that in fact there are *more* 'pregnant' young men on the scheme than pregnant young women. What is YTS contributing to their consciousness of their responsibility as fathers or to their ability to handle it? By the time they leave school most young women have learned from mothers and sisters, as well as in domestic-science and child-development classes, a good deal about the care of children. Young men of YTS age today however are usually as far from this kind of knowledge as they have ever been. They have almost universally refused domestic subjects at school. Their culture rejects domesticity and femininity with a fury that leaves the odd one who *is* drawn to caring for children exposed to humiliation and scorn.

The experience of nursery work had given Nick and Andy abilities that are rare in a boy. Andy said of himself:

> I'm glad I did it. Because for me, my own children, and in future, its learned me how to come close to children. Like if our children cry or are upset. Friends come round with their little children and the mum'll be shouting at them. I want to say to her 'No, don't do that, do it this way.' But she'd say 'How do *you* know, you're a bloke.'

He felt he was able to cope with his own children better than other men coped with theirs. 'It's not that I spoil them. I just know how to cope with them. One of me mates, he's got a little girl and he just loses his temper and says "Sod yer" and "Go upstairs". I suppose, yeah, I've got more patience.' He himself felt proud, he said, of wheeling a pram. But he had noticed that his friends did not like being associated with little children. 'If they see a little baby and it's given to them, they're embarrassed to hold it. Because it's the macho bit, isn't it?' He felt that if more men had had his experience of working with children:

> there'd be more families staying together. There's a lot of break-ups now especially in our bit of London, over children. It's seen as the woman's job to look after children. But if both of them was to do it there'd be a lot of marriages saved.

And male violence would certainly become less of a peril to women and children. 'There's a lot of kids do get beaten up round here. Like I had from my dad and what I saw my little brothers and sisters go through.'

Support for young men?

The question arises of course: should the strategy be to win positive action for women, to help women enter male-dominated occupations? Or should it go further and include positive action to break up sexual apartheid altogether? There is a respectable case for confining it to the former. It is argued, with good reason, that it is against women's interests to encourage men into those few areas of work in which they do not have to compete with men at present. If men were to enter secretarial work, hairdressing and other female ghettoes in any numbers they might deprive women of jobs and would certainly tend to climb quickly over them and win the better jobs, pushing women down. This research has led me to believe that we would do better to limit our efforts to positive action for women with one exception: 'caring' work.

'Caring' work gets done in two places: at home, unpaid; and in paid employment. In neither place are many men found doing it. Getting men to take their full share of domestic caring work is a minimum

Men often climb to the top

condition for women's equality in paid work. Yet if domestic specialisation is to be broken down, men have to develop new capabilities, interests and needs: most men are not well-equipped to look after babies, the elderly, the ill. The skills that women have in connection with those activities are real skills that do not develop overnight. One way for more men to learn them is in paid employment in the caring professions. This is why I believe the MSC should be urged to undertake positive action to get more young men into *OTF-10: community and health service occupations*.

We have seen the extent of the problems that beset YTS schemes even when they are keen to get young men into 'caring' placements. We have had reports of resistance and diversionary tactics by teachers and careers officers. How much more resistance – less visible to outsiders – must there be from YTS managing agents and employers providing YTS work-experience? MSC's 'special groups' unit however does not hold a remit for young men – who after all are not a 'special group'. As a result they have done nothing to confront the reluctance of the patriarchy to see its sons slip away from masculine status and deal with nappies and bedpans. Consciousness-raising work is needed among managing agents and in the Careers Service, and those already aware and willing to act need help with outreach to young men, parents and schools.

Essentially, MSC needs to bring within the scope of 'positive action for women', the issue of the domestic division of labour and, so far as this implies action about young men, to bring them into the picture too. One step should be to offer financial support for nurseries. Certain large YTS schemes in busy centres might advertise themselves as offering nursery places to YTS trainees who otherwise could not come on the Scheme because they have babies. These nurseries could themselves be places of training for young men.

Young men who are attracted into 'caring' placements need to be given support. The teasing and comments which young men receive from young women as the lone male trainee in 'caring' placements is harassment of a sort. It is not the same in kind as the harassment which young women receive in the all-male workplace. What Andy said of his experience points up this difference:

> I did get teasing, yes. But you don't usually get girls asking blokes to go out with them, so I was all right there. I got chatted up a couple of times, I always do, but that's life, isn't it? I had a girl-friend at the time anyway so I wasn't interested. But a girl in a workshop, especially if she was a pretty girl, she'd have all the blokes saying 'I could pull her', and that. She'd have all that to deal with.

Male harassment of lone women is directly sexual. It emanates from men's power and plays on women's subordination. The authority to which it refers is present in the workplace itself: in the males there. In the woman-dominated workplace women do not very often harass the young man sexually. They tease by making reference to an outside authority feared by the young man: other men. The women act as the bearers of expectations the world has of him: that he will prove himself better than women. Nonetheless, even if the predicament of the lone boy is qualitatively different from that of the lone girl, it can be sufficient to distress and deter him. It merits some effort to group boys together and also to design and provide structures of support beyond the occasional chat with an overworked scheme coordinator.

The content of MSC's 'life and social skills' requirement in YTS off-the-job training has been the subject of a tug-of-war in some schemes. MSC like to see it as preparation for job-getting; schemes have been forbidden to include politicising discussion of the causes of unemployment. Personal politics, equally inflammatory, nonetheless evades the ban and a few schemes have tried to use 'life and social skills' time to organise single-sex groups of young men to talk through issues of sexism and of gendered expectations and behaviour. This use of the social experience of YTS for 'male awareness training' should be developed and could make the needed connection between the actual experience of many male YTS trainees as fathers or almost-fathers and their choice of occupation within YTS and after YTS. It should also of course be used to support homosexual young men. We have no way of telling how many of the young men like Andy, Nick and William, who have chosen to do training for 'women's work', identify themselves as heterosexual men trying to redefine the male role, and how many are gay, making a statement about their sexuality. Both groups need recognising, understanding and supporting.

The question is sometimes raised: if single-sex training provision in non-traditional areas is sometimes appropriate for young women, would it be appropriate for young men? As suggested at the beginning of this chapter, the situations of the sexes are never symmetrical. Both men and men's jobs have high status relative to women and women's jobs. Young men entering women's jobs are expected to *climb* out of them. Young women entering men's jobs are expected to *drop* out of them. Wherever men are together they tend to create a culture that reinforces masculinity and denigrates women and women's values. Around men and 'their' technologies has been generated a competitive masculine culture that has a powerful effect in repelling women and excluding them – but is unnecessary to the acquisition of skills. In nursery work or nursing the values embodied in the culture of the workplace – gentleness, consideration, supportiveness – may be associated with womanliness but they are intrinsic and necessary to the skills. It makes sense therefore to proceed differently for the two sexes. Young men would probably benefit less from single-sex training than from ensuring that they are not an isolated one of the minority sex, and from making it possible for several to train together, along with young women and with women staff. Quotas might be desirable in this context. The problem of isolation should be given special attention on the college courses which such trainees attend as off-the-job training.

The young men described in this chapter represent very rare instances of occupational gender-innovation in caring work within the

Youth Training Scheme. The overwhelming majority of their peers look with uneasy disbelief on the likes of these three. They commit all their wit and energy into building an impregnable masculine gender-identity, using their occupation to reinforce it. Young men characteristically distance themselves by all the means available to them from the things these few embrace: from little children, from disability, illness and age, from other people's distress, vulnerability and need. They fantasise and act out a predatory relationship (it barely deserves the word relationship) with young women, and look on women's world and women's culture with derision. So routine is sexual exploitation and violence by men that the accounts given above of William, for instance, bathing elderly women patients and Nick toilet-training pre-school children awaken – along with surprised delight that such a thing is possible – fear for how many men might abuse such situations.

Most young women today are led to believe they can have enduring relationships with young men built on mutual respect, understanding and equality. Given the gender-system that prevails, this is a cruel deception. There are however factors working for women. Changes in the pattern of employment have brought more women an independent income. The efforts of the women's movement have brought improvement in women's legal standing. It is marginally more possible today for women to survive and rear children without being dependent on men. There are more examples of autonomous, self-determining women for girls to see and emulate. Besides, some men, some of the time, escape from the worst aspects of the culture of masculinity. What research can never show is the intimacy of relationships between young women and young men when they are going well. There is something in many men that wants and needs the more human qualities of women's world and values. Although they cannot admit it to each other, some men want to share in the love of women and children. In transforming gender-relationships there is already something to build on. Making possible different and better experiences for little boys and young men is a good place to start building. And why not in YTS?

Note

1. It is significant that the verb 'to mother' refers to a social activity, while the verb 'to father' refers to a biological one. I use 'fathering' here in a social sense.

9

Beyond Equal Opportunity

The case-studies in Chapters 5–8 have shown that there is not one factor tending to gender-conformity in the Youth Training Scheme but many, and that they are interrelated and unlikely to be corrected by superficial measures. Simply exhorting young women to widen their aspirations, as MSC have done in the past, is certainly not enough. Indeed, in the absence of understanding support by adults, such appeals may incur trouble for young people who take them seriously.

One cause of occupational sex-segregation in YTS is undeniably some incidence of unlawful discrimination. The law of equal opportunity has always been invoked by the MSC but it has not always been observed down the line where the Scheme takes concrete form. To be fair to the Manpower Services Commission this is largely because the actual provision of youth training is beyond its control and indeed is also beyond the control of any elected authority. The only way the Commission could hope to deliver up to half a million youth-training places so rapidly was by opening it up to private enterprise. As we have seen, YTS provision is consequently in the hands of a myriad inadequately-supervised managing agents and sponsoring employers, many of whom have profit as a first aim, quality of training inevitably running second.

Discrimination against young women as women has possible expression in YTS at four levels: in the careers guidance process; among managing agents; among employers; and on the part of trade unions. Asian and Afro-Caribbean women also experience racial discrimination at these same points. In the main, the sexual discrimination that occurs is passive rather than active and in many cases it is unconscious. There is however clearly *some* conscious and active sex-specific selection going on in recruitment to YTS.

The Careers Service as we have seen is an important agent in recruitment of young people to YTS. The Service is hard-pressed. It is inadequately staffed, so that its officers do not have the time they would wish to go into schools and explore with young people individually early in their secondary school careers the options open to them in their working lives, the implications of different choices. Because employers have highly sex-typed preferences in recruitment, because jobs are scarce and young people hungry for any opportunity that offers, careers officers have little wish to cause confusion by challenging prejudices on anyone's part.

Managing agents, for their part, are in some cases employers in their own right, taking on trainees for training in their own firms. Some are private training agencies or 'umbrella' agencies who use private firms for work experience for their trainees. Some are local authorities and other public-sector bodies. Some (it is a declining minority) are community projects and training workshops of various kinds. In all these guises managing agents are involved in recruiting trainees. Though a few YTS places are broadly defined, most are occupationally specific. They are located within an 'occupational training family' and have training plans that define the content in closer detail. It is clear enough, then, whether the place is 'about' typing, computers, carpentry. Some managing agents are undoubtedly allowing their own prejudices to determine the sex of trainee they encourage or discourage with regard to these different kinds of trainee place. Others are unconsciously swimming with the current of market practice. Others still are worried about sex-typing yet taking no action to reduce it. Managing agents who openly challenge employers' prejudices and actively explore alternatives with YTS candidates are rare.

The majority of youth trainees spend all but a few weeks of their time on the Scheme working on employers' premises. Few of these employers have changed their practices in any fundamental way since the introduction of the Sex Discrimination legislation in 1975. Though they may be aware that it is unwise actually to state their preference for one sex or another, they are confident that they can get away with sex-typed recruitment simply by choosing the one they want from a mixed bunch at interview. That their workplaces are staffed almost entirely with female typists, female cleaners and cooks, male technicians, sales staff and managers, goes to confirm the advantage employers have always seen in a sexual division of labour. Even where a recruit evades gender-conformity on entry to the workplace, therefore, she or he is almost invariably faced, once there, with a sex-stereotyped employment structure and internal labour market. The career paths laid out ahead are clearly signposted 'his' and 'hers'.

Neither are trade unions altogether innocent of sex discrimination. Some have made cogent criticisms of YTS and have acted on them by boycotting the scheme. The National Graphical Association is one of these. The paradoxical effect has been that YTS has opened up some training possibilities for young women in skill areas from which they have historically been excluded – but only in non-unionised print shops. Their progress has been in spite of, not through the agency of, the union. The Society of Graphical and Allied Trades is a union that, while it has serious doubts about YTS, has cooperated while laying down rules that ensure apprentice status for trainees. Yet its traditional demarcation practices are continuing to disadvantage women. One female trainee I interviewed was not permitted to carry out the same tasks in the workplace as her male counterpart, nor was she receiving the same off-the-job training. This was not because her employer said so, nor because the managing agent who had sent her to this firm was negligent. It was simply because trade-union practice would not permit it. The men in the work place would not allow women to do 'men's work' and the employer saw no purpose in training this young woman for activities for which he would not be allowed to employ her.

Male trade unionists of course have motives for this exclusion, both social and economic. They have long gained by keeping a functional separation and pay differential between women and themselves (Cockburn, 1983). Today the unions of the printing industry, at national level, proclaim equal opportunity. Equal opportunity, however, is not enough to reverse historical disadvantage. Now the NGA, SOGAT and the British Printing Industries Federation, through their Joint Training Council, are embarking on an industry-wide cooperation in the Youth Training Scheme. Yet no positive action is planned within this scheme to counteract the years of disadvantage girls have experienced in the matter of skilled work and training in the print. 'We believe the biggest impediment to increasing the number of women entering the industry to train for skilled occupations is their perception of printing as "men's work" ' says the JTC's

Training Adviser. 'We have therefore put a major effort into our careers information package.' Again the burden of change is being put back on young women.

At its inception the Youth Training Scheme was not covered by the provisions of the Sex Discrimination Act 1975. On 21 July 1983, by order of the Minister, it was brought within the Act for purposes of recruitment. Once on the Scheme however trainees' legal rights still fall short of those of full employees. Strengthening sex-discrimination law and the race-discrimination law therefore – ensuring that they cover youth trainees in all circumstances, educating those involved in YTS in all their provisions, making recourse to the law easier for the individual and seeing it rigorously and universally applied in youth training – these are steps that have to be a first priority.

'Young women are their own worst enemies'

I have argued that occupational sex-segregation in YTS, the widespread tendency we have seen for young women to conform to feminine job stereotypes while young men follow their own sex-typed path, is a form of current inequality because it presages a future inequality between women and men. Occupational segregation by sex is in fact *the* sex-equality issue within YTS. That it is an equality issue however is by no means obvious to everyone concerned. It is often represented as a case of 'different but equal'. It is also often said to be simply a matter of trainee choice. Undeniably the great majority of trainees have stated firmly sex-typed preferences on leaving school and joining the Scheme. This being so, toughening-up on sex discrimination will not go all the way to solve the problem.

Many of the adults involved in running YTS were sorry to see so much gender-conformity but they did not feel responsible. 'Young women are their own worst enemies' they said. 'Young women come to us *asking* for office jobs, nursery work, hairdressing. What can we do about it? We can't force them to do something they don't want to do.' Almost everyone with whom I discussed the problem was of the opinion that parents, television, school had all conspired already to form in young people the most rigidly gendered expectations and desires. *'At 16 it's too late.'*

Of course, substantial change is needed in school curricula and the gender-relations of school and home. But can nothing be done for young adults? There have developed in Britain these last several years a score of women-only training workshops in which women can learn 'male skills' in the absence of men. They are mainly funded by the European Social Fund, local authorities and voluntary organisations and have received 'designation' by the Secretary of State under Section 47 of the Sex Discrimination Act to allow them to discriminate positively in favour of women. These workshops are normally for women over 25 years of age and are in particular open to single parents, providing nursery provision in one form or another. They have proved immensely popular. One such exercise is described in a booklet *New Styles of Training for Women* (South Glamorgan Women's Workshop, 1986). When I pointed out to my informants in YTS that these women-only adult technical training courses had a long queue of women, eager to obtain access to men's skills, especially in computer technology, they said, 'Ah, yes. But that is older women. Youth trainees haven't yet had the experience of a couple of children and some rotten low-paid jobs. *At 16 it's too early.*' So there we were, stuck with a problem that it was both too early and too late to do anything about.

As the research progressed I became more and more certain this diagnosis was wrong. Something can be done for young women in YTS. Young people are not irredeemably fixed in their gender-mould. Though it will not be every young woman who will want to train as a computer specialist or a civil engineering technician, nor every young man who will show a leaning towards the caring professions, some will certainly be evading the pressures to conform. We have seen a few of them in the foregoing chapters.

There is in fact a curious double-think apparent among young people today. The atmosphere of 'equal opportunity' that developed along with the growth of the new women's movement beginning in the late 1960s appears to have appealed to young people's sturdy sense of fair play. Most of the trainees I interviewed had been keen for others to break out of gender conformity, to 'have a go'. They were firmly committed to the principle that it is anyone's right to choose for themselves. 'It's up to her', they were saying, or, 'It's up to him.' But this openness at the level of ideas coexists with an actual behaviour that is almost always conformist. When it came to it, for themselves, young people were making cautious, practical decisions. Especially in a time of high unemployment the important principle seemed to be 'a job at any price'.

On the other hand there was a minority of young women who, as we have seen, wanted to break out of what they saw as boring and unrewarding 'feminine' occupations. Some achieved it. But others were deterred by the high price of stepping out of line. In earlier chapters we have noted women's realism over and again. Women know what trouble lies in store for those who defy the rules of gender. If they are the 'wrong' gender for the job they will meet with discomfort, isolation and even harassment in the place of training. They will have difficulty in obtaining work afterwards. They will not find it easy to sustain further skill development and continuous careers.

Peggy Newton and Janette Brocklesby in their study of women engineering apprentices found that on beginning work they were:

> faced with curiosity, disbelief and sometimes open opposition from the men who were to work with them. They needed to prove that they could do the job, and they also needed to work out their position as women in a strongly male environment... Many women found the attitudes and behaviour of their male workmates confusing. Some men treated them as 'one of the lads', but others behaved in a paternalistic way towards them. Women who joined the men during tea and dinner breaks often found that they were only partially accepted as group members and that they were sometimes 'told' to behave in a more feminine way.

Being a lone woman working among men made good relations with women colleagues difficult. 'Many women engineers felt that they were envied and resented by other female workers; there was often tension with older women who worked as operatives on the shop floor... secretaries also presented problems for some women' (Newton and Brocklesby, 1983, p.35). There is now plentiful evidence of these painful effects occurring wherever women try to enter men's workplaces on equal and similar terms.[1] Occupational sex-segregation is partly gender-demarcation, in which lines are drawn by one set of workers and a price paid by others who ignore them. Much of the energy of such women, energy that should be free for dealing with the demands of the work itself, is deflected into implementing strategies for social survival.

Women, then, may outflank the prejudicial workings of the labour market and the job market, they may outface the discriminatory practices of recruitment, but they know they will not escape the gruelling necessity of living out their decision once made. From one work-ing day to the next it promises to be a lifetime of adapting, compensating, competing, challenging, defying – and explaining the perverse choice they made. I have argued that an understanding of the relations of training and work feeds back to young women and acts as a deterrent from making gender-contrary choices. It drives others, who do go so far as to give it a try, quickly away again. The experiences which young people are having on YTS today are having an effect on their future work and training decisions.

Throughout this book, whenever the words 'occupational choice' have occurred, the 'choice' has been in inverted commas. This was to prevent us forgetting just how restricted the choice of job for working-class young people really is. The choice as it exists in the imaginations of occupational psychologists theorising about the school-to-work transition is a fiction. A working-class 16-year-old, leaving school at the first opportunity, makes a heavily constrained and often reluctant decision, not a free choice. It is constrained by social class. But for a young woman, especially if she is black, other limitations curb her initiative, not least her own perception of the rewards and penalties dealt out in the 'real world'. We should recognise this – neither taking her choice at face value, nor dismissing it as wrong-headed. We should keep in mind that young women are capable of performing every bit as well and often better than young men in most kinds of work. Those 'suffering' from being black or being women are not comparable with those suffering from mental and physical disabilities. Race and sex are only disabilities when they are made to be so in someone else's interests. Young women's practices will change when we change their circumstances.

Towards similar achievements

Ending the sexual division of labour in paid employment is not a question simply of opening doors that are closed, removing barriers of discrimination. The door was open to Angie and Karen – they even passed through it. What they encountered in the engineering workshop however drove them out again. What should be aimed for, in and through the Youth Training Scheme, is not merely equality of opportunity but something more far-reaching. We should take responsibility for *similarity of achievement* between the sexes. It is not enough to evaluate our performance in training young people against a benchmark that measures access. We have to do more than ask 'Are women free to apply?' We have to evaluate YTS against a standard that measures outcomes. We have to ask 'Are young women taking up the opportunities that are offered? Are they leaving the Scheme with the *same kind* of qualifications as their male counterparts? Are they getting *similar* jobs? Are they set to progress as well within them?'

Similarity of achievement has two features that distinguish it from equality of opportunity. First, it is concerned with what a woman actually gets to do rather than what she is free to attempt. It assumes that not all failures are the individual's fault. It takes some responsibility for outcomes. Second, it contradicts the assertion that women may be doing something different from men but that they are nonetheless equal. It proposes instead that women and men as sexes, overall, may reasonably be expected to have similar activities, live similar lives, distribute themselves over all available occupations in a broadly similar curve.[2] It anticipates that the gendered nature of jobs can be ended in time, along with our own imprisonment in a limiting and deforming gender-dichotomy.

For women and men, black and white, to experience similar achievement, means, it will be clear, structural changes within systems of school, careers guidance, training and employment. In the meantime inputs must compensate by being pitched in favour of those for whom the outcomes are currently most disadvantaging. In other words, positive action for women, doubly positive for black women, is called for. Many of the adults to whom I spoke who were responsible for the delivery of YTS gagged on the notion of 'positive discrimination'. Discrimination of any kind, they felt, was bound to be unfair. To give something to women at the expense of men, or black people at the expense of white, was somehow to perpetuate inequality in another form. Positive discrimination is not wrong. It would need to go a long, long way before it could begin to tip the balance beyond equality.

During 1986, the Manpower Services Commission, as we have seen, showed signs of being ready to act on positive discrimination for women in YTS. Whether the Commission, given its nature and political context, can ever find the will to make a thorough job of it remains to be seen. It is however worth considering, in the light of this research, what principles might guide positive action.

The first is clearly that we should acknowledge the significance of the gender-dynamic in outcomes in YTS. This means recognising that sexual identity and sexual relations matter powerfully to young people and that whether a 'proper' gender-persona is sought or whether it is rejected a gender-dynamic is always a factor in occupational choice and behaviour. It means recognising that young women and, in a different way, young men do not make gender-contrary moves scot-free. It means recognising the adverse effect that men, as managers, instructors, supervisors and as trainees, can have on the achievement of women in YTS. The effect occurs both through weight of numbers in areas defined as male but also by masculine attitudes and behaviour.

Second, we need to accept that it is not only women who have to do the adapting. 'Male awareness training' directed towards change in the practices of men, adult and young, in YTS is specially urgent. In fact, the most productive positive action for women in the YTS would be positive action on and about men. The material and ideological content of some courses may need adapting. Would young women have been more motivated to learn about 'engineering' at Pond Close, for instance, if it had been less wrapped up in a male craft culture, conventional workshop products; if it had included getting access to a car or van, learning to drive, and learning to maintain it perhaps? Would carpentry and plumbing seem more relevant to young women if these skills were clearly part of gaining control of their own environment? The relationship and structuring of different occupational sections may need changing. At the City Street ITeC, should office technology have been dropped from the Centre's programme? Or should typing have been made part of all technical options?

A third principle for positive action is to recognise that the sexual division of labour in employment and at home are interdependent. Part of the realism with which young women approach decisions about employment is their anticipation that domestic roles will not be equally shared with men. 'Home' needs to enter YTS in several ways. First, we need to acknowledge how many 16- and 17-year-old young women are pregnant or, indeed, mothers. Nursery provision may be appropriate in many schemes. Second, we should realise that a similar number of young men of this age are on the point of being fathers. All young men will have a bearing on young women's lives by their attitude to women and to child care and other caring responsibilities. More young men in YTS should be encouraged into formal training for the caring professions. The issues need dealing with in consciousness-raising activities among all men, young and old, on the Scheme. Young women may need comparable support in holding out for what they most want: a sustained career combined with a full family life.

Finally, we need to recognise that young people on YTS are looking forward, not only in terms of their domestic lives, but also in terms of their job prospects. We need to link action against sex-segregation in youth training to action against the sexual division of labour in employment. What young people want most out of YTS is jobs. They will not make a decision that risks their chances of getting work. Almost all the firms used for work-experience in YTS have traditional employment structures with sex-typed occupations and unequal career prospects for 'women's jobs' and 'men's jobs'. Training for business studies integrated with office skills, for example, is little use to a trainee if on work-experience placement she or he is obliged to specialise typing *or* accounts. Designing training placements to integrate male and female roles and skills is, again, little use if the real jobs to which the trainee can move are specialised and sex-typed. The Scheme could use the very thing for which it is often criticised – its closeness to employers – to challenge their practices and influence them to change patterns of recruitment, relations of work and in particular, the gendering of jobs. This of course runs directly counter to Conservative policies based on 'business knows best'. A form of 'contract compliance' however, as developed by some Labour local authorities might be appropriate. Voluntary organisations, local authorities and other public-sector employers of YTS trainees may be the more ready to give a lead. Post-YTS employment possibilities such as women's cooperatives might be associated with ITeCs and other technical-training workshops, too. It is only when women can be assured of genuine employment possibilities ahead of them outside those that are stereotyped female that it will be legitimate to put full weight behind encouraging them to train for such work.

Developments within the MSC and its Scheme

Much more powerful and precisely directed external pressure on behalf of women in YTS is needed, if any such principles are to be adopted. The pressure has to come from the Equal Opportunities Commission, from trade unions, women in political parties and from autonomous women's organisations. Women need to express politically something of the anger and determination shown by some racial pressure-groups. For there is much that could be done by MSC in response.

Much more consciousness of sex and gender issues is needed within all divisions and departments of the Commission. Much more public information is needed about the achievements and non-achievements of women, including statistical reviews – and in particular these should be cross-specified by race. Work against racism in YTS too should be increased. It might be helpful however if MSC were to give more distinct articulation to race- and sex-equality work, so as to avoid the situation where the race issue, because of its political saliency, tends to obscure the sex issue.

The 'special groups' unit, YP-3, should be strengthened and expanded. It could well take on a concern with work among men on sexism. Sex/gender issues and in particular the problem of occupational sex-segregation should become a component of all in-service training for MSC officers. Much more guidance from Moorfoot on the subject is needed in Area Offices. Local statistical analysis urgently needs developing, using the Training and Occupation Classification (TOC) now developed by MSC in place of 'occupational training families'. The curriculum in use for the Youth Trainers' Award ought to be expanded to include sex/gender issues. Intensive educational and consciousness-raising work with managing agents, organised by locality, is needed on these issues. Courses dealing with 'women in YTS' should be offered by all Accredited Training Centres, and this topic should be mandatory in MSC's contract with its ATCs. Local development activities with work-experience providing firms are urgently needed to ensure that training plans do not 'play into' sex-typed assumptions and that all the occupations with which YTS placements are associated and to which they may lead offer substantial career possibilities.

Regional and local sex-equality officers should be appointed by MSC. After all, the Department of Employment under which MSC falls has Regional Race Relations Officers; and MSC has already funded twenty Youth Development Officers to work on the race issue. They are fielded by the Commission for Racial Equality and other bodies. Though there is a danger that sex equality posts serve merely as a public relations front, if combined with external pressure they could be useful to women.

The exploratory positive action proposals that have now been issued by MSC should be implemented quickly. It is specially important to strengthen the commitment to women-only training in many situations where women are failing to enter male-dominated occupations. Women need 'women's space', especially in technology. Provision of single-sex technical training for adult women is now well beyond the experimental stage and its advantages are well proven. In the long run however the challenge remains to make mixed-sex training possible without disadvantage to young women. It is important to enable women to enter non-traditional areas in groups, rather than individually. Quotas are helpful in this respect. But we need to recognise their need for support and counselling. They should not have to 'go it alone'.

Because sex-segregation is not symmetrical it is not experienced by women and men in the same way. Single-sex schemes are not appropriate therefore for young men in YTS. Though logically sex segregation can only end by men moving into female-stereotyped areas while women move into men's, there are dangers in encouraging

Young women need their own space

young men to encroach on those few occupations in which women at present are free from competition with men. On the other hand it is urgent that more men learn caring and nurturing skills. Encouragement should be given to young men to take training in *OTF-10: community and health service*. Holding quotas of places for males in such schemes, and offering counselling and support, as well as doing 'outreach' work to boys in school would all help to achieve this.

A pre-YTS taster period of eight to thirteen weeks should be considered for young women wanting to try training for 'male' skills and young men wanting to enter training for the caring professions. They should be paid at the rate of the normal YTS allowance. There is a precedent for this in the thirteen-week preparatory period allowed to the disabled. The disabled also have a right in two-year YTS to take the twenty-four-months training at any time up to the age of 21. Why not extend this right to young women entering gender-contrary occupations and young men entering caring work?

One factor holding back young women has been the lack of adult women teachers of 'male' subjects. The natural movement of women into and through technical training courses, though marginally more evident today than in the past, is still excruciatingly slow. Money should be committed urgently to organising local and regional programmes of technical training for adult women in order to break through this barrier and rapidly produce a generation of skilled qualified women to staff training schemes and teach technical courses in further education.

It is in computer and information technology that the best technical-career possibilities today lie, and women are losing out badly in this field in YTS. Women in ITeCs should be invited by the MSC to get together to consider possibilities for changing in the organisational structure, and the training practices and internal relations in ITeCs. It is clear enough that something is going very wrong there. Financial support should be offered to the group to develop strategies for eradicating the powerful masculine bias both in ITeCs and in computer skills and information technology teaching in YTS generally, and their recommendations should be heeded by MSC. Women in the Careers Service, likewise, ought to be encouraged and funded by MSC to organise to develop strategies for breaking down sex-segregation through careers work. There is no lack of women who would be committed to this kind of activity. Their recommendations should guide the Careers Service, local education authorities and the MSC. The Commission should offer time off to adult and young women in YTS to organise locally and nationally to explore and develop these and other strategies. There have been occasional national meetings of women in YTS, and for a year a research and action project existed in London, funded by the Greater London Council. Women however are already hard-worked and underpaid in YTS and financial support is needed if they are to find a voice and get it heard by policy-makers.

Part of a wider movement

These suggestions are made in a positive, some would say too optimistic, spirit. They are about changes that are achievable in the here and now. They could be implemented tomorrow by a Manpower Services Commission as it exists, in a Youth Training Scheme as presently conceived. There are, however, already too many analyses of YTS content and too few of the Scheme's context. YTS as devised and implemented by a monetarist government inevitably represents a struggle between frank Conservative intentions (with a large 'C') and the aspirations of liberal professionals (small 'l') within the Manpower Services Commission and the Youth Training Board. Though the published policy statements on YTS often reflect the latter, the former are there as its hidden agenda and largely determine the outcome. Some of the widely-heard criticisms of YTS were reviewed in Chapter 1. A youth training scheme cannot become the resource it ought to be for young people without changes in the wider political economy. For a start, YTS could only cease to be a sham in an economy where work was available to everyone, where the purpose of a scheme for 16- and 17-year-olds was not to keep people out of the job-market but to ensure that leaving school and going to work did not mean the end of learning.

So we need full employment in an economy rebuilt on the basis of the production of socially useful, socially chosen goods and services. We need a redefinition of work, besides, so that currently-unpaid domestic labour is redistributed and becomes part of the economic calculation (Phillips, 1983). A Labour 'alternative economic strategy' however that created employment for everyone who wants it yet had no impact on the relations of work and the relative power and powerlessness of people seeking work would not of itself achieve equality between women and men. True equality means an end to occupational segregation by sex, and that in turn is predicated on two specific innovations. It cannot be achieved without them. It cannot be won by women's will power, however strong. The two developments are, first, a restructuring of internal labour markets, the jobs themselves; and second, a unification of external labour markets, of competition for jobs.

We saw in Chapter 1 the tendency of capitalist enterprise to generate a demand for sharply differentiated kinds of labour power with skilled, permanent, well-rewarded workers on the one hand and semi- and unskilled, insecure and expendable workers on the other. We saw how within those groups, the core and periphery workers, exist other subdivisions. The barriers between them are hard to cross and there are few routes that lead from the bottom to the top. It is not only in capitalist firms that occupations are continually subdivided and regrouped. Public authorities show the same tendency and in state institutions very often the hierarchical ranking of jobs produces even more baroque inequalities. Such a system creates endlessly renewed opportunities for the strong, in particular adult white men, to bear on the weak, avoiding the worst of exploitation themselves while participating in the exploitation of others. Caught up in a process like this what can an unqualified 16-year-old ever be but part of the now-hired, now-fired disposable secondary labour force? Where can women be but on the edge?

We need social and economic strategies that prefigure a more ideal world. We are unlikely to get them from any except a left Labour government. Yet it may be worth thinking through what would be entailed, since they could colour Labour Party and trade-union strategies even today. An employment strategy by which young people, women and other disadvantaged groups in the workforce would be well served must involve employers in restructuring the relations of employment, sharing responsibilities more evenly, enriching poor-quality jobs, spreading technical knowledge, levelling out hierarchies, reducing pay differentials and equalising legal rights and working conditions. This is not impossible. Even today, cooperatives attempt some of it. Even profit-oriented firms have been persuaded to experiment – for instance, with training women machine-operatives in the skills needed to maintain and repair their own machines (Sinclair, forthcoming). David Ashton and his colleagues in their examination of internal and external labour markets found firms in which they were astonished by the extent to which managers had been able to bring about quite radical changes in the organisation of the internal structure of employment. 'What had been dead-end clerical work had been reorganised to provide all those who entered the organisation with the chance of a career progression.' It showed, they concluded, 'how internal labour markets are not just the result of technological or organisational imperatives but are socially generated' (Ashton *et al.*, 1982). What is required is a political environment in which employers would have the incentive to bring about such changes. Public-sector employers, including local authorities, are obvious places to begin.

The second prerequisite of sex-equality is a set of social policies that tend towards unifying the labour market, measures that would tend to bring women and men, black and white, into the search for work on equal terms, similarly employable for similar jobs. It would also aim to adjust the relationship between adults and young people in the labour market in such a way that adult experience and skills were not undervalued but neither were youthfulness and inexperience exploited.

For either of these things to happen the notion of the 'family wage' must finally be abandoned. For years women have argued that it is wrong that men should be paid more than women simply on the basis that they are expected to keep a wife and children (Rathbone, 1949; Land, 1980). The concept of the male breadwinner has always had the effect of keeping married women's earnings low, forcing women who support themselves and dependents onto poverty wages, and giving an unwarranted privilege to men, many of whom in reality have no dependents or live in families in which there is more than one income. The Equal Pay Act of 1970 did not dispatch the 'family wage' differential, it simply forced it to lodge within occupational sex divisions. Men just made sure they were doing different work from women.

The low youth wage and, today, the lower-than-low youth training allowance, are part of the family-wage syndrome. By policy of trade unions, as well as employers, apprentice wages have always been very much lower than those of qualified journeymen. A steep differential has been energetically maintained by those it benefited most, adult white men. Men of course paid a price for their uncontested status as head of household: the family man was expected to subsidise his young workers in the way he was expected to keep 'his' womenfolk. Both groups have often worked for the employer at less than the true cost of their reproduction. The present Tory government, in cutting the value of student grants, has taken steps to ensure that even middle-class families today spend more of their own resources on equipping sons and daughters for the labour market. It is not surprising that the YTS system is predicated on working-class families partially supporting their young economically for several years after they leave school.

The shape of the average family in Britain is changing however. The irony is that many of the parents who are contributing to the support of young workers today (as we saw in Chapter 2) are not high-earning fathers but low-paid mothers, often living without men or with unemployed men and often working part-time precisely because they have children.

Migrant labour from the Caribbean, Asia and East Africa has also been employed by capital and the state on the cheap. The cost of its production – the upbringing, education and training of workers when young – has been borne not in Britain but in their country of origin. Today, as a new generation of British-born black workers is entering the labour market, racist discrimination continues to serve as an alternative mechanism to force down wages (Counter Information Services, 1978; Phizacklea, 1983; Castles, 1984). Black people, especially black women, are driven into positions where they can be super-exploited, inside and outside the family. Really effective measures against racial discrimination therefore are an integral part of any social strategy to unify the labour market.

Finally, women – the adult women that today's young women YTS trainees will soon become – need to be freed from domestic constraints, so that they no longer come looking for paid work 'with one hand tied behind them'. Or rather, in so far as their hands are tied, men's should be so tied as well. Greatly increased social provision for the care of young, elderly, ill and disabled is needed; and better provision for maternity and compassionate leave, for flexibility in working hours and working years, combined with an expectation that both men and women sometimes need time away from work to tend others. Working hours need to be reduced in all kinds of work so that there is no longer the sharp divide between full-time career jobs and part-time casual jobs. In such a supportive market-context a youth training scheme could look very different. Young women and young men within it would look much more like each other, their prospects would match, equality would go more than skin-deep.

'Occupational segregation by sex' is a term with a fixed and static ring about it. It makes it sound as though what we are faced with is a given world, compartmentalised, in which women and men are simply found, lodged in one place or another, the problem being how to shift them. The reality is different, as we have seen: we make our world and we make each other. When jobs and people are seen as the dynamic system of relations they really do comprise it becomes clear that the points of intervention are many.

Notes

1. Much of the recent research on the experience of women entering 'men's work' and on the gendering of jobs has been done in the USA and Scandinavian countries. American sources of interest in this connection include Wetherby, 1977; Walshok, 1981; Hacker, 1981; O'Farrell and Harlan, 1982; and Lembright and Riemer, 1982. Interesting work has been done in Sweden by Berner, 1983; and currently by Fürst, Göteburg University, and Walden, Linköping University.
2. This is a widely articulated aim in the women's movement. I was interested to find the following in a report on male and female roles in Sweden:

    The goal of equality – what does it look like? The sex roles have been upheld because women and men have specialised in different tasks. They have complemented one another. But seldom has attention been paid to the destructive feature of this complementarity... if equality is to be realised, women and men must have access to the *same* life areas. In the family, equal parents. In working life, two breadwinners. In society, two citizens. In leisure, two individuals (Liljeström, 1978, pp.19–20).

References

Allum, C. and Quigley, J. (1983) 'Bricks in the Wall: the Youth Training Scheme', *Capital and Class*, no. 21.

Amsden, A. H. (ed.) (1980) *The Economics of Women and Work* (Harmondsworth: Penguin).

Arnot, M. (1983) 'A Cloud over Co-education: an Analysis of the Forms of Transmission of Class and Gender Relations', in S. Walker and L. Barton (eds).

Ashton, D. N. *et al.* (1982) *Youth in the Labour Market*, Research Paper no.34, Department of Employment.

Atkinson, J. (1984) *Flexibility, Uncertainty and Manpower Management*, Report no.89, Institute of Manpower Studies (University of Sussex).

Ball, C. and Ball, M. (1979) *Fit for Work? Youth, School and (Un)employment* (London: Chameleon Books, Writers and Readers Publishing Collective).

Barker, D. L. and Allen, S. (eds) (1976) *Dependence and Exploitation in Work and Marriage* (London: Longman).

Barrett, M. and McIntosh, M. (1980) 'The Family Wage: Some Problems for Socialist-Feminists', *Capital and Class*, no.11.

Barron, R. D. and Norris, G. M. (1976) 'Sexual Divisions and the Dual Labour Market', in D. L. Barker and S. Allen (eds).

Bates, I. (1984) 'From Vocational Guidance to Life Skills: Historical Perspectives on Careers Education', in I. Bates *et al.*

Bates, I. *et al.* (1984) *Schooling for the Dole? The New Vocationalism*, Youth Questions Series (London: Macmillan).

Batsleer, J. (1985/6) 'Life Skills and Social Education', *Youth and Policy*, no.15, Tyne and Wear.

Bedeman, T. and Courtenay, G. (1983) *One in Three: The Second National Survey of Young People on YOP*, Research and Development Series no.13, Manpower Services Commission.

Beechey, V. and Whitelegg, E. (eds) (1986) *Women in Britain Today* (Milton Keynes: Open University Press).

Benett, Y. and Carter, D. (1982) *Sidetracked? A Look at the Careers Advice Given to Fifth Form Girls*, Equal Opportunities Commission.

Benett, Y. and Carter, D. (1983) *Day Release for Girls*, Equal Opportunities Commission.

Benn, C. and Fairley, J. (eds) (1986) *Challenging the MSC on Jobs, Education and Training: Enquiry into a National Disaster* (London: Pluto).

Berner, B. (1983) 'Women, Power and Ideology in Technical Education and Work', paper to the International Conference on the Role of Women in the History of Science, Technology and Medicine in the Nineteenth and Twentieth Centuries, Hungary.

Blau, P. *et al.* (1963) 'Occupational Choice: a Conceptual Framework', in N. J. Smelser and W. T. Smelser (eds).

Blaxall, M. and Reagan, B. (eds) (1976) *Women and the Workplace: the Implications of Occupational Segregation* (University of Chicago Press).

Brah, A. and Golding, P. (1983) 'The Transition from School to Work among Young Asians in Leicester', Centre for Mass Communication Research (Leicester University).

Braham, P. *et al.* (1981) *Discrimination and Disadvantage in Employment: The Experience of Black Workers* (London: Harper & Row).

Brake, M. (1980) *The Sociology of Youth and Youth Subcultures* (London: Routledge & Kegan Paul).

Brelsford, P. *et al.* (1982) *Give us a Break: Widening Opportunities for Young Women within YOP/YTS*, Research and Development Series no.11, Manpower Services Commission.

Brooks, D. and Singh, K. (1978/9) 'Ethnic Commitment Versus Structural Reality: South Asian Immigrant Workers in Britain', *New Community*, vol. VII, no. 1.

Bryan, B. *et al.* (1985) *The Heart of the Race: Black Women's Lives in Britain* (London: Virago).

CAITS (Centre for Alternative Industrial and Technology Systems) (1986) *Flexibility: Who Needs It?* (Polytechnic of North London).

Carby, H. (1982) 'White Women Listen! Black Feminism and the Boundaries of Sisterhood', in Centre for Contemporary Cultural Studies (ed.).

Castles, S. (1984) *Here For Good: W.Europe's New Ethnic Minorities* (London: Pluto).

Centre for Contemporary Cultural Studies (ed.) (1982) *The Empire Strikes Back: Race and Racism in Seventies Britain*, University of Birmingham (London: Hutchinson).

Chapkis, W. and Enloe, C. (1983) *Of Common Cloth: Women in the Global Textile Industry* (Amsterdam and Washington: Transnational Institute).

Chisholm, L. (1984) 'Occupational Choice Processes: American Girls at School in W.Germany', unpublished paper, Institute of Education (London University).

Clarke, J. *et al.* (1975) 'Subcultures, Cultures and Class', in S. Hall and T. Jefferson (eds).

Clarke, L. (1980) *Occupational Choice: a Critical Review of Research in the*

214   *References*

United Kingdom, Careers Service Branch, Department of Employment (London: HMSO).

Clarricoates, K. (1978) ' "Dinosaurs in the Classroom" – a Re-examination of Some Aspects of the "Hidden Curriculum" in Primary Schools', *Women's Studies International Quarterly*, vol.1.

Cockburn, C. (1983) *Brothers: Male Dominance and Technological Change* (London: Pluto).

Cockburn, C. (1985) *Machinery of Dominance: Women, Men and Technical Know-how* (London: Pluto).

Coffield, F. *et al.* (1986) *Growing Up on the Margins* (Milton Keynes: Open University Press).

Cohen, P. (1984) 'Against the New Vocationalism', in I. Bates *et al.*.

Cole, M. and Skelton, B. (eds) (1980) *Blind Alley: Youth in a Crisis of Capital* (Ormskirk: G.W. and A. Hesketh).

Commission for Racial Equality (1978) , *Looking for Work: Black and White School-Leavers in Lewisham*.

Commission for Racial Equality (1984) *Racial Equality and the Youth Training Scheme*.

Connell, R. W. *et al.* (1982) *Making the Difference: Schools, Families and Social Division* (Sydney and London: Allen & Unwin).

Corrigan, P. (1979) *Schooling the Smash Street Kids* (London: Macmillan).

Coulson, M. A. *et al.* (1967) 'Towards a Sociological Theory of Occupational Choice: a Critique', *Sociological Review*, vol.15, no.3.

Counter Information Services (1978) *Racism: Who Profits?*, Anti-Report no.16.

Curran, M. M. (1985) *Stereotypes and Selection: Gender and Family in the Recruitment Process*, Equal Opportunities Commission (London: HMSO).

Dahlberg, G. and Holland, J. (1984) 'Children, Class and Ideology: a Cross-cultural Investigation of Children's Understanding of Work and the Social Division of Labour', unpublished paper, Institute of Education (London University).

Dale, R. (1985) *Education, Training and Employment: Towards a New Vocationalism* (Milton Keynes: Open University Press and Pergamon).

Davies, B. (1986) *Threatening Youth: Towards a National Youth Policy* (Milton Keynes: Open University Press).

Deem, R. (ed.) (1980) *Schooling for Women's Work* (London: Routledge & Kegan Paul).

Deem, R. (ed.) (1984) *Co-education Reconsidered* (Milton Keynes: Open University Press).

Department of Education and Science (1975) *Curricular Differences for Boys and Girls*, Education Survey no.21 (London: HMSO).

Department of Education and Science (1985) *Statistical Bulletin*, no.5/85, February.

Department of Employment (1974) *Unqualified, Untrained and Unemployed*, Report of a Working Party set up by the National Youth

Employment Council (London: HMSO).

Department of Employment (1983) Press Notice, 17 January.

Department of Employment (1985) 'A Survey of Youth Training Scheme Providers', *Employment Gazette*, August.

Department of Employment (1986) *Equal Opportunities for Girls and Boys*, Careers Service Branch.

Dex, S. (1982) *Black and White School Leavers: the First Five Years of Work,* Research Paper no.33, Department of Employment.

Dickens, M. (1983) 'Women and the Adult Training Strategy', *Unemployment Unit Bulletin*, no.9, August.

Doeringer, P. B. and Piore, M. J. (1971) *Internal Labor Markets and Manpower Analysis* (Massachusetts: D. C. Heath).

Dunn, J. and Grimwood, H. (1984) 'Changing Perspectives: Careers Officers, Social Control and Transition Problems', in C. Varlaam (ed.).

Eden, C. and Aubrey, K. (1986) 'YTS and Gender: Continuity or Challenge?', Paper to BERA Conference, Bristol University, September (Bath College of Higher Education).

Edmond, N. (1986) 'Women and YTS', in Labour Movement National Inquiry.

Edwards, R. (1979) *Contested Terrain: The Transformation of the Workplace in the Twentieth Century* (London: Heinemann).

Eisenstein, Z. R. (ed.) (1979) *Capitalist Patriarchy and the Case for Socialist Feminism* (New York: Monthly Review Press).

Equal Opportunities Commission (1981) 'Response to the MSC Consultative Document: "A New Training Initiative" ', unpublished paper, September.

Equal Opportunities Commission (1983) 'Positive Discrimination in the Youth Training Scheme', unpublished paper.

Equal Opportunities Commission (1986) *Women and Men in Britain: a Statistical Profile* (London: HMSO).

Esland, G. *et al.* (1975) *People and Work* (Edinburgh: Homes McDougall).

Evans, J. M. *et al.* (1984) 'Youth Labour Market Dynamics and Unemployment: and Overview', in Organisation for Economic Co-operation and Development.

Eversley, J. (1986) 'Trade Union Responses to the MSC', in C. Benn and J. Fairley (eds).

Faulkner, W. and Arnold, E. (eds) (1985) *Smothered by Invention: Technology in Women's Lives* (London: Pluto).

Fawcett Society (1985) *The Class of '84: a Study of Girls on the First Year of the Youth Training Scheme*, National Joint Committee of Working Women's Organisations.

Finn, D. (1984) 'Leaving School and Growing Up: Work Experience in the Juvenile Labour Market', in I. Bates *et al.*

Finn, D. (1985) 'The Development of the Community Programme: Has it "Proved its Worth"?' *Unemployment Unit Bulletin*, no.16. April.

Finn, D. (1986) 'YTS: the Jewel in the MSC's Crown?', in C. Benn and J. Fairley (eds).

216   References

Finn, D. (1987) *Training without Jobs: New Deals and Broken Promises*, Youth Questions Series (London: Macmillan).

Ford, J. (1969) *Social Class and the Comprehensive School* (London: Routledge & Kegan Paul).

Ford, J. and Box, S. (1967) 'Sociological Theory and Occupational Choice', *Sociological Review*, vol.15, no.3.

Friedman, A. (1977) *Industry and Labour: Class Struggle at Work and Monopoly Capitalism* (London: Macmillan).

Fuller, M. (1980) 'Black Girls in a London Comprehensive School', in R. Deem (ed.).

Fürst, G. (1986) 'The Retreat from Male Jobs: a Study of Female Industrial Workers and the Division of Labour in an Internal Labour Market'; a paper on Swedish experiences of women entering male jobs, in preparation, Department of Sociology, University of Göteborg, Sweden.

Game, A. and Pringle, R. (1983) *Gender at Work* (London: Pluto).

Ginzberg, E. *et al*. (1946) *Occupational Choice: an Approach to a General Theory* (New York: Columbia University Press).

Goldstein, N. (1984) 'The New Training Initiative: a Great Leap Backwards', *Capital and Class*, no.23.

Gorz, A. (ed.) (1976) *The Division of Labour: the Labour Process and Class Struggle in Modern Capitalism* (Brighton: Harvester).

Greater London Council (1986) *The London Labour Plan*. Greater London Training Board (1983) 'The Youth Training Scheme in London at September 1983', Report TB 85, by the Director of Industry and Employment and the Chief Economic Adviser, Greater London Council, 14 November.

Griffin, C. (1985) *Typical Girls? Young Women from School to the Job Market* (London: Routledge & Kegan Paul).

Griffin, C. (1986) *Black and White Youth in a Declining Job Market: Unemployment amongst Asian, Afro-Caribbean and White Young People in Leicester*, Centre for Mass Communication Research (Leicester University).

Hacker, S. (1981) 'The Culture of Engineering: Woman, Workplace and Machine', *Woman's Studies International Quarterly*, vol.4, no.3.

Hakim, C. (1979) *Occupational Segregation*, Research Paper no.9, Department of Employment.

Hakim, C. (1981) 'Job Segregation: Trends in the 1970s', *Employment Gazette*, December, Department of Employment.

Hall, S. and Jefferson, T. (eds) (1975) *Resistance through Rituals: Youth Subcultures in Post-war Britain*, Centre for Contemporary Cultural Studies (London: Hutchinson).

Hansard (1985) 20 March (London: HMSO).

Hartmann, H. (1979) 'Capitalism, Patriarchy and Job Segregation by Sex', in Z. R. Eisenstein (ed.).

Hartnett, O. *et al*. (1979) *Sex-Role Stereotyping* (London: Tavistock).

Hayes, C. *et al*. (1983) 'YTS and Training for Skill Ownership', *Employment Gazette*, August, Department of Employment.

Hayes, C. and Fonda, N. (1983) 'Delivering Occupational Training

Families', *Manpower Studies*, no.6, Spring/Summer.

Hebdige, D. (1979) *Subculture: the Meaning of Style* (London: Methuen).

Hill, J. M. M. and Scharff, D.E. (1976) *Between Two Worlds: Aspects of the Transition from School to Work*, Careers Consultants.

Himmelweit, H. T. *et al.* (1952) 'The Views of Adolescents on Some Aspects of the Social Class Structure', *British Journal of Sociology*, no.2, June.

HM Stationery Office (1973) *The Employment and Training Act* (London: HMSO).

HM Stationery Office (1981) *The New Training Initiative*, Cmnd 8455 (London: HMSO).

HM Stationery Office (1984) *Training for Jobs*, Cmnd 9135 (London: HMSO).

HM Stationery Office (1985) *Education and Training for Young People*, Cmnd.9482 (London: HMSO).

Holland, J. (1981) *Work and Women*, Bedford Way Papers no.6, Institute of Education (London University).

Holland, J. and Varnava-Skouras, G. (1979) 'Investigation of Adolescent's Conceptions of Features of the Social Division of Labour', Sociological Research Unit, Institute of Education, unpublished paper (London University).

Hunt, A. (1975) *Management Attitudes and Practices Towards Women at Work*, Office of Population Censuses and Surveys, Social Survey Division (London: HMSO).

Incomes Data Services (1983) *The Youth Training Scheme*, Study no.293, July.

Institute for Employment Research (1982) *Women's Working Lives: Evidence from the National Training Survey*, Research Report, (University of Warwick).

Jackson, M. (1985) *Youth Unemployment* (London: Croom Helm).

Kaneti-Barry, M. *et al.* (1971) *2100 Sixth Formers: a Study of Sixth Form Boys and Girls with Particular Reference to their Subject Specialisation, Educational Aims, Vocational Choice, and Careers Prospects*, Brunel Further Education Monographs no.2 (London: Hutchinson).

Kelly, A. *et al.* (1984) *Girls into Science and Technology Project: Final Report* (University of Manchester).

Kenrick, J. (1981) 'Politics and the Construction of Women as Second-class Workers', in F. Wilkinson (ed.).

Kessler, S. J. and McKenna, W. (1978) *Gender: an Ethnomethodological Approach* (New York: Wiley).

Kraft, P. and Dubnoff, S. (1984) 'Software for Women means a Lower Status', *Computing*, 9 February.

Labour Movement National Inquiry into Youth Unemployment and Training (1986) *Youth Unemployment and Training: A Report*, Available from TURC Publishing, 7 Frederick St, Birmingham, B1 3HE.

Labour Research Department (1985) 'YTS in Practice', *Bargaining Report*, no.41, June.

Labour Research Department (1986) 'Young Workers' Pay', *Bargaining Report*, no.52, May.

Land, H. (1980) 'The Family Wage', *Feminist Review*, no.6.

Laws, J. L. (1976) 'Work Aspiration of Women: False Leads and New Starts', in M. Blaxall and B. Reagan (eds).

Lee, G. *et al*. (1982) 'Jobs for White Girls; Jobs for Black Girls?', paper presented at the British Sociological Association conference.

Lees, S. (1984) 'Nice Girls Don't', *New Society*, March/April.

Lees, S. (1986) *Losing Out: Sexuality and Adolescent Girls* (London: Hutchinson).

Lembright, M. and Riemer, J. (1982) 'Women Truckers' Problems and the Impact of Sponsorship', *Work and Occupations*, vol.9, no.4, November.

Liljeström, R. *et al*. (1978) *Roles in Transition*, Report of an Investigation for the Advisory Council on Equality between Men and Women, Stockholm, Sweden.

Lloyd, A. and Newell L. (1985) 'Women and Computers', in W. Faulkner and E. Arnold (eds).

London Careers Workers Action Group (1982) *Better Training Real Jobs* (Campaign Bulletin published from 24 Montpelier Road, London NW5 2XD.)

London Women in Youth Training Research and Support Project (forthcoming) *Women in the Youth Training Scheme* (London Strategic Policy Unit).

McRobbie, A. (1978) 'Working Class Girls and the Culture of Femininity', in Women's Studies Group, Centre for Contemporary Cultural Studies (ed.).

McRobbie, A. (1984) 'Dance and Social Fantasy', in A. McRobbie and M. Nava (eds).

McRobbie, A. and Garber, J. (1975) 'Girls and Subcultures', in S. Hall and T. Jefferson (eds).

McRobbie, A. and Nava, M. (eds) (1984) *Gender and Generation*, Youth Questions Series (London: Macmillan).

Mahony, P. (1985) *Schools for the Boys?: Co-education Reassessed* (London: Hutchinson and the Explorations in Feminism Collective).

Maizels, J. (1970) *Adolescent Needs and the Transition from School to Work* (Athlone Press).

Makeham, P. (1980) *Youth Unemployment*, Research Paper no.10, Department of Employment.

Manpower Services Commission (1977) *Young People and Work: Report on the Feasibility of a New Programme of Opportunities for Young People* (The Holland Report).

Manpower Services Commission (1979) *Opportunities for Girls and Women in the MSC Special Programmes for the Unemployed*.

Manpower Services Commission (1981a) *The New Training Initiative: a Consultative Document*, May.

Manpower Services Commission (1981b) *The New Training Initiative: Agenda for Action*, December.

Manpower Services Commission (1982) *Report of the Youth Task Group*, April.

Manpower Services Commission (1983a) 'Positive Action for Women: a Summary of Training Division's Activities', AT-2 unpublished paper, November.

Manpower Services Commission (1983b) *Wider Opportunities for Young Women within YTS: a Resource Guide for Sponsors' Staff Training*, November.

Manpower Services Commission (1983c) *Guide to the Work of Area Manpower Boards*, March.

Manpower Services Commission (1984) *Youth Training Scheme Review 1984*, YTS L 60, September.

Manpower Services Commission (1985a) 'Equal Opportunities for Young Women in YTS', YTB/85/27, unpublished paper.

Manpower Services Commission (1985b) 'Equal Opportunities for Young Women in YTS: Follow-up Paper to YTB/85/27', YTB/85/38, unpublished paper.

Manpower Services Commission (1985c) *Development of the Youth Training Scheme*, July.

Manpower Services Commission (1985d) *Approved Training Organisations: an Information Paper*, November.

Manpower Services Commission (1985e) 'Review of Area Manpower Boards', unpublished paper, October.

Manpower Services Commission (1986a) Form TFS-1, Section 11.

Manpower Services Commission (1986b) *Training for Skills YTS*, TFSL 12, publicity booklet, January.

Manpower Services Commission (1986c) *Training for Skills: Managing Agents' Handbook*.

Manpower Services Commission (1986d) 'Ethnic Minorities and YTS', paper by the Youth Training Directorate, YTB/86/14.

Martin, J. and Roberts, C. (1984) *Women and Employment: a Lifetime Perspective*, Department of Employment and Office of Population Censuses and Surveys (London: HMSO).

Musgrave, P. W. (1967) 'Towards a Sociological Theory of Occupational Choice', *Sociological Review*, vol.15, no.1.

National Association of Teachers in Further and Higher Education (NATFHE) (1984) *The Great Training Robbery*.

National Union of Students, Women's Unit (1985) *Women and YTS: A Report*, December.

National Youth Bureau (1984) *Trainee Participation in the Youth Training Scheme: Principles and Practice*, Youth Opportunities Development Unit.

Nemerowicz, G. M. (1979) *Children's Perceptions of Gender and Work Roles* (New York: Praeger).

Newton, P. and Brocklesby, J. (1983) *Getting on in Engineering: Becoming a Woman Technician*, Report to the Engineering Industry Training Board, the Equal Opportunities Commission and the Social Science Research Council (Huddersfield Polytechnic).

220   *References*

Oakley, A. (1972) *Sex, Gender and Society* (London: Temple Smith).
O'Farrell, B. and Harlan, S. (1982) 'Craftworkers and Clerks: the Effect of Male Co-worker Hostility on Women's Satisfaction with Non-traditional Jobs', *Social Problems*, vol.29, no.3, February.
Organisation for Economic Cooperation and Development (OECD) (1977) *Youth Unemployment*, A Report on the High Level Conference, vol.1, 15–16 December (Paris).
Organisation for Economic Cooperation and Development (1984) *The Nature of Youth Unemployment* (Paris).
Organisation for Economic Cooperation and Development (1985) *New Policies for the Young* (Paris).
Ormerod, M. B. (1975) 'Subject Preference and Choice in Co-educational Single-sex Secondary Schools', *British Journal of Educational Psychology*, no.45.
Osterman, P. (1980) *Getting Started: The Youth Labour Market*, (Cambridge, Massachusetts: MIT Press).
Phillips, A. (1983) *Hidden Hands* (London: Pluto).
Phillips, A. and Taylor, B. (1980) 'Sex and Skill: Notes Towards a Feminist Economics', *Feminist Review*, no.6.
Phizacklea, A. (ed.) (1983) *One Way Ticket: Migration and Female Labour* (London: Routledge & Kegan Paul).
Pitcher, E. G. and Schultz, L. H. (1983) *Boys and Girls at Play: the Development of Sex Roles* (Brighton: Harvester).
Pollert, A. (1986) 'Sex-stereotyping in YTS: the Case of the Private Training Agencies in Birmingham', in Labour Movement National Inquiry.
Psathas, G. (1968) 'Towards a Theory of Occupational Choice for Women' *Sociology and Social Research*, vol.52, January.
Ramazanoglu, C. (1986) 'Ethnocentrism and Socialist-feminist Theory: a Response to Barrett and McIntosh', *Feminist Review*, no.22, Spring.
Randall, C. (1985) Report for the Centre for a Working World, Bath, and the School of Advanced Urban Studies, University of Bristol, 1985, cited in *Youth Workers Bulletin* no.15, August 1986.
Rathbone, E. (1949) *Family Allowances* (London: Allen & Unwin).
Rauta, I. and Hunt, A. (1975) *Fifth Form Girls: Their Hopes for the Future* (London: HMSO).
Rees, T. L. (1984) 'Reproducing Gender Inequality in the Labour Force: the Role of the State', Paper no.84/27e for the Standing Conference on the Sociology of Further Education (University College, Cardiff).
Rees, T. L. and Atkinson, P. (1982) *Youth Unemployment and State Intervention* (London: Routledge & Kegan Paul).
Reich, M. *et al.* (1980) 'A Theory of Labour Market Segmentation', in A. H. Amsden (ed.).
Roberts, K. (1972) *From School to Work: a Study of the Youth Employment Service* (Newton Abbott: David & Charles).
Roberts, K. (1975) 'The Developmental Theory of Occupational Choice: a Critique', in G. Esland *et al.*
Roberts, K. (1980) 'Occupational Choice: a Historical Romance', *Youth in Society*, vol.89.

Robins, D. and Cohen, P. (1978) *Knuckle Sandwich: Growing Up in the Working Class City* (Harmondsworth: Penguin).

Rubery, J. (1980) 'Structured Labour Markets, Worker Organisation and Low Pay', in A. H. Amsden (ed.).

Sarah, E. *et al.* (1980) 'The Education of Feminists: the Case for Single-sex Schools', in D. Spender and E. Sarah (eds).

Scofield, P. *et al.* (1983) *Youth Training: the Tories' Poisoned Apple*, Independent Labour Party.

Searle, C. (1984) 'Some Trends in YTS Curriculum Theory', unpublished paper, Garnett College.

Sharpe, S. (1976) *Just Like A Girl: How Girls Learn to be Women* (Harmondsworth: Penguin).

Shaw, J. (1980) 'Education and the Individual: Schooling for Girls or Mixed Schooling – a Mixed Blessing?' in R. Deem (ed.).

Sherratt, N. (1983) 'Girls, Jobs and Glamour', *Feminist Review*, no.15, Winter.

Simons, G. L. (1981) *Women in Computing*, The National Computing Centre Publications.

Sinclair, E. (forthcoming) 'Retraining women operators for technical skill shortages', Manpower Services Commission.

Smelser, N. J. and Smelser, W. T. (1963) *Personality and Social Systems* (New York: Wiley).

Socialist Society (1983) *The Youth Training Scheme: a Strategy for the Labour Movement'.*

South Glamorgan Women's Workshop (1986) *New Styles of Training for Women: an Evaluation of South Glamorgan Women's Workshop*, Equal Opportunities Commission.

Spender, D. and Sarah, E. (eds) (1980) *Learning to Lose* (London: The Women's Press).

Stafford, A. (1986) 'Trying Work: Participant Observation of a Scheme for the Young Unemployed', Ph.D. thesis, University of Edinburgh.

Stanworth, M. (1981) *Gender and Schooling: a Study of Sexual Divisions in the Classroom* (London: Hutchinson with Explorations in Feminism Collective).

Super, D. (1953) 'A Theory of Vocational Development', *American Psychologist*, no.8.

Super, D. (1957) *The Psychology of Careers* (New York: Harper & Row).

Thorpe, S. (1986) 'Girls and Computer Literacy/Information Technology on the Youth Training Scheme', in Labour Movement National Inquiry.

United Nations (1980) *The Economic Role of Women in the ECE Region*, E/ECE/1013.

Varlaam, C. (ed.) (1984) *Rethinking Transition: Educational Innovation and the Transition to Adult Life* (Lewes: Falmer).

Venness, T. (1962) *School Leavers: Their Aspirations and Expectations* (London: Methuen).

Walden, L. (1986) and others involved in the project 'Female Culture, Male Culture, Technological Culture', University of Linköping, Sweden.

222 *References*

Walden, R. and Walkerdine, V. (1985) *Girls and Mathematics: From Primary to Secondary Schooling*, Bedford Way Papers no.24, Insitute of Education (London University).
Walker, S. and Barton, L. (eds) (1983) *Gender, Class and Education* (Lewes: Falmer).
Walkerdine, V. (1984) 'Some Day my Prince Will Come: Young Girls and the Preparation for Adolescent Sexuality', in A. McRobbie and M. Nava (eds).
Walsall Council for Community Relations (1978) *Aspirations versus Opportunities: Asian and White School-leavers in the Midlands*, with the Leicester Council for Community Relations and the Commission for Racial Equality.
Walshok, M. L. (1981) *Blue Collar Women: Pioneers on the Male Frontier* (New York: Anchor Books).
West, M. and Newton, P. (1983) *The Transition from School to Work* (London: Croom Helm).
West Midlands County Council (1985) *The Great Training Robbery Continues*, Trade Union Resources Centre (Birmingham).
West Midlands YTS Research Project (1985) *Unequal Opportunities: Racial Discrimination and the Youth Training Scheme*, Trade Union Resources Centre, Birmingham.
Westwood, S. (1984) *All Day, Every Day: Factory and Family in the Making of Women's Lives* (London: Pluto).
Wetherby, T. (1977) *Conversations: Working Women Talk about Doing a Man's Job*, (New York: Les Femmes).
Wickham, A. (1985) 'Gender Divisions, Training and the State', in R. Dale (ed.).
Wickham, A. (1986) *Women and Training* (Milton Keynes: Open University Press).
Wilkinson, F. (ed.) (1981) *The Dynamics of Labour Market Segmentation* (New York: Academic Press).
Williams, W. M. (ed.) (1974) *Occupational Choice* (London: Allen & Unwin).
Willis, P. (1977) *Learning to Labour: How Working Class Kids Get Working Class Jobs* (London: Saxon House).
Wilson, A. (1978) *Finding a Voice: Asian Women in Britain* (London: Virago).
Winship, J. (1985) 'A Girl Needs to Get Street-wise: Magazines for the 1980s', *Feminist Review*, no.21, Winter.
Women in YTS (1983), Report of a Conference, Manchester, November.
Women's Studies Group, Centre for Contemporary Cultural Studies (ed.) (1978) *Women Take Issue: Aspects of Women's Subordination* (London: Hutchinson).
Young Women's Plastering Project (1986) 'Young Women and Training in the Construction Industry: the Experience of the Young Women's Plastering Project', unpublished paper, Sheffield.

Index

223